PATTERN OF MEXICO

BOOKS ILLUSTRATED BY E. H. SUYDAM

BOSTON AND THE BOSTON LEGEND
  By Lucius Beebe

LOS ANGELES: CITY OF DREAMS
  By Harry Carr

SAN FRANCISCO: A PAGEANT
  By Charles Caldwell Dobie

SAN FRANCISCO'S CHINATOWN
  By Charles Caldwell Dobie

HAWAII: ISLES OF ENCHANTMENT
  By Clifford Gessler

PATTERN OF MEXICO
  By Clifford Gessler

ROMANTIC CITIES OF CALIFORNIA
  By Hildegarde Hawthorne

WILLIAMSBURG: OLD AND NEW
  By Hildegarde Hawthorne

HIGHLIGHTS OF MANHATTAN
  By Will Irwin

ANYBODY'S GOLD: THE STORY OF
  CALIFORNIA'S MINING TOWNS
  By Joseph Henry Jackson

WASHINGTON, PAST AND PRESENT
  By Charles Moore

DETROIT: DYNAMIC CITY
  By Arthur Pound

VIRGINIA: THE NEW DOMINION
  By Agnes Rothery

FABULOUS NEW ORLEANS
  By Lyle Saxon

LAFITTE THE PIRATE
  By Lyle Saxon

OLD LOUISIANA
  By Lyle Saxon

CHICAGO: A PORTRAIT
  By Henry Justin Smith

LOOKING ACROSS THE ZÓCALO IN MÉXICO, D. F., TO THE
CATHEDRAL AND THE SAGRARIO

PATTERN
OF MEXICO

By CLIFFORD GESSLER

Illustrated by

E. H. SUYDAM

D. APPLETON-CENTURY COMPANY
INCORPORATED
NEW YORK   1941   LONDON

917.2

Gessler

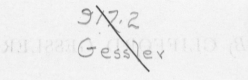
PRINTED IN THE UNITED STATES OF AMERICA

Word came, as the last pages of this manuscript were being written, of the death of Edward Howard Suydam, gifted illustrator of this Series. A valued collaborator and friend is gone; in this book and in its companion volumes, his work remains.

CLIFFORD GESSLER

ACKNOWLEDGMENTS

PARTS of the chapters entitled "Guadalajara Lives Merrily," "Little Mornings of Jalisco," "The Haunted Lake," and "Pictured Walls" appeared in *Travel*. The verses attached to "Dark Madonna" are included by permission of *The Commonweal;* those at the end of "Rain Comes to Uruápan," by courtesy of *The American Mercury;* those closing the Tehuantepec chapter are from *Poetry: A Magazine of Verse*. The author acknowledges with gratitude the aid of Margaret Gessler, whose keen critical judgment and analysis of art values have been of great assistance in the writing of this book.

CONTENTS

Contents

Contents

ILLUSTRATIONS

xiii

Illustrations

PATTERN OF MEXICO

THESE MANY MEXICOS

MEXICO, even to one whose feet have trodden the earth of many lands, is an adventure. A spiritual rather than a physical adventure, for although one can readily believe that anything whatever may happen, the things that do happen are rarely very hazardous.

You cross a bridge, or walk through a gate in a metal fence. The ground under your feet is the same dry, sun-baked earth; the hills in the distance the same puckered brown barrows of semi-desert. The wind whisks freely back and forth, and as dust settles at one side or the other of an imaginary line, it is United States or Mexican soil. So much for the artificialities of geographical boundaries.

But the spiritual borders: "the latitudes of the mind, the

I

longitudes of the blood," are something else. It is not wholly a matter of language, architecture, dress. There is a different feeling, evasive of definition, but inescapable to the inward sense, about this country that sprawls toward the earth's belt-line from the margins of Texas, New Mexico, Arizona, California.

Throughout that country, one is conscious of the weight of age: of a land that has been tilled and fought over for many centuries, a land whose soil has not been enriched by the blood that has sunk into it since the wars of Indian nations before recorded time.

The "New World" here is old; and in spirit it is a blend, a not yet fully coherent blend: the Old World and the ancient New; Asia and Europe, both transmuted by slow, inescapable influences of climate and soil; the American Indian and the Latin—and it is difficult, often, to determine where one begins and the other leaves off.

It is a diverse country, varied in climate and scene, in resources and in humanity. It is many countries, with their local languages and customs and costumes, with isolated villages often knowing little of what goes on beyond the next sierra; a multitude of little worlds, thrown together somehow in the twenty-eight states, two territories, and federal district that make up the Republic of Mexico.

Here are snow-crowned volcano cones and quiet mountain lakes; stupendous gorges and cañons; bewildering forests; gardens of tropical fruits; vast deserts; palm-feathered, gracefully curving beaches; vistas of time-mellowed cathedral towers through massive arches; the deep, tenacious throb of life in plaza and patio and market-place; death, and the suffering which is life, and music in the streets by night.

The Capital, with its cosmopolitan modernity, is one Mexico; the dusty, cactus-fenced adobe villages around their plaza squares, another. The provincial cities, stately with age and steeped in history; the hulking ruined temples of older

These Many Mexicos

cultures: they too are Mexico. The plateau with its miles of bristling maguey; the enchanted lake country of Michoacán; the west country of strolling singers, old pirate ports, and thatched fishing villages; the soft tropical Gulf coast; mountain-seamed Oaxaca; dreamy Tehuantepec of the flower-filled painted bowls, embroidered tunics, and bronze-statue women: these are more Mexicos. And Yucatán, even more detached, whose people say in mild rebuke: "We are not Mexicans, we are Yucatecos"—strangest, perhaps, and most fascinating of all.

And many more: there is no end to the variety and charm—mingled though it may be, at times, with vexations—of these many Mexicos that make up that sprawling, slowly integrating country that is nearest to us of all truly foreign lands.

Mexico: old and new, primitive and modern, infinitely varied—how shall one tell of it, how reduce it to an intelligible synthesis? By fragments, perhaps, as one sees it: fragments of moonlight on cobbled streets, petals drifting down to tiled patio floors among fragrant shrubs and singing birds, many-colored cubes and cones of produce in canopied markets, sculptured walls of ancient temples and tombs, the diverse face of humanity in plaza and in street—innumerable bits of color and life that form a mosaic, a tapestry: the pattern of Mexico.

Here the present is rooted in the past. One can not begin to understand what one sees until one knows something of the story behind it. That is history. A good half of what one sees in Mexico is history. So I begin with the bare essentials of that past which shapes the present. Not a complete, detailed history, but a sketch of significant movements, concentrating on a few of the more dramatic or dynamic sequences.

Hence the arrangement of this book. First, this brief historical background. Then chapters describing representative sections of Mexico as I saw them, followed by elementary discussion of some current problems of Mexico and some thoughts

3

on Mexican art. A few "practical considerations" for travelers have been included in an appendix.

I can avoid repetition—although references to these things will occur incidentally at times—by mentioning at the start a few virtually universal features. A Mexican town usually has its plaza or great square, partly bordered by arcades (called *portales*); its open-air markets where fruit and vegetables, pottery and all manner of merchandise are displayed in geometrical compositions as they were in American Indian markets of the country before the Spanish conquest; its Colonial churches with elaborately carved façades; its streets of residences stuccoed in pastel shades, blank-walled or with iron-grilled windows, their home life facing inward upon the patio.

So much for the general physical pattern, in which moves an unhurried rhythm of living.

The pyramidal mountains confront the smoking mirror of heaven: across that mirror move shadowy figures of the past.

I · Roots of a Nation

I · "PRAISE THEN THE SINGERS"

STONE-AGE men from Asia, it is thought, crossed the northern strait, filtered through the continent of the Americas: hunting, fishing, gathering wild seeds. They became the American "Indians."

Somewhere in Mexico or perhaps, as some think, farther south, grew the grass they called "grain of the gods." Some one, thousands of years ago, dropped a kernel, and, when the plant fruited, remembered. Thus was born American civilization. For from the "grain of the gods" or some other wild grass developed maize, which European settlers named "Indian corn." It changed the whole life of a people.

They settled down, then, among their fields; in time, they built cities. Leisure was created; there was time at last for men to think. The new economy brought new needs: pottery, textiles, metalwork. The tending of the grain brought a more intense worship of the gods of sun and rain and earth. That meant poetry, music, sculpture, painting, the dance; it meant noble architecture, for the temples of the gods must transcend the humble homes of men.

Tribes continued to drift down from the north; others doubled back from the south. The earliest people of whom anything is known, in Central Mexico, have been called, for want of a more specific name, the "Archaics." A tribe known in history to-day as Toltecs later occupied the fields of these early people, probably absorbing the survivors, and building an empire that crumbled in its turn, leaving as its chief monuments the so-called pyramids of Cholula and Teotihuacan.

Another tribe, the Mayas, whose origins are not entirely clear, had developed a great civilization in Central America and in the peninsula of Yucatán. Some of their dated monuments are the earliest fairly definite chronological milestones that have been found in the hemisphere; Dr. Spinden has traced the Maya calendar system back to 613 B.C. A relatively late period of this people was contemporary with the ascendancy, in central Mexico, of the Toltecs. The two were in contact in the late twelfth century A.D., and influenced each other.

Meanwhile in the Valley of Oaxaca, in southern Mexico, had developed the civilization of the Zapotec and Mixtec tribes, whose monuments the visitor sees at Mitla and Monte Alban. There were still other important peoples in various parts of Mexico, at various periods, whose names are omitted here in order to minimize confusion.

And still the tribes came down from the north. These late, comparatively uncivilized intruders bear, collectively, the name, in history, of Chichimeca, which means something like "barbarian." On the ruins of the Toltec culture in the central highland the invaders founded, however, a culture that endured until it was overthrown by the Spaniards, the strange white "gods" from overseas.

Last to arrive of the Chichimeca tribes who emerged from the legendary "Seven Caves" was a poor, weak, but aggressive folk known to history as Aztecs. From another name of the same people is derived the word "Mexico." Finding the best lands occupied, they were driven from place to place until their chief, on an island in the lake of Texcoco, saw the prophesied sign: a nopal cactus, on which perched an eagle, in its claws a snake.

This was the site on which arose later the center of the City of Mexico. The year, as nearly as we can know, was A.D. 1325.

There they built their huts of mud and reeds, planted their "floating gardens"; so poor were they that for tribute to the neighboring lord of Atzcapotzalco they could pay only frogs and a few fish. But they prospered. Taking advantage of dissensions among their neighbors, and making favorable alliances through royal marriages, they built power.

These, then, were the principal pre-Spanish civilizations in Mexico: in the central highland, the Toltecs, and later, the Aztecs. Farther south, around Oaxaca, the Zapotecs and Mixtecs. In Yucatán and neighboring Central American countries, the Mayas. There were many other tribes, such as the Totonacs, toward the Gulf Coast, and the Tarascans in what is now the State of Michoacán, but the ones who have left the most notable ruins for the delight of archæologists and the wonderment of tourists are these four: Toltec, Aztec, Maya, and Zapotec with some Mixtec additions.

All these tribes still live in Mexico, in many cases around the ruins of their former splendor. Of them, only the Toltecs have disappeared as a separate people, having merged with other tribes. All were victims of the Spanish conquest, but the ones who figure most prominently in the story of that conquest are the Aztecs.

Successive Aztec chiefs extended the empire to the Gulf and

to the Pacific and to outposts beyond the Guatemala border, resisted here and there by such intransigents as their relatives the warriors of Tlaxcala, the Tarascans of Michoacán, and the Zapotec lords who guarded the passes of Oaxaca.

The Mayas, meanwhile, had declined through civil war and perhaps other causes not fully known, and in part had retired from Yucatán to the interior of Honduras and Guatemala.

The Aztec empire was at its height, though already seeds of decay were sprouting, when in 1502 Moctézuma Xocoyotzin laid down the broom with which he was sweeping the temple courts and took up the royal sword of his ancestors.

Tenochtitlán, the Aztec city in the lake, had grown with the centuries. Around the great square rose colossal step-pyramids, which were foundations for temples. Along canals that served as streets stood stone palaces, murmurous with running water, fragrant with roof-gardens. In the market-place, products of every part of Mexico were displayed. Hundreds of tribes paid tribute—in cotton and skins, in cacao and vanilla, in quills of gold dust, jewels of obsidian and turquoise, jade and pearls. Plumed armies returned with plunder and new pledges of vassalage, bringing captives to be slain in sacred rites, the heart torn out on the sacrificial stone to feed the gods.

Stone causeways connected the city with neighboring towns that gleamed white among the groves on the borders of the lake. Military roads led to garrison posts in tributary cities. Aqueducts carried water from the mountains. Sons of priests and nobles learned, in organized schools, the wisdom of their forefathers. Zoölogical and botanical gardens conserved knowledge of the various environments of Mexico; libraries of picture-writing recounted deeds of heroes or of gods; carved and painted scenes adorned temple walls; gold and silver, turquoise and obsidian and jade were cunningly worked to deck the person or to honor the deities.

This was the city whose ruins form the foundations for to-day's City of Mexico.

"Praise Then the Singers"

It was a barbaric but magnificent city, an uneven but richly cultured civilization, not without its philosophy, its poetry, its strivings toward the finer spiritual values of which man, rude and predatory as he still is, can be capable.

"Not with a heap of treasure," wrote Nezahualcóyotl, "shall you enliven your vassalage, for treasures are but smoke; praise rather the singers, and the flowers that cover the earth, for they will intoxicate your soul."

Moctézuma (for so Mexican historians of to-day spell the ancient name) walked in his gardens, or looked from his temple towers to the shimmering lakes and clustered white-walled palaces, the checkered groves and fields. The greater part of the land now known as Mexico was his.

His merchants, protected by the threat of his obsidian-sworded legions, traveled far beyond his borders. He dwelt in a palace of three hundred rooms; the highest nobles entered his presence barefoot, with cords about their necks in homage and with eyes downcast, for none might look the Son of Heaven in the face. He might visit, if he chose, a thousand concubines. In all the world, as he knew of it, there was not his equal. Surely his piety, his innumerable blood sacrifices, were recognized in the halls of heaven. The gods' favor was his.

But neither sacrifice nor prayer can stay the march of destiny—the insubstantial reality of economic forces, the irresistible drive in man himself which set afoot the great march east and west from the forgotten cradle of life; the two opposite waves of migration that were to meet on Mexican soil in a whirl of confusion from which recovery even yet is not complete.

Already the signs hung in the sky, pushed up out of the earth, floated on the sea. Moctézuma read them, and the fresh fish from the Gulf coast, the juicy venison from midland forests, the chocolate from southern valleys, turned bitter in his mouth with fear.

II · THE SMOKING STARS

"LET me not be angry," chanted a poet seer, "that the grandeur of Mexico must perish. The smoking stars gather against it; the lover of flowers shall be destroyed."

Had rumor, perhaps, reached the Mexican highland of the Spaniards in the Caribbean?

For adventurers from Spain were pushing from island to island, seeking gold and finding little or none, then turning to the enslavement of Indians on the land, as they had been doing since Columbus' ships sighted the palm-fringed shore of Guanahaní in 1492.

The tribes of the Indies did not thrive in slavery. Colonists and late comers pushed farther west, determined to seize new serfs, or lured by the evasive gleam of gold. To disappointment and tragedy, they colonized Darien.

A ship of discouraged colonists from that isthmian settlement crashed on a reef of Yucatán. Two survived the wreck and the sacrificial knife, to remain as slaves among the Indians. In such humble circumstances the first Spaniards arrived within the present boundaries of Mexico.

Slave raiders from Cuba, under Francisco Hernández de Córdoba, suffered thirst and wounds along the Yucatán coast in 1517. Indian prisoners told them of the two Spanish captives in the jungle. The next year, Juan de Grijalva coasted as far as the region of Vera Cruz, hearing of richer countries inland and bringing back samples of gold that whetted the Spaniards' greed.

These were forerunners, some of their men companions, of Cortés.

Hernán Cortés had come to the Indies athirst for adventure and fortune. Legend gossips that his departure from Spain was delayed by a fall from a lady's window when a husband unexpectedly returned. In Haiti, he told the governor, "I came not for work, but for gold."

In Cuba, becoming involved with Catalina Suárez, sister of the governor's lady, he was imprisoned for a plot, escaped, was recaptured, patched up his differences with the governor by marrying the girl. Through shrewd intrigue in the governor's court, he obtained command of the third expedition to the Mexican mainland.

Governor Diego Velázquez, however, wasn't quite sure he could trust Cortés. Thinking the matter over, he sent messengers to recall the expedition and depose its commander. But the wily adventurer had sailed before the governor's message could reach him.

Cortés had ten ships, about five hundred fighting men, a hundred and twenty workmen and sailors, sixteen horses, fourteen pieces of artillery, and two hundred servants, mostly Indians, with a few Negroes. With this force he approached a continent inhabited by millions of warlike Indians.

His instructions from the governor are characteristic of the times. Among other things, members of the expedition were to refrain from blasphemy, cards, and dice; to more practical purpose, they were to rescue the two enslaved castaways of the Conde de Valdivia's party, survey the coasts, induce the natives to submit to Spain and the Church—and get gold.

Shift the scene to Moctézuma's palace in the high valley of the lakes. His world, that had been so securely closed in by the great sea, was cracking.

Ten years before the Spaniards came, according to native traditions gathered by Fray Bernardino de Sahagún, "appeared in the sky a marvelous and frightful thing . . . a great and shining flame of fire . . . and the point of it reached to the middle of the sky."

A temple burned; another was struck by lightning; "three stars together, with long tails," appeared; the lake flooded the city; hunters brought a bird with a "mirror" in its head "in which appeared the sky and stars . . . and the second time Moctézuma looked in the mirror he saw a multitude of people who came armed and on beasts"—and the bird vanished before astrologers could come to interpret the vision. A voice as of a woman was heard by night mourning: "Oh, my sons, we are lost."

"I have discovered a great truth," Nezahualpilli, astrologer king of Texcoco, told his lord Moctézuma. "A few years hence our cities will be destroyed."

"And in the third year of the Rabbit they saw ships, and Moctézuma sent men to receive Quetzalcóatl, for he thought it was he who came."

The emperor remembered a troublesome prophecy that Quetzalcóatl, the blond and bearded Feathered Serpent of the Toltecs, would return to overthrow the Aztec rule.

The Smoking Stars

Receiving the messengers' report of the strangers' power, Moctézuma, more alarmed than ever, "sent sorcerers to cast a spell...that they might sicken and die"—but the sorcerers reported: "This is a strong people; we can do nothing."

There was no hope, declared Nezahualpilli, gloomily consulting the stars. But the pious Moctézuma still believed that prayer and sacrifice could avert disaster. Blood of new hundreds—thousands, some say—flowed from the stone of sacrifice. Taxgatherers went forth to demand increased tribute: the great temple was to be encrusted throughout with gold and precious stones.

"The vassals can pay no more," warned the lord of the treasury. And Moctézuma had him killed.

The subject tribes, taxed beyond endurance, bled thin by sacrifice, were ready to grasp at any hope of revolt, follow any leader, be he god, man, or demon, who might free them from the Aztec dominion.

In the midst of this terror and confusion, the white strangers advanced.

Cortés had halted first in Yucatán. Of the two Spanish captives, Gonzalo Guerrero refused to be rescued. He had a wife and family among his adopted tribe, and had become a chief. The other, the priest Jerónimo Aguilar, joined Cortés and served as interpreter in Maya-speaking country.

In Tabasco, Indians attacked in a great wave. The Spaniards, even with their better armor and weapons, might well have been overwhelmed. But the Indians had never before seen horses; the sixteen mounted Spaniards seemed to them supernatural centaur-like monsters. The natives fled.

They made peace with gifts: gold, ornaments, food. But, wrote Bernal Díaz, "this present was worth nothing in comparison with the twenty women who were given us, among them one very excellent woman called Doña Marina, for so she was named when she became a Christian...a great chief-

15

tainess, and the daughter of great caciques, and the mistress of vassals, and this her appearance clearly showed."

Malinali, as she seems to have been called in her own language, was the daughter of a chief near Coatzacoalcos, the modern Puerto México. After her father's death, the story goes, her mother bore a son to another chief, and that this son might be the heir, she gave Malinali to some Indians of Xicalango, who sold her in turn to the Tabasco people, from whom she came into the possession of Cortés.

"And Doña Marina, as she was good looking and intelligent, and without embarrassment, he gave to Alonzo Hernández Puertocarrero ... but afterward Doña Marina lived with Cortés and bore him a son, named Don Martín."

At San Juan de Ulua (Vera Cruz), the Spaniards met the emissaries of Moctézuma—the "clever painters ... to make pictures true to the nature of the face and body of Cortés and all his captains. ..."

There Doña Marina took over the interpretation in place of Aguilar, who did not understand the language of the Aztec ambassadors.

"This was the great beginning of our conquests," wrote Díaz. "I have made a point of explaining this, because without Doña Marina we could not have understood the language of New Spain."

Marina's help went beyond interpreting. She knew Indian customs, Indian rivalries and enmities, and could aid Cortés to take advantage of them. By her rank and personality she exerted an important influence. "She was obeyed," Díaz notes, "without question by the Indians throughout New Spain." Several times she warned Cortés of plots; no doubt she coached his speeches and improved upon them in translation.

Years afterward, when she accompanied Cortés to Honduras, in a town along the way her half-brother and the mother who had sold her into slavery were brought before her. "They thought she had sent for them to put them to death, and they were weeping." But Doña Marina sent them home with gold and jewels.

What became of Marina? This, too, is going ahead of the main story, but it is not without interest. Cortés' wife, Doña Catalina, eventually caught up with him. The chronicles are not entirely clear, but in Orizaba it is said Doña Marina never lived with Captain Juan Jaramillo, to whom she was married there. And Doña Catalina died suddenly in Cortés' house at Coyoacan, of "asthma" induced, according to gossip of the day, by pressure of her husband's hands on her throat after she had taunted him about Marina.

"Malintzin," Lady Malin, the Indians called her, and applied the name to Cortés as well: Malin-tzin, "Mr." Malin. To the Spaniards, it sounded like "Malinche," and that is what Cortés is called whenever Díaz quotes the Indians, throughout his *True History of the Conquest*.

A little girl stood at the desk of the San Francisco library as I drew out a source book on Mexican history. Noting the title, she volunteered: "I'm from Mexico. I was born in Guadalajara. I know the names of the capitals of all the states of Mexico. There are twenty-eight states, two territories, and one district federal."

She showed me a tattered school history of Mexico. As I turned over the pages, my glance fell on the words: *"El pusilánimo Moctézuma...."*

The Aztec emperor's irresolution seems, however, to have been caused not by cowardice but by superstition. If Cortés and his men were gods, or representatives of gods, he could not fight them. But perhaps he could bribe them. He sent gifts: "a wheel like the sun, as big as a cartwheel, with many sorts of pictures on it, the whole of fine gold ... which those who afterward weighed it said was worth ten thousand dollars" —and other objects nearly as rich. At the same time he urged Cortés not to attempt the difficult and dangerous journey to the capital, as the emperor could not bear to have anything untoward happen to such distinguished visitors.

The more numerous and the richer the bribes sent to induce Cortés to go away, the more reason the Spaniard saw for penetrating to the source of this wealth. An old Spanish helmet was brought back full of gold dust to the value of three thousand dollars and "worth more to us than if it contained twenty thousand, because it showed us that there were mines."

In return, Cortés sent Moctézuma a glass cup, three shirts, an armchair, and a red cap.

Now Cortés cut loose for good from Diego Velázquez, the Cuban governor. Founding a "city" on the sand, he had himself elected captain general of the "Villa Rica de la Vera Cruz"—and thus became independent of the governor, subject only to the king, and entitled to one-fifth of the loot. Lest any of his men falter, he scuttled the ships, except for one which he sent back to inform the king.

The Totonacs of Cempoala, unwilling vassals of the Aztecs, were his first allies. Thence, by a march in hunger and cold over mountain passes, the Spaniards came to Tlaxcala, fought there, then made new allies of those antagonists.

Moctézuma, more and more desperate, sent word: "Come, then, if you will. Come by way of Cholula."

For the oracle had spoken: "Cholula shall be the grave of strangers."

To Cholula they came, with six thousand Tlaxcalan allies. They were made welcome in that city of many temples; two thousand porters were assigned to carry their supplies. But Doña Marina, the chroniclers relate, learned of a plot: the porters, bearing hidden arms, were to massacre the Spaniards.

Cortés struck first. Luring the porters and the Cholula nobles into the plaza, he and his men cut off the exits. Swords flashed in the sunlight; Cortés wrote to his sovereign: "Three thousand died."

The Smoking Stars

Moctézuma came out to meet the "white gods" on the causeway that led into the Capital; he lodged them in a palace on the great square.

It was a good life in that city, wrote Díaz: food and drink and women brought to the hand (though he complained that the officers, as ever, took the handsomest)—and yet there was a smoldering menace in that island town; they guarded the doors in the time of sleep.

They must have a hostage. So they seized Moctézuma, and held him captive in his father's palace. Cortés ruled the land through Moctézuma, who acted as his mouthpiece, while he sent explorers to smell out gold.

Back in Cuba, Governor Velázquez had not been idle. Word came to the Aztec capital from Vera Cruz that Pánfilo de Narváez had landed there, with three times Cortés' force, to subdue that "outlaw" and take New Spain for the Cuban governor.

Cortés sent messengers to bribe Narváez' men, and himself marched toward the coast with an armed party, leaving Pedro de Alvarado in command in the Aztec city.

At night, in rain, Cortés stormed Narváez' camp at Cempoala. The men who remained loyal to Narváez said later that they had mistaken fireflies for matchlights of a great host. It was an easy victory. Narváez, at bay on a temple pyramid, fell wounded down the stair, crying out, *"Válgame Dios,* they have killed me and put out my eye!"

Adding Narváez' men to his own forces, Cortés hurried back to Tenochtitlán. Entering silent, ominous, empty streets, he found Alvarado besieged within.

For Alvarado, suspecting a plot when the priests and nobles prepared a religious festival, had hemmed them in the temple square and massacred them, as his master had done at Cholula. Blood of thousands, it is said, dyed the ceremonial raiment of the dance.

Now the city was still, and that stillness held menace of doom.

The aroused Indians apparently had been waiting for Cortés to return, that they might have all the Spaniards entrapped. In the late watch, arrows and sling-stones whined; roofs burned; the fighting was harsh at the wall-tops; in the lulls the Spaniards snatched sleep under shelters thatched with Aztec spears.

Cuitláhuac, the emperor's brother, had been a prisoner with Moctézuma; the Spaniards released him now, hoping he would calm the people. But soon the attackers were back, more furious than ever, with Cuitláhuac shrilling the war-cry at their head.

Days passed thus; mounted Spaniards sortied, hoofs slipping on the stones; they stormed the temple but could not hold it. Food and water supplies were cut off. Powder was running low.

Moctézuma, urged by Cortés, mounted the wall to speak to his people, in an effort to pacify them. A shower of stones answered; he fell—"and when we least expected it, they came to say that he was dead. Cortés wept. . . ."

The Spaniards' plight was desperate. The causeways to the mainland had been cut; the invaders were besieged on a hostile island.

Cortés, to gain time, tried to negotiate, offering to return the treasure and depart. Meanwhile he had his carpenters make a portable bridge, with which to cross the gaps in the causeways. On a rainy night, the Spaniards stole out into the deserted streets, bearing the bridge and all they could carry of the gold.

Some say a woman, dipping up water from a canal, screamed the alarm. The portable bridge jammed at the first breach, and the Indians were upon them by water and land—thrusting, hacking, pulling armored Spaniards into the water to drown, weighted as they were with gold and jewels.

Survivors crossed on bodies of the dead. Alvarado, commanding the rear guard, was cut off at the last breach—and hence arose the legend of his "leap." According to the tale, Alvarado, fighting furiously, broke through the Aztec ranks and leaped or vaulted on a spear over the gap.

Alvarado himself said later that he crossed on a beam. Wrote Bernal Díaz: "In Mexico there was a certain soldier called Ocampo . . . a gossiping fellow," who invented the story that Alvarado "abandoned his companion Juan Velázquez de León, leaving him to die with more than two hundred soldiers and horsemen . . . and that he saved himself by the great jump."

Under a huge tree which still stands at Popotla, Cortés rested, the tale tells, and wept. The night of June 30, 1520, has been remembered since as the "Sad Night."

He had lost more than half his Spaniards, a thousand of his Tlaxcalan allies, most of the treasure, all the guns. Every survivor bore wounds. Harassed still, the Spaniards circled and fought desperately through to refuge at Tlaxcala.

They came back in the spring with reinforcements and with swift sailing boats for the lake. Three months the siege endured; famine and disease ravaged the city, where Cuauhtémoc, the Falling Eagle, ruled since Cuitláhuac had died of the smallpox that came in the ships of Narváez.

House by house the Spaniards pulled down that city, raiding by day and returning to their bases at nightfall, to raid farther the next day. The defenders at last were besieged in the northeast quarter, wounded, starving, ill. The Aztec warriors, in their last stand, broke before the charge of Gonzalo de Sandoval, and fled into the lake.

Sea fighters, surrounding a canoe, captured Cuauhtémoc, the Eagle now indeed fallen.

"Then Guatemoc [sic] said to Cortés: 'Señor Malinche, I have done my duty in defense of my city and I can do no more. . . . Take that dagger at your belt and kill me at once.' And when he said this he wept tears and sobbed, and other great lords with him also wept."

Pattern of Mexico

Not so, replied Cortés; he would love him as a brother. So later he roasted Cuauhtémoc's feet to force him to reveal the hiding-place of the Aztec treasure; and in the end hanged him, on the march to Honduras, for an alleged plot. As far as is known, the treasure never was found.

Each year, on the day of the city's fall, his people gather at the Cuauhtémoc monument in the Paseo de la Reforma to reënact, in dance and pantomime, his heroic deeds.

Cortés has no public monument in the city that he won.

III · A CRY IN THE NIGHT

THERE was not really very much gold for anybody. Cortés and his companions, and later comers who followed the lure of loot, returned to the West Indies practice of extracting wealth from labor of Indians on the land. Wide tracts, and hordes of slaves, were allotted.

Slavery, even when forbidden in name, continued in fact. In our own time, the struggle was still being fought to end it.

Servitude was not new to the Indians. Apologists for the economic system inherited from the Conquest contend, not without reason, that the common Indian worked as hard, and got as little, under lords of his own race as under the lash of Spanish overseers. There is, however, a psychological difference. And the heritage of slavery remained a source of

Pattern of Mexico

Mexico's major ills long after Spain had ceased to rule the New World.

The exploiters quarreled among themselves. Interests of *criollos*—those born in Mexico of unmixed Spanish descent—clashed with those of *gachupines*—Spaniards from Spain. Both groups despised and victimized the *mestizo,* man of mixed race, true child of the Conquest. And the Indian was at the bottom of the heap.

Humane viceroys and kings in Madrid, urged by conscientious friars and priests, enacted laws to protect the Indians, but the immediate masters, then as often in our own time, ignored or evaded such restrictions. Mexico was sown with seeds of conflict, and it was only a question of time before the harvest should mature.

Liberal doctrines from revolutionary Europe filtered through censorship to an articulate minority in New Spain. Creole and *mestizo* revived half-abandoned dreams of ousting the *gachupín*. The Napoleonic wars, forcing abdication of Charles IV and imprisonment of his son Ferdinand, brought the conflict in Mexico to a head, for the confusion in Spain was reflected in the colonies.

It was a priest, a friend of the Indians, who led the revolution for independence, and it was a wealthy landowner who actually brought independence about and turned the revolution from its course.

At midnight on the fifteenth of each September the president of Mexico steps out on a balcony of the National Palace and rings a bell, with a shout of *"Viva México!"* That bell, on that date in 1810, hung in the parish church at Dolores, now called Dolores Hidalgo in memory of Father Miguel Hidalgo y Costilla, who rang it to call his parishioners to fight for freedom.

Hidalgo and other fathers of the revolution died before firing squads. By 1820 the cause was all but lost; the royalists were largely in control.

A Cry in the Night

A few rebel bands still held out in the mountains. Agustín de Iturbide was sent by the viceroy to suppress Vicente Guerrero, who was keeping the revolution alive in the state that now bears his name. Iturbide was ambitious. After a rather half-hearted battle, he entered into an agreement with Guerrero, known in history as the "Three Guarantees" of independence, religion, and union of Spaniards and *mestizos.*

The helpless viceroy resigned. His successor, Juan O'Donojú, signed at Córdoba, in 1821, the treaty that recognized Mexican independence. It was repudiated in Spain, but the Spaniards could hold only the fort of San Juan de Ulua, off Vera Cruz.

The next year Iturbide was proclaimed emperor of Mexico.

After seven years' struggle with a chronically empty treasury, he was overthrown and exiled by survivors of the old revolutionary group and by a new figure in history, Antonio López de Santa Anna, who appeared frequently in the story of his country from then on, and who several times served as its president. Iturbide, unwisely returning from Italy, was "courteously tried and executed."

In the decades that followed, the republic acquired the reputation of a land of perpetual revolution and banditry, which more sober later years have failed to live entirely down. As Don Pablo Martínez del Río has phrased it, "the vice president always considered it his duty to rebel against the president, and often the president considered it his duty to rebel against himself."

In the course of this turbulent period the struggling republic clashed with the expansion of the rising United States. Americans settling in the Mexican territory of Texas proved, from the Mexican point of view, an unruly lot. Demanding greater home rule and not getting it, they followed the fashion and rebelled. Texas became an independent republic for a few years, until it could obtain annexation to the United States.

Mexico was not pleased. Boundary difficulties led to Mexican occupation of disputed territory. This led in turn to the North American invasion of 1847. United States troops marched across Mexico without much serious opposition from a disunited nation. The resulting peace stripped Mexico of almost half its territory, which later became the southwestern states of the Union.

Meanwhile, the internal difficulties that had grown out of the sixteenth century Conquest persisted. Pomp in the Capital contrasted with discontent and disorder in the countryside. There was almost continuous strife. The rebel aims broadened. The Wars of Reform began.

Benito Juárez was a Zapotec Indian from the state of Oaxaca. Orphaned at four, he herded goats for an uncle. Fleeing from a scolding, he went to relatives in the city of Oaxaca. A member of the clergy educated him, and he became a lawyer, minister of justice, and vice-president of the republic.

When President Comonfort joined a counter-revolutionary movement "in rebellion against himself," Juárez set up a rival government. War raged three years, between clericals and conservatives in the Capital and Juárez in Vera Cruz. Early in 1861 the victorious Juárez entered Mexico City to preside over a devastated country, an empty treasury, and an assortment of domestic and foreign debts. With the victory, he inherited the causes of the French Intervention.

The first phase of this trouble had already occurred: the episode of 1838 dubbed the Pastry War. Among the French claims was one for pastry ravished by Mexican officers, on a spree, from a café operated by a Frenchman in Tacubaya. Not only the lives and herds of Frenchmen, it appeared, but even their pastry was not safe. The outraged Gauls sent an expedition to Vera Cruz.

López de Santa Anna rode from his hacienda to the walled city of the True Cross to repel the invaders single-handed if necessary. They landed before he was up. As Santa Anna, awakened, rushed out in night attire, a French officer asked, "Where is Santa Anna?"

The general pointed up the stairs. As the French dashed to the room he had just left, Santa Anna donned uniform and sword and hurried to lead the defense, behind barricades that included bird-cages—with the birds still in them.

Leading a counter-attack, Santa Anna got in the way of a grapeshot, losing the leg that was to become famous in two nations. The French retreated to their ships and later, after collecting their claim, sailed home. Thus Santa Anna became "the Saviour of Mexico."

Santa Anna had poor luck with his legs. The original, interred with pomp in the Capital, failed to remain entombed; a mob exhumed it in a later uprising and dragged it through the streets. The wooden member which replaced it on the general's person was captured and used as a baseball bat by North American soldiers in the invasion of 1847. I am told it rests in a museum in Illinois.

When Juárez organized his government in 1861, not only France but also Great Britain and Spain wanted to collect. Juárez' treasury couldn't even pay interest.

Mexican clergy and fugitive conservatives were intriguing abroad, especially at the court of Napoleon III. Juárez had closed convents and monasteries and had dispossessed the Church of lands. The time was favorable for a counter-attack with European help, since the United States was too busy fighting its own Civil War to interfere.

The three creditor powers agreed on a joint expedition, but Britain and Spain withdrew when they began to suspect that the venture was to be largely for French benefit. A French army landed and marched on the Capital.

The fifth of May is celebrated everywhere in Mexico, and streets are named for it, even in remote villages, in memory of the battle in which General Zaragoza and young Porfirio

Pattern of Mexico

Díaz hurled back the French troops at Puebla in 1862. It was only a temporary victory. The French entered the Capital and sent for the Austrian Archduke Maximilian to become emperor.

Maximilian was not altogether readily recruited, though he had no idea how thankless was the task to which he was invited. The Archduke, in his confused way, cherished ideals; he insisted on a popular demand for his services.

With the principal cities under military occupation, a "plebiscite" was easily managed. The "vote" was overwhelming. Maximilian, with all nobility of intention and weakness of practical execution, responded to the "call."

The emperor and his bride Carlota imported briefly the pomp of European royalty to the little court at Chapultepec and the Borda palace at Cuernavaca. Not without small disillusionments: the "welcome" at Vera Cruz was little more cheerful than the aspect of the vultures that blackened every roof; and even in the Capital (I quote from a letter of the time):

"We had better luck than Max. His quarters in the Palacio Nacional were verminous, and he had to get up and sleep on a billiard table."

There were more serious omens. The gaiety and brilliance of that court, webbed with intrigue, must have felt, often, the cold encroaching shadow of doom.

Though French generals continued to assure Maximilian that Juárez was defeated, the little Zapotec in the frock coat stubbornly refused to remain so. Maximilian had authority only where there were French troops. Even there, the Juaristas raided.

Maximilian, honest, well meaning but irresolute, moving in a fog of good intentions, disappointed practically everybody. The Mexican masses, whom he fancied he was destined to lead to a new and enlightened freedom, would have none of him. The clergy fumed because he refused to restore the lands

A Cry in the Night

Juárez had seized. The French were exasperated by his upright "impracticality."

Then the Civil War in the United States ended—to the chagrin of Napoleon III, who, it is believed, had expected the Confederacy to win. Secretary of State Seward demanded recall of French troops from Mexico. They withdrew, and Maximilian was left to defend what he fondly called his country with the few Mexican conservative regiments of Tomás Mejía and Miguel Miramón.

Carlota refused to give up. She sailed for France to demand aid from Napoleon III, from the Pope, from any one who would listen. Her mind cracked under the strain. Many years later the world was reminded briefly of an all but forgotten woman when news went forth from a castle in Belgium that Carlota was dead.

Maximilian was about to follow her to Europe. As usual, he had difficulty in making up his mind. At last, yielding to the entreaties of a few loyal conservatives, he remained.

The end came in Querétaro, whither he had gone to lead, in his own impressive person, the loyal troops—revising, between battles, his manual of court etiquette.

Querétaro was besieged. The Juarist General Escobedo offered Maximilian safe conduct if he would just go away. The noble Hapsburg would not consider it. His duty, he thought, was to stay with his followers and take what might come. The defenders, as a last hope, planned a midnight sortie to join Mejía's Otomí tribe in the mountains. According to the records, Miguel López persuaded Maximilian to delay, and then let the enemy into the town.

López, too, connived for Maximilian to escape. But the Hapsburg still thought flight would be dishonorable.

He must have known what would happen. Marshal Bazaine had persuaded him, when the French troops were still upholding his shaky throne, to sign a decree under which any Mexican caught bearing arms against the imperial government was to be shot. And the firing squads had been busy. Juárez, despite pleas of Mexicans and of foreign rulers, condemned Maximilian to the same fate.

To the Princess Salm, on her knees before him, replied the stern little man from Oaxaca: "If all the kings and queens of Europe were at your side, I could not spare his life."

Even yet, Maximilian might have escaped if he would. Many of the Juaristas, it appears, didn't really want his blood. They would have preferred, secretly, to let him go, if it could be done without openly implicating themselves. Prince Salm bribed the guards. Princess Salm offered Colonel Palacio a hundred thousand pesos; then, finding the colonel incorruptible, attempted, according to a contemporary memoir, to win him over by offering herself. The colonel, however, had as rigid a code of duty as Maximilian. As the princess, tearing off her clothes, approached, he threatened to leap out of the window.

In any case, Maximilian would not go unless Miramón and Mejía, who had refused any pardon excluding him, could also be saved. Nor would he compromise his dignity by shaving his beard to conceal his identity in flight.

The court martial, meeting to confirm Juárez' judgment, divided, three and three. The presiding officer cast the deciding vote for death.

Maximilian asked only that good shots be chosen for the execution squad, and that they shoot him in the heart rather than in the head. He couldn't bear to have his beauty spoiled.

One can not say just how accurate are the traditions preserved of historic scenes. Probably they are mainly true in principle, if not in actual detail.

"Are you ready, gentlemen?" Count Egon Corti, relying upon contemporary memoirs, quotes Maximilian. And, embracing Mejía and Miramón: "We shall meet in the other world." Then, pausing on the last step of the stair: "What a glorious day! I have always wanted to die on such a day."

A bugle sounded in the sunlit place.

A Cry in the Night

"Well, Tomás, is that the signal?" another chronicler quotes the imperial victim, addressing Mejía.

"I can't say, Señor. I've never been executed before."

To Miramón: "General, a brave man must be honored by his monarch even in the face of death. Allow me to give you the place of honor"—indicating his right side.

To Mejía: "General, what is not rewarded on earth will surely be rewarded in heaven."

Many years afterward, an old man in a North American city held on his knee a little girl who was later to become my wife.

"I was the officer of that firing squad," Colonel John Sobieski was wont, in those days, to relate.

" 'I regret that I have to do this,' I told him.

" 'You are a soldier,' he answered. 'You must do your duty.'

"He gave an ounce of gold to each soldier, saying, 'Shoot straight.'

"Then he wiped his forehead, for he was weak with dysentery, and gave his handkerchief to his servant, Tudos.

"He spoke, then, in Spanish: 'I forgive everybody, and I hope that everybody will forgive me. My blood is to be shed; I wish that it may be for the good of my country. *Viva México! Viva la independencia!*'

"I gave the signal with my sword. The shots sounded. Maximilian fell. His lips moved. I thought I could catch the word *'hombre.'* ...

"I handed my pistol to the sergeant for the finishing shot. It was in the heart."

IV · DARK WAVE

A MINING engineer recently told this story. He was riding over a mountain trail when he overtook a group of Indians, walking to town with loads of pineapples. Attempting to buy one of the fruit, he entered into conversation and learned their mission.

They were from a remote village, and they were on their way to town to send a protest to the President. The government of the state had taxed them, as they thought, exorbitantly; they wanted the governor removed or restrained. So the village scribe, the one man who could write, had drafted a letter.

They showed the engineer the letter. It was addressed to "Don Porfirio Díaz."

Dark Wave

When one realizes the isolation of some of those villages, and recalls the length of time Díaz ruled, the story is not so incredible as it may at first appear. It is not impossible to believe that the events of an entire generation had passed them by and that to them Don Porfirio, who had been president nearly half a life-time, was still head of their nation.

In the gloomy salon of the American Club in Mexico City hangs a portrait of Porfirio Díaz, perhaps the most successful example of that Latin-American type, the *caudillo*. The portrait is viewed with reverence. Under it, or more often in the adjoining bar, North American businessmen lament the "good old days" of Don Porfirio.

The *hacendados* lament him, too, but among the deepest mourners are the foreign capitalists and industrialists to whom, many Mexicans complain, he sold the country.

The Mexican republic, after its reëstablishment at the fall of Maximilian, was long to remain a republic only in name. Juárez struggled with debts and a hostile congress. In a mistaken effort to end militarism, he sent home two-thirds of the troops, who promptly became bandits or rebels. Just after suppressing a revolt, he died. Porfirio Díaz, who had been an able general against Maximilian and the French, overthrew Juárez' successor and began a dictatorship which was to endure for thirty-four years.

Except for one administration by a puppet executive, Manuel González, Díaz was president of Mexico until the revolution of 1910.

"Bread or a club," in the Mexican phrase, was his policy. He ruled with the firm hand that appeared necessary in the Mexico of his time. He enforced peace, ruthlessly but efficiently. There was "order"—or if that order was disturbed, disorder didn't last long. He bought off enemies if he could; if not, he crushed them. And he "developed" the country—by

33

granting profitable concessions to foreign exploiters. Practically anything in Mexico could be had, for a price.

Officials and foreigners and friends of the administration amassed wealth. The condition of the people reverted to or remained that of the Colonial period. Díaz suspended enforcement of anti-clerical laws, and then adroitly controlled what, in a political party, is called "patronage"—the church appointments.

Dummy governors and dummy legislatures ruled the states, under Díaz and a dummy congress. The Indians lost much of the little land they had retained. Labor organization was suppressed, with shooting if necessary. Schools were for children of the wealthy. The press took orders from Díaz.

These were the years to which many of my good friends of the business type look back with longing. Mexico was safe for North American enterprise. Of course, there were bribes to be paid to officials, but labor was incredibly cheap and well under heel; there was no serious objection to shooting any obstreperous peon who got out of hand, and, in short, business of the "rugged individualist" school flourished and paid handsome dividends.

Meanwhile Díaz erected an impressive façade of "progress" and "national prosperity." He built those architectural atrocities which still stand in the Capital as memorials of his régime. His rural police patrolled the roads, not only hunting down runaway hacienda laborers and discouraging any attempts by Indians to regain their communal lands, but also making bandits more scarce than ever before in the nation's history. Mexico acquired railroads, factories, credit; in 1894 it achieved its first balanced budget.

Díaz, says the economist Edward Alsworth Ross, was "really a great man and had the good of Mexico at heart. Political stability was his first concern. In attaining and maintaining that, his confidence was abused by selfish associates, and he was blamed for their crimes."

Dark Wave

The basic daily wage was the equivalent of twelve and a half cents a day.

The situation couldn't last forever, though Díaz and the group of advisers who are known in history as *"científicos"* seem to have believed it would.

As the master grew old, his followers quarreled over who was to be his successor. Díaz refused to name one. He had so long kept every one subordinate; he couldn't change now, to raise up a potential rival.

Díaz made a blunder—or perhaps, as some have suggested, it was only the old dictator's sense of humor. To conciliate United States opinion, as some have assumed, he told a North American newspaperman that he would retire in 1910 and turn Mexico over to the people. When the interview leaked back into Mexico from the United States, some Mexicans took it seriously.

Among these was a little man with a brown beard and a squeaky voice, and a flame of idealism in his heart: Francisco I. Madero. He went up and down the land making speeches. He was imprisoned, but his wealthy family, loyal to kinship if embarrassed by his subversive doctrines, manœuvered his release, and he crossed the border to send forth another high-pitched *grito* of rebellion.

Madero alone wasn't the Revolution. He was, says the historian Teja Zabre, "not the cause, but the danger signal ... spokesman of the exasperation of the oppressed populace."

Living costs had doubled, and the basic wage was still twelve and a half cents a day.

The initial uprising, in November of 1910, fizzled feebly in an aroma of stale powder smoke. Madero was on the point of sailing for Europe.

But hard-riding cowboy *guerrilleros* in the state of Chihuahua took up the cry with more effect. Abraham Gonzáles, Pascual Orozco, and the former cattle-rustler who had adopted the name of an earlier bandit, Pancho Villa, rode formidably if motion-picturesquely over the cactus-studded plains. They began to cut railroads, blow up bridges, defeat federal troops, capture towns.

In the south, Emiliano Zapata stirred the peons of Morelos with his cry of "Land and Liberty." By spring, rebel bands were active in eleven states. And Mexico, as Anita Brenner has epitomized it, "rose in a great dark wave to die."

Díaz, according to analytical interpreters of the history of that period, had played off one military or civil officer against another so long, and weakened them all so much, that he had scarcely any left who were efficient and whom he could trust. Most of his generals, most of his state governors, were old men, fogged in bureaucracy, fat with graft. Even the army, on which his power largely depended, had deteriorated: it was poorly armed since so many officials had dipped their hands into military funds, and it is said that two-thirds of the payroll was on paper only.

José Ives Limantour, chief of Díaz' advisers—the so-called *científicos*—whose financial skill had lifted the government out of bankruptcy in 1894, returned from Europe. On him, Díaz mainly relied.

Limantour had noted that the United States had twenty thousand soldiers on the border. Perhaps they were there just to keep disturbances from spilling over the boundary. And yet . . . perhaps Washington thought Díaz had been over-kind to British oil interests.

Limantour negotiated with the rebels. He offered compromises.

Madero, listening to his landed relatives, was willing. But the movement had gone beyond compromise. Francisco Vázquez Gómez took over the negotiations for the rebels, with sterner demands. Díaz and the cynical *científicos* must go; revolutionary governors must be named in eighteen states; the government must reimburse the revolutionists.

Dark Wave

Limantour couldn't accept such terms. If he did, he would be out of a job.

Orozco and Villa grew impatient with all this talk. What was needed, said Villa, was a *golpe terrífico,* a terrific stroke. They dynamited their way into Ciudad Juárez, and the federal General Navarro, mercifully aided by Madero, fled across the border.

Zapata stormed Cuautla. Mobs, or rebel bands from the mountains, seized one state capital after another. The Díaz power crumbled. Vásquez Gómez' terms were accepted. Díaz resigned and left the country.

Madero, more effective as an orator than as an administrator, and involved in the difficulties of a disorganized country, was a lost sheep among the wolves that gathered around him. Entering the Capital as a symbol of the people's hopes, he seems to have found that his popularity had declined among thoughtful revolutionists as it became evident that he had a political rather than an economic vision. As often happens, the movement had progressed beyond him. And while he lost the confidence of some sincere supporters, selfish associates manœuvered to divert the revolution to their own purposes.

Zapata held out uncompromisingly for literal fulfilment of his program of "land and liberty." A bloc in the congress demanded agrarian reform. Madero fumblingly tried to satisfy them, thus incurring the hostility of foreign capital. A series of counter-rebellions failed, and still treachery coiled to strike.

Victoriano Huerta, drunken and blustering—as Edith O'Shaughnessy called him, "a somber Indian Cæsar"—betrayed both sides. Madero was forced to resign, then was kidnapped and assassinated under the convenient subterfuge: "accidentally shot during a street riot" while being transferred to the penitentiary "for protection."

The Huerta dictatorship, an orgy of assassination and loot, proved unpalatable to the United States as to Mexico.

Venustiano Carranza, behind his benevolent beard and blue

spectacles, rose up, in dignified, scholarly, and somewhat inept fashion, in the north. Pancho Villa, his tough cowboys singing "La Cucaracha," galloped furiously over the desert. "Cruel to the point of brutality," said a man who had served with him, "dominating to the point of absolute possession. His personality was like the bow of a ship, dividing the wave of passions: either one hated him, or one surrendered one's will, never to recover it. His look seemed to lay bare one's soul." But Villa and Zapata remain popular heroes, accredited by many with being the two sincere military leaders of the Revolution.

Zapata still crusaded through the Morelos and Guerrero countryside, at the head of his ragged fighting peons, writing on the pillars of the Borda Garden at Cuernavaca: "It is more honorable to die on your feet than to live on your knees," and singing, "If they're going to kill me to-morrow, they might as well do it to-day." Alvaro Obregón, the chick-pea merchant of Sonora, stormed southward, winning battle after battle without a single defeat.

President Woodrow Wilson embargoed arms to the Huerta federals and let guns and supplies pass the border to the rebels; demanded a salute to the American flag on the pretext that Huerta's men had arrested some American sailors at Tampico; seized Vera Cruz in an attempt to intercept German munitions destined for Huerta. Strong with North American arms and ammunition, Villa and Obregón advanced. Huerta fled. Obregón entered the Capital. Carranza, "First Chief of the Revolution," ruled. But the cold, vain, slightly ridiculous figure behind the blue spectacles was another disappointment. His ideas, too, were political rather than social. He was considered too close to the landed proprietors.

Obregón and Villa drove him in turn out of the Capital and to his death. Obregón rode back north to suppress Villa, who suspected his sincerity. But from then on, the Revolution was regarded as established.

Dark Wave

It was still stronger on paper than in fact. One after another, revolutionary heroes found the practical difficulties too perplexing, or abandoned in greater or less part the principles for which they had fought. Many of them grew rich, and the peon still did not have land. Spokesmen for the deprived millions often declared that they had but exchanged old exploiters for new.

Nevertheless, the constructive phase of the Revolution is held by several historians to have begun with Obregón, who, having lost an arm at the battle of La Trinidad, is said to have jested that he was an ideal president because, having only one arm, he could "steal only half as much."

There were still counter-risings. Thirty-six generals joined Adolfo de la Huerta's rebellion when Obregón passed the presidency on to his associate Plutarco Elías Calles. Munitions from across the border are credited with having put down this movement.

Calles began auspiciously, from the revolutionary viewpoint —distributing land, lending money to small farmers, encouraging labor organization. About midway in his term, however, he seems to have swung over to the conservative side—at least, those elements of it which had political influence; and some Díaz practices reappeared. He began to encourage North American capital to some extent, and his friends were acquiring wealth.

It appeared that Obregón and Calles were to bat the presidency back and forth between them, thus holding power in a perpetual duumvirate while complying outwardly with the constitutional requirement of "no reëlection." This neat plan was interrupted by the assassination of Obregón—at the instigation, the government contended, of some of the clergy, with whom Calles had quarreled.

Calles set up a series of presidents, more or less under his domination: Emilio Portes Gil, Pascual Órtiz Rubio, Abelardo

39

Rodríguez—and one who refused to be a Calles-operated robot, Lázaro Cárdenas.

The evidence appears to indicate that when Cárdenas showed signs of independence, Calles intrigued against him. Cárdenas thereupon put him on a plane and shipped him over the border.

Cárdenas seems to have regarded the presidency not as an opportunity for personal profit (though it appears that, as usual, some of the president's associates did not neglect such opportunities), but as a mandate actually to enforce the Constitution—the one drawn up in 1917, embodying the principles for which, on paper at least, the revolutionary generals had turned out Díaz and, after him, Carranza.

Even Cárdenas' enemies conceded his honesty. The worst that was said of him in opposition headquarters in Mexico was that he was "mistaken," or addicted to impractical social notions, and that some of those about him lacked his own uprightness.

Cárdenas had as a program not only the Constitution, but also a party declaration, drawn up before he assumed office, for application of that Constitution: a platform known as the Six-Year Plan. Among other things it envisaged not only distribution of land, but irrigation works, government loans and machinery to make the land fruitful; reassertion of collective bargaining and security of the working-man in his job; development of roads, harbors, and other productive public works; universal education; improved public hygiene—in general theory, exploitation of resources for the benefit of the many rather than of the few, whether those few were local feudal lords or foreign industrialists. It has been described as "a Mexican New Deal."

Like most attempts at social reform, it became the subject of much controversy, both at home and abroad. Even the provisions for education were fought. In the last year of Cárdenas' administration, rural teachers were still being assas-

PASEO OLAS ATLAS, MAZATLÁN

sinated—at the instigation, it was alleged, of landowners, industrialists, and conservative clergy.

Expropriation in 1938 of foreign-operated oil properties, to deal with a situation created by a labor dispute, provoked a crisis in foreign relations, producing a virtual boycott on Mexican oil. The next year, war in Europe, with the resultant blockade, cut off many remaining markets, and the government had to deprive the workers of much that they had gained by the expropriation.

A right-wing revolt had threatened in 1938, at about the time of the expropriation, when Saturnino Cedillo—encouraged, according to report, by foreign oil companies and by Nazi Germany—was suspected of fomenting a Fascist *coup*. Whatever the truth behind the rumors, it appears that Cárdenas beat Cedillo to the draw. Suppression of Cedillo's touted "private army" proved to be little more than a police operation.

It would be incorrect to assume that Mexico's problems were solved or the objects of the revolutionary movement entirely attained. Fulfilment fell short of aims, since the government was forced to operate under the handicaps of insufficient funds for the projects attempted, hostility of conservative Mexican elements as well as of foreign interests, sabotage by opponents, and diversion of funds to their own selfish purposes by ostensible supporters. But it seems clear that the revolutionary program (considered without regard to its basic virtues or defects, and without qualifications of approval or disapproval) made more actual progress under Cárdenas than ever before. He distributed more land, founded more schools, than any of his predecessors; reformed the party system to make it somewhat more representative; was, for a Latin-American executive, remarkably lenient to opponents, and initiated many of the vast and urgently needed public works envisioned by the Plan.

Throughout Mexico, I found considerable discontent. I

heard complaints that the armed agrarians were not careful whom they shot; that some local officials were as grasping as they had been in the time of Díaz; that industry and business were paralyzed by lack of foreign markets and by government interference with the economic system; that investors were frightened away by insecurity of title; there were still crime, disease, ignorance, poverty.

Some denounced the administration's policies as going too far; others complained that they didn't go far enough, or that promised reforms moved too slowly. But it was clear that Cárdenas himself was loved by the plain people. They liked his simplicity, his directness, his preference for spending time about the countryside, among the people, rather than in the Capital. He would go out to the adobe villages and sit down at the edge of the cobbles, and the townspeople would gather around him to tell him their troubles, as one man to another.

Back in his headquarters (so I was told) the president would call in a secretary. "See that a school is established at San Andrés; a water and sewer system at San Bártolo. Do so and so for Juan Pérez at Santa María, and thus and thus for Pedro Martínez at San Benito de la Montaña."

Lázaro Cárdenas didn't forget. To be sure, he couldn't be everywhere at once; he couldn't always be certain that the things he wanted done would not be perverted by local officials. But, for the most part, even his opponents admitted that he did his best.

Cárdenas (or Cárdenas and the group around him) as most Mexican presidents have done or attempted to do, in effect named his own successor. General Manuel Ávila Camacho, candidate of the administration party, was officially declared to have defeated his opponent, General Juan Andreu Almazán, in the election of 1940. Avila Camacho was pledged, with certain reservations induced by troubled world conditions and the advisability of placating the United States, to follow the general line of Cárdenas' policies. As he put it, his task was to conserve

Dark Wave

the gains of the Revolution and at the same time to promote stability and prosperity, and to accelerate recovery from the effects of earlier destruction, under which the nation was still suffering.

A Mexican of what might be called the lower middle class said to me, summing up the whole controversial situation: "Foreigners are too impatient with Mexico. Mexicans themselves are too impatient. A country that has first been ground down for centuries in slavery, then ravaged by decades of civil war, can't be rebuilt in a few years. Let us alone, give us time, and we'll work things out."

Many learned volumes have said no more than that.

II · The Gates of Mexico

This section deals with three principal approaches to Mexico from the United States:

First, by the west coast. This may be done in several ways; the route traced here crosses the border at Nogales and continues by rail to Mazatlán, which is considered, for the purposes of this book, as representative of the west coast ports; thence inland via Guadalajara.

Second, from the north, crossing the border at Laredo or at El Paso.

Third, the east coast approach, from the Gulf port of Vera Cruz.

All these routes bring us to the City of Mexico. A later section of the book branches out from that center to other regions.

V · FLOOD OF SUN

THE gates of Mexico are several. One must begin somewhere, and I know no better beginning than the enchanted West Coast.

All day our train moved southward over sun-scorched plains between low, savage hills, on which gaunt cactus-fingers pointed in mute prophecy to a burnished empty sky. The monotone of that dry brownness was broken here and there by shabby ranches that seemed infinitely small in the bleak immensity of the landscape, and drab little railroad towns where shawled women peered from box-car dwellings, and bare toes of children peeped between sandal-thongs.

So through the wide-spaced oases of more favored cities to the pearl-endowed gulf and the ancient port of Guaymas, dreamy beneath worn tawny mountains curving around a cobalt bay. The colors of those ridged slopes shifted with the changing light: mauve and rose and gold, deepening to lilac and purple, under an intense and polished sky.

Across the gulf, where the barren mountains of Baja California slope ruggedly to the sea, are the pearl fisheries that produced royal jewels for ancient Mexico and medieval Spain. Many tales of conquest and piracy cluster about that ragged shore, but none, I think, is stranger than one that was told me in Guaymas—the story of the Pearl Without Shame.

In La Paz, the tale runs, in the early eighteenth century, lived Doña Consuelo, only daughter of a Spaniard whose house is still pointed out in that "ghost town" on the bay.

"Beautiful she was, but pale—and she never smiled," related Don Guillermo, teller of the tale. "Men wooed her, and always she answered: 'If you love me, bring me a pearl.' For she loved pearls with a love that was a kind of madness, and would wear no other jewels. It was whispered that when the pearl was brought she paid as Pharaoh's daughter paid for the stones of the great pyramid of Egypt.

"There came a young prince—a prince without a kingdom: Don Francisco, descendant of a princess of Moctézuma's line who had married a Spaniard in the Conquest time. He wanted to marry Doña Consuelo. Unsmiling as ever, she answered, 'Bring me a pearl.'

"The prince had no money to buy pearls. But he was determined. He joined the native divers. Slowly, painfully, he learned to dive. He found pearls. But this one was irregular of shape; that one defective of color. He must have for Doña Consuelo the perfect pearl.

"At last he found two—one pink, one of a color unlike that of any pearl seen before or since. When he first looked at it, it was purple, and when he looked again it was silvery gray.

" 'Throw it away,' warned his Indian companion. 'It is a

leper pearl, accursed; a pearl spreading disease of pearls—a pearl without shame.'

"But Don Francisco kept it, separate from the other.

"When he returned to La Paz, he found that Doña Consuelo had married Don Severiano, a wealthy Spaniard. So he kept the pink pearl and gave her the accursed leper pearl. Big as a thumb nail it was, but evil. She wore it with her others, and the curse fell upon them, dulling their luster.

" 'The sickness of the pearls,' Don Francisco told her, 'comes from your own lost honor.'

"Don Francisco sold the pink pearl, and with its price he went into business, becoming a wealthy merchant."

"What became of the leper pearl?" I inquired.

"Don Severiano, the husband, crushed it and threw the dust of it into the sea.

"But they say, in La Paz, that the *perla sin vergüenza* could not be destroyed. The ghost of Doña Consuelo wears it at her throat as she walks, in her wedding gown, in the plaza on moonlight nights, weeping for her shame."

There are two opinions as to the wisest way of approaching Mexico. One school holds it best to plunge directly in, for the sake of savoring in all its fresh newness the sharp impact of the foreign life. The other favors a more gradual advance, allowing time in a comparatively neutral atmosphere to begin adjustment to these new horizons.

My wife and I chose the latter procedure, relaxing in the sun-drenched patios and vine-hung balconies of Playa de Cortés, just out of Guaymas, looking toward jagged brown islands over the indigo Bacochibampo Bay.

Playa de Cortés is a happy blend of Mexico and the United States, a luxurious American resort in a Mexican setting. Atmosphere within and without is Mexican; operation and standards of service American, though northern briskness must sometimes make compromises—as when the servants keep the managers "broke" by borrowing money. One of them had borrowed so much that the manager decided the practice had gone far enough and sternly refused the man's next request. The young man accepted the refusal without complaint. But, as he turned to go: "Please, Señor, may I pick flowers from the garden? My Jesusita has just died." The manager was so overcome that he gave the man a larger amount than he had asked.

The Playa is a famous starting point for expeditions in quest of monstrous fish. While we were there, no day passed but some tanned sportsman brought in a swordfish that looked as big as a boat, and the table never lacked deliciously prepared sea food.

For our own part, it was a place for lazy days, watching reflected light from the pool as it danced on walls of deep, cool balconies, and on surfaces of sun-umbrellas; swimming in the warm salt water, letting the sunlight of Mexico flood our being; absorbing rest and peace. It may be also, for those who do not adhere strictly to principal cities, a memorable contact with plumbing that works, salads that can be eaten without anxiety, and water of which one need not ask whether it has been boiled. Some regions of Mexico have not yet acquired the comforts that are commonplaces at Playa de Cortés.

The young boy at the desk looked very small and lonely as we went down to the shadowy lobby at one o'clock in the morning to leave the dim, silent hotel for the railway junction a few miles away. The hour, the silence, the strangeness of the vast, unfamiliar country coiled around us—and no doubt, too, the faint subconscious reflection of tales told by travelers in less peaceful times.

"I have a man to stay with me," he explained. "But—he didn't come to-night."

The car, guided by a silent driver, lurched through darkness over a rough trail, to halt in a big, dim open space at some distance from the feebly lighted station. Two muffled figures, shapeless under sarapes and looking prodigiously tall, suddenly materialized from the darkness at either side, and stood silent near the car.

The mysterious figures, still without a word, shouldered our bags and ambled toward the station. Our "bandits" were only hard-working carriers, trying to earn a few cents.

Again the way wound through desert spotted with scrawny cattle, ranchers in big hats, and women, their heads swathed in rebozos against savage sun, bent over rude brooms, sweeping the bare dust in front of earth-floored shacks, separating dust from dust that swirled in clouds around them. We wondered why they were doing it, if not merely for some activity to relieve the monotony of that arid life.

Indians at stations along the way offered gaudy baskets and blankets, garishly striped hammocks, innumerable bulky and tawdry souvenirs. Some of our fellow-travelers couldn't wait. They rushed out to buy at the first stop, returning loaded down with tasteless curios which at first they exhibited with pride and then viewed with growing dislike, as they discovered better things farther on, to throw their early acquisitions away in disgust before reaching the Capital.

And then, through a more clothed and fruitful country, to that jewel of cities, Mazatlán.

A promontory, terminating in a rugged hill, reaches seaward like a lion's paw between two curving bays. The water is of a startlingly deep blue; the slashed and furrowed and heaped-up coastline forms a magnificent scene, through which the sea-wind moves, wafting away one's cares.

On the slopes of the peninsula, and to either side, lies the piled, irregular, tinted town.

Business streets and the better residential quarters we found impressively clean. Men in sandals were plying brooms of coarse fiber; they were always sweeping Mazatlán. To the poorer streets, that straggled up precipitous hillsides, this organized service of neatness did not extend. Here, more informally, men and women stood in doorways, tossing water from earthen bowls or tin cans on to the cobbles, for coolness and for laying the dust.

Rain falls of course, at times, in Mazatlán, but I remember the city drenched with sun, from the time we awakened amid low, fluty conversation of pigeons on roof-tiles, to the hour when the far ball of red-gold fire plunged suddenly into the Pacific.

"You will be homesick for Mazatlán," said a teacher who had spent many years in the girls' school on the height. We often walked there in the late afternoon and early evening to look down on the huddled roofs and on the cobbled streets down which, urged on by a gentle hissing from their drivers, ambled burros loaded with charcoal for household fires.

The teacher was right. Although there are comparatively few "sights" in Mazatlán, the beauty of its situation and the general atmosphere of the place have an unusual appeal. We were to look back, often, with nostalgic affection, on its indefinable charm.

The easeful spirit of the West Coast ports conquers even North American restlessness. In many cities, especially in the nerve-tautening altitude of the plateau, most visitors feel they must be continually going, "using their time." In Mazatlán it didn't seem to matter whether we did anything or not; it was enough just to sit in the shade and watch life go by.

Of course one does become dutiful and rouse one's self at times. An absurd little *araña* cart took us up and down the seaside promenade, over the hill pierced with the hopeful tunnels of adventurers in quest of fabled pirate treasure; to the harbor on which the government had been spending many pesos, constructing a long mole made of huge concrete cubes that stood piled up like the building-blocks of a giant child; and to

FISHING VILLAGE, MAZATLÁN

the thatched fishing village that is one of the chief "points of interest" if one is not too depressed by its poverty and apparently complete lack of sanitation. The shacks, surrounded by a ragged barbed-wire fence, were crowded together under tattered coconut palms in a scene of picturesque squalor. Nets, hung to dry, made accidental butterfly designs; boats lay offshore or drawn up on the broad beach.

There are farther excursions, too: to islands in the bay or to palm-shadowed lagoons, for excellent fishing or for picnics, where Indian boys walk up tall palms to toss down cool, delicious drinking-nuts. And there are beaches: shell-strewn, golden with sun.

That sun beat down right mightily at midday, firing inland streets to oven heat. But in the arcade facing the Paseo Olas Altas, it was always agreeably cool, or rather of the mild, satiny temperature of warm air fanned into cooling circulation. It was pleasant to sit there, looking out at the ever-fresh beauty of the Pacific, which in season piles against the sea wall the high waves that give the street its name; or to watch the varied human procession—for the Olas Altas is a favorite promenade in late afternoon or twilight hours.

It would be peaceful there, were it not for the swarm of bootblacks persistently importuning, and the equally annoying vendors of small, misshapen pearls, picture post-cards, belts and purses of alligator hide—which last, indeed, if one is interested in them, can be bought more reasonably there than in inland cities. Words make no impression on these pests. We learned, much later, a deprecatory jerk of the thumb, a sidewise and outward flutter of the hand, that deterred them somewhat, and a phrase in Spanish, "God will reward you," that seemed unaccountably to satisfy the beggars that infested other cities.

Over dull-red roofs the Temple of the Immaculate Conception lifted blue-tiled towers whose color changed glowingly as day advanced, through a dazzling scale of jewel-like tones.

Pattern of Mexico

Black-shawled women prayed silently in the cool, dim interior, beneath the inscription: "For thy crown, the emeralds and rubies are all our tears."

Mazatlán was as good a place as any in which to become accustomed to the atmosphere of a Mexican city: the differences in everyday custom that are the breath and spirit of a country and of a people. The grayish cubes of imperfectly refined sugar; the leisurely pace of life, with the day split into two parts by the noon siesta and meal hours on a later schedule than with us; the vendors of food and soft drinks in the streets —a Mazatlán specialty is fresh oysters in the shell; the huge burdens carried on the head, with the quick, catlike Indian walk; the bread-peddler kneeling at door after door with the broad tray balanced on his skull—and all the other sights and sounds that mean Mexico.

The West ports: Mazatlán, Manzanillo, Acapulco. Although each has its individual character, all have certain qualities in common: beauty of natural scene, Old World atmosphere, tropical ease. The principal distinction of Mazatlán is its relative neatness; Manzanillo and Acapulco, farther south, are somewhat more unkempt, more dilapidated, and hence, in the sightseer's vocabulary, more "picturesque."

But from each the slanting palms beckon to sun-embraced beaches, between eroded mountain and amazingly blue, crisply ruffled sea. And the country roundabout is redolent of warm, heavy fragrances of earth and growing things, murmurous with surf and the voices of gaudy hot-country birds. The ports are places in which to rest uncounted lazy hours in caress of sun or shade and soft sand; to watch spear- and net-fishermen on sable rocks; to dip into coolness of sea by night when the moon irradiates the curling surf. Places to sit of afternoons under the arcades, sipping beer and watching the pageant of passing life.

San Blas, in the state of Nayarit, south of Mazatlán, was one of those ports in Colonial times, when Fray Junípero

PALMS SLANT SUNWARD ALONG THE STRANDS OF INDIGO BAYS
IN MEXICO'S WEST COAST PORTS

Flood of Sun

Serra planned there his expedition to California, and the founders of San Blas, according to local tradition, cast bells for the California missions. Few go now to that all-but-forgotten port, save for a history-minded pilgrim now and then who makes his way to the ruined monastery that looks drowsily toward the sea.

Too few visit Colima, that palm-bowered, gardened city of color, inland from Manzanillo. It lies in the shadow of its tall volcanic peaks, and the scenic tropical mountain country around it is one of the most spectacular regions of Mexico. It may be reached by rail either from Manzanillo or from the more inland city of Guadalajara.

Don Ángel, who manufactured candy of appallingly poisonous appearance, was quite agitated as we sat in an outdoor café overlooking the bay of Mazatlán.

"I have just heard," he reported, "of an incredible barbarity. At Chametla, not far from here, is the first church ever built in the state of Sinaloa. It was from Chametla that Nuño de Guzmán explored the Pacific coast. There was found recently at Chametla a bell which had been on one of Guzmán's ships, the *Santo Juan Nepomuceno*—and that bell was cast in Spain in 1442—half a century, mind you, before Cristóbal Colón discovered America. And would you believe it, a boy sold the bell for sixty centavos as old iron!"

It was Don Ángel who told me the story of the bandit Marcos Díaz, who flourished in the mountains behind Mazatlán some years ago.

"The Comandante," he related, "sent word to Don Marcos to come to town and surrender. The bandit replied, 'Come and get me.'

"The Comandante was a clever man. He arrested the bandit's mother, grandmother, and four children. Then he sent word that he would shoot one of them each day until Don Marcos surrendered.

"So Don Marcos rode into town and gave himself up. Preparations were made to shoot him—courteously, of course, and with all due ceremony. The Comandante confessed that he hadn't really intended to shoot Don Marcos' grandmother. And Don Marcos, on his part, was such a frank and engaging fellow, and the Comandante so pleased with his own strategy, that they didn't shoot the bandit, either. He confided that banditry hadn't been paying very well of late, and he was tired of it and ready to enter some other profession.

"So Don Marcos was pardoned, and got a job with a mine owner, carrying the pay-roll from the bank to the mine. He was especially qualified for such work. Wasn't he accustomed to handling large sums of money, and in fact, hadn't he often robbed that very pay-roll!"

"How did he get along on the new job?"

"Splendidly, the last I heard. Don Marcos was such a great *bandido,* and had such a reputation, that the pay-roll was quite safe in his care. All the other *bandidos* were afraid to touch it."

VI · NOBLE AND LOYAL CITY

THE "Noble and Very Loyal City of Tepíc," as a
king of Spain entitled it in 1811, has, apart from its
bold mountain setting, little to attract any visitors
save those who wish, as I did, to enjoy for a time the atmosphere of a Mexican provincial town.

Around it, brown mountains pricked with sparse green
change with the hours to lavender, mauve, écru, and indefinable shades. Towering above it, the ancient volcano Sangangüey lifts its shattered bowl to the golden cascade of the
sun.

The cobbled streets slope downward from either side to a
row of flat slabs in the center. Those streets are gracious in the
late afternoon, when the declining sun mellows the faded blues

57

and pinks and dull reds of the low houses; citizens with sarapes flung jauntily over their shoulders stroll or loaf in the plaza; sidewalk merchants do a desultory business in cigarettes, candy, and soft drinks; there is laughter of children's voices; trees are lyric with bird song.

The huge, arcade-bordered main plaza is adorned with the usual monuments to the inexhaustible supply of revolutionary heroes. Fronting it, the plain dignified façade of the cathedral lifts graceful twin towers, in which the bells are rung by climbing up and tipping them by hand. Roundabout the city are numerous smaller plazas, where women come for water, to the choiring of the birds.

Street musicians, four or five to a group, carry stringed instruments and voices from *cantina* to *cantina*, singing for a free-will offering or a stated fee. *Mariachis*, as these minstrels are called, affect gay jackets embroidered with designs such as the Mexican eagle, and low-crowned sombreros banded with tooled leather and sometimes embellished with silver ornaments.

The stranger often imagines that all *mariachi* songs are "folk songs." They are, in the sense that they are a popular song literature somewhat similar in origin and purpose to our own. When I inquired by whom these songs were composed, the answer was, *"Pues, por todos"*—by everybody.

From all sources—radio, recordings, cinema—the strolling musicians collect what suits their fancy, perhaps remolding it to their own taste. Occasionally a talented *mariachi* composes a song. Not all of them become a permanent folk expression. A few go on year after year: "The Four Fields" and "Rancho Grande"—both, I was told, composed in Tepíc—probably will always be sung. But many songs change with the seasons, as the public and the musicians themselves tire of them. These are permanent only as a type, in which *amor* and *pasión* rime with *flor*, *dolor*, and *corazón*, like the "moon, croon, spoon" of their counterparts in the United States.

MAIN PLAZA AT TEPÍC

Noble and Loyal City

It is the *mariachis,* more than anything else, that impart an air of gaiety to the West Country towns. Somehow one feels that where there are music and singing in the streets, life can not be all poverty and sorrow and grime.

I enjoyed Tepíc: its daily life, unexciting but tranquilly agreeable, full of little sights and sounds that make up the aroma of Mexico. Even the hotel, primitive as it was in some respects, became a homelike, friendly place. Like most Mexican provincial hostelries, it had an unimpressive façade, indistinguishable from other buildings in the street save that its massive door stood open until midnight when others were barred. Through that doorway, into a very large patio, a train of burros trotted each morning with fuel for the kitchen fires. Plants in green-painted kegs stood about. One had to be watchful in leaving the shelter of inner balconies to cross the open space, for the maids hung wet mops over upper railings to drain, leaving them to drip grimily on to the tiles below.

The fare, in the alcove that served as dining-room, offered no cause for complaint. At every breakfast eggs, steak, and *frijoles* ("seven times," as Pancho the waiter boasted, "re-fried"). Each noon and evening, choice of steak or chicken, excellent *tacos,* and again and always, the seven-times-refried black beans.

My room was large, high and bare, with one barred window set like an embrasure in a wall four feet thick; tiled floor, blue and white plastered walls, and a heavy door with an ancient Spanish lock so complicated that the first night I had to call the porter to let me in. Later I learned that the lock meant little, since the maid, after cleaning the room, always left the key in the door.

The bars may have kept out night prowlers, but they were no discouragement to mosquitoes. I believe it had never occurred to the host that a guest might want to sleep with the wooden shutter open.

59

Pattern of Mexico

The Calle de Vera Cruz, in Tepíc, might well be called, in its outer blocks, the Street of Sewing Women, for nearly every open door disclosed one or more women bending over the machine known in that country as "Seeng-gair."

The cobbles fail; a road, ankle deep in dust, leads upward, between walls of broken adobe above which bananas wave tattered fronds, to the Temple of the Holy Cross: a humble chapel, whose blackened walls enclose an interior shabbily redecorated in blue and gold, opening upon a garden court where pigs browsed, and a dog lay across the worn threshold.

The miraculous Cross of Grass occupies the center of a small plot of ground enclosed in a high, pink-plastered wall and separated from the church interior by an iron grille, before which women kneel in mute adoration, candles burning at left and right.

It is a bit disappointing, at first, this dry figure of herbage, faintly cruciform, with traces of pious spadework trenching its outlines—but when one reflects upon the faith that has clustered around it these four centuries and more, the innumerable knees that have pressed the worn pavement before it, one must admit that in the lives of these humble and devout people it stands for something.

A naked electric bulb on a long cord hangs over it, and ragged paper decorations cross the little court.

Señor Sánchez, my host, told me the story, somewhat apologetically but with evident belief.

"On the night of May second, 1540, a friar, weary with journeying, lay down to rest on a barren hillock. When he awoke, zacate grass had grown, in the form of a cross, where his body had lain and where he had stretched out his tired arms. Since this was clearly a sign from heaven, a chapel was built around the cross of grass. It has been venerated ever since, and many miracles are attributed to it.

"At the time of the Revolution, soldiers pastured their horses there, thinking to destroy the cross. The horses cropped away all the grass—but next day the cross reappeared exactly as before."

Lettered roughly across the ruined wall of an adjoining structure which was evidently a part of the church or of a connected monastery, I read the words: "50th Battalion of Cavalry."

A clatter of firecrackers and bells awoke me on the first of May. This date was celebrated as International Labor Day with as much *éclat* as the somewhat frowned-upon labor movement of Tepíc could muster. Breakfast was a matter of snatch as snatch can, and the hotel was tidied up in haste such as I had not seen before in all my stay. Men appeared with huge red flags, and the help marched off to the parade.

The market was busy, with unusually varied sarapes on early morning shoulders. Women thronged the place, carrying large baskets on rebozo-wrapped heads. The town, except for the public market, was closed up; even the doors of *cantinas* were barred. The procession moved down the narrow main street: red flags, platoons of teachers marshaling files of children; girls in white uniforms with gilt buttons; squads of workmen from the various unions; young women with sunshades; men in shining new sombreros; bugles, drums.

They moved to the plaza, where faulty or poorly adjusted loudspeakers translated into squeaks and squawks what no doubt were eloquent speeches.

"How many did they kill in Chicago?" inquired Don Jesús, who stood beside me, as the last speaker finished in a burst of crackling oratory.

"In Chicago?" For the moment I was at a loss.

"Yes, in 1886. That's what they are protesting to-day."

I had forgotten the "Haymarket massacre," as have most people, though it is one of the things every American should know. I certainly hadn't expected to be reminded of it in Mexico.

Pattern of Mexico

There could be no thought of the midday Mexican dinner for some time, as all the hotel help was assisting in the ceremonies. Don Jesús tilted his head toward the door of Don José's *cantina,* discreetly ajar.

"It is forbidden—but he will give a present to the chief of police. They are good friends."

At the tables sat a group of hotel guests and a few townsmen. Manuel the bartender had a black eye.

"Last night he said, 'To hell with the unions,' and the chief of the *sindicato* let him have it. Better watch out, Manuelito!"

Don Pablo, the salesman from Guanajuato, exhibited a broken watch crystal. "The watch got drunk," he explained. And from that moment he kept pace with the afternoon-long procession of beer ordered by other patrons, matching drink for drink with double jiggers of tequila mixed with orange soda-water.

A musician entered—no *mariachi,* this Don Gonzalo, but a wandering soloist, jaunty in white shirt and cream-colored trousers; lean, nervous, sensitive, with the haunted look of a poet in his delicate face. Unpacking a large pearl-inlaid guitar, he planted a foot on a chair. Head tilted back, eyes half closed, his long hands stroked the strings with a ready artistry, as his voice soared with an ecstasy foreign to the casual air of the *mariachis.*

He shook his head to a proffered drink. His intoxication was no vulgar thing of the juice distilled from the agave, but a diviner drunkenness, proceeding from the wine of poetry and song. Only at the end of the afternoon did he step to the bar, and even then it was a gourd of water that he lifted to his lips.

He accepted five pesos for twenty songs. The recital began. The *Patrón* and his bartender joined us; bystanders crowded about; all business was suspended. Toward the end even Pancho, the hotel waiter, shambled in to sit in silent fascination.

Song after song glided forth as the afternoon mellowed

RUINS OF MONASTERY AT SAN BLAS, STATE OF NAYARIT

away: full of the tropic splendor and haunted longing of Mexico—songs of *"pasión"* and *"amor,"* of far places, of the bull ring; chants of the Yaqui and Mayo tribes; a Mexican "Prisoner's Song": "Last year you loved me—that was a year ago."

He paused to rest. Don Pablo took the guitar gently from his hand and sang, his dark eyes dancing, a song of his beloved Hill of the Frog.

A group of *mariachis* entered, drawn by the sound. Don Gonzalo, who had recovered his guitar, laid it aside with an air of grave boredom, as if to say: "What have I in common with these mere street musicians?" Their merry music, however, softened his stern mood: a little later he seized his instrument and called to them to give him the chord for "Jalisco." After that they alternated, while the afternoon drifted away on waves of song.

The *mariachis* pocketed their tips and left; Don Gonzalo put away his guitar; Don Pablo drained one more fiery draught, and we crossed the street to Pancho's fried chicken and *frijoles*.

"What were you celebrating to-day?" I inquired.

Pancho had no idea. "The *sindicato* told us to march," he replied. "It was a grand demonstration. Very pretty, wasn't it, señor?"

VII · MOONLIGHT IN IXTLÁN

THE mixed train rattled through the midnight from Tepíc into the little station of Ixtlán del Río. The swineherds in the slatted cars forward were asleep in gunnysack hammocks, swinging to the motion of the train, above their snuffling charges. The crammed Pullman was dark; the lighted first- and second-class coaches bulged with passengers and luggage—crates, baskets, bales, bundles, huge melons, square and round bottles of tequila.

Swinging to the ground, I made off in the direction of shouts that indicated the whereabouts of Ixtlán's only "taxi." It was a battered "fordito" (or "fotingo," as the word is sometimes rendered), manned by two ragged, barefoot boys. The eight of us who were passengers for Ixtlán wedged ourselves in, perching on one another's laps. One boy piled the luggage on the hood; the other tied the door shut with binder twine.

"*Se cierra automático,*" he remarked—it shuts automatically!—and a wave of laughter arose from the packed humanity inside.

His companion cranked laboriously by hand; the car sputtered and we lurched down the cobbled road, stopping every few yards to retrieve the baggage from the dust alongside.

There is a feeling of mystery and adventure about entering an unknown foreign town at night. Streets that may be prosaic enough in sunlight gather romance with the shadows; one speculates on what secrets may lie concealed in the dark alleys, what possible perils may lurk under the trees that bulk so much larger and darker than by day.

In the jammed *fordito,* I was cozily compressed between a plump Mexican woman and a traveling salesman who was spreading that which is alleged to be next to godliness. I had seen his posters in every town on the line, proclaiming in correct Castilian that assorted motion-picture stars used no other soap than the brand which he purveyed.

The Mexican woman chattered along as if we were not strangers at all. I was a Norte Americano, no? Ah, she was *muy simpático* to North Americans. Her sister had married one, and lived in Phoenix, Arizona; I had been in Phoenix, no doubt? Truly, *los Estados Unidos* was a great country. She was on her way to visit another sister in Jala, a cactus-hedged village a few hours' ride across the dusty plain from Ixtlán.

Lights of the town bloomed dimly and infrequently, scarcely illuminating the cobbles over which we rocked, to the imminent peril of decrepit tires. We groaned around a dark corner and stopped before a blank wall like a fortress, whence issued no ray of light.

The driver battered at the heavy door; the hollow sound boomed in the space behind. A bent and shambling porter opened it only a crack at first, conferred in low tones with the driver, then swung the great door back.

Bustling about, he lighted a dim bulb. I stood in a tiled patio that was open to the sky. Flowering plants loomed in the shadows; singing birds stirred drowsily in suspended cages; a circular fountain—which, as far as I could observe, was connected with no water supply—stood silent in the center.

At Ixtlán they don't ask you whether you want a room with bath. There are no rooms with bath. Without a word, the porter creaked open another thick door and ushered me into a large, bare, cell-like room, feebly lighted by one anemic lamp.

The single window, without glass, was set high in the yard-thick wall; it was crossed with bars, and a wooden shutter swung on warped hinges. In a corner stood a severe washstand with bowl and pitcher; on the floor beside it, a pail. The efforts of my fellow-traveler, the salesman, had not yet borne fruit here: there was no soap. A chair stood stiffly near the door; a ragged rug of indeterminate color and texture lay in front of a sagging bed over which was spread a sheet gray with years of futile laundering.

Above the bed, from a hook in the ceiling, hung a rope, its end looped in a noose. Probably it had at some time supported a no longer existent mosquito net, but at that hour, in those rather somber surroundings, it had a strikingly ominous aspect. Evidently, if a guest wanted to hang himself, the hotel furnished the equipment.

There was laughter in the patio when I mentioned this to my fellow-guests next day.

"Todo servicio!" exclaimed Don Manuel. Every service!

The hardship was more apparent than real. I have slept, for months of tropic nights, on a pandanus-leaf mat laid on a floor of pebbles; in a wooden bunk in the "fo'c'sle" of a sampan amid the fumes of a Diesel engine; on the counter of a Japanese store in a Hawaiian plantation village; I have burrowed, shielding my face from mosquitoes with a newspaper,

OUTSKIRTS OF TEPÍC, LOOKING TOWARD MOUNT SANGANGÜEY

Moonlight in Ixtlán

in the Barking Sands of Maná on the island of Kauai. There have been nights I have spent rolled in a blanket on the pilot-house roof of a South Sea ship, and others on a mat under a coconut palm on the broken coral of a Tuamotuan atoll.

In the cell-like room of the hotel at Ixtlán, then, I sank quickly into dreamlike unconsciousness until the church bells awakened me at six.

The patio looked more cheerful in the morning light. The flowers had awakened; birds skirled in their cages; their wild cousins chattered from the *arrayán* tree that towered above the tiled roof. Doña María, the slender, sweet-faced proprietress, neat in widow's black, was swishing—with that rhythmic motion that is the very breath and atmosphere of Mexico —a square black mop-rag, tied to a stick by one corner, over the tiles. (I asked once, in another city, why this apparently rather ineffective method of cleaning was so much in vogue. "They enjoy it, Señor; they enjoy the motion. And besides, it is the custom.") From the kitchen in the rear came the slap, slap of firm hands patting tortillas, to accompaniment of soft singing.

The toilet, as in most small-town hostelries of Mexico, was just off the kitchen, and, like most, it boasted modern plumbing with nothing to make it "plumb." It was flushed, I gathered— when any one thought of it—with a bowl of water from the concrete tank next door in which Rosita washed the dishes. Beside it stood an oil-tin to receive the torn squares of old newspapers impaled on a nail above.

The *señora* in the front room was ordering a bath. The bathroom, adjoining the toilet, was a cement-floored shower apartment, with a door that wouldn't close, under a roof-tank. The *mozo* was preparing to start the bath. He was setting up a crude ladder, up and down which, if I understood correctly, he would climb all morning, bearing bucket after bucket of water to fill the tank. The *señora's* bath would be ready by noon.

Pattern of Mexico

"The *camión* for Jala and Jomulco leaves at nine o'clock," reported Doña María, after a conference with the *mozo* and the *portero*. I learned, almost too late, that it left at eight. But the mistake wasn't their fault. Time has a degree of unreality in Ixtlán.

Slowly the kitchen staff got under way. The guests, and Doña María, sat at the neat table in the alcove. Rosita, plump and smiling, emerged from the kitchen, bearing on her flattened palm a high stack of tortillas, which she dealt off, with her free hand, like cards around the table. A boy entered from the street with a saucer of semi-liquid, cloudy-colored butter, suggesting, in appearance, some kind of axle-grease. This was evidently for my benefit, as I was the only foreigner present; nobody else had any use for butter.

Rosita, parrying thrusts of wit from the salesmen, distributed lavish plates of fried eggs, mutilated but tasty steaks, brown mounds of fried beans, and tall glasses of creamy milk. Doña María herself arose to serve a glass of it to her blind mother, who sat rocking in the patio under the *arrayán*.

Rosita unlocked the tall cupboard and brought out little brown slabs of sweet *ate* fruit paste, casually brushing ants from them as she laid them on our plates. They went well with the hot, strong, bitter-roasted Mexican coffee.

The boy whom I had sent, in precaution, to the bus station, returned, breathless. The bus was loaded, would leave "instantly." Abandoning my unfinished *frijoles,* to the evident dismay of Rosita and Doña María, I dashed over the cobbles to the bus. Though bare and hard, it was clean and smooth-running, under the management of the local bus-drivers' union. Wooden seats had been installed crosswise on a long truck. Passengers were already seated, surrounded by baskets, bundles, and miscellaneous luggage.

Off we plunged, between gray-brown adobe walls, over cactus-punctuated hills, and into a wide, flat-floored valley rimmed with scarred volcanic mountains. Clouds of dust rolled

chokingly across the brown countryside. The road became a
faint track over the scorched immensity of the plain; it petered
out, and the *camión* continued apparently cross-country, with
dust swirling ever thicker around us, like waterspouts at sea.

Hour after hour we jolted on; at last the driver, operating
seemingly by instinct, swerved sharply into a high, narrow valley shut between tremendous mountains, and clattered up to a
tall gate in a dense wall of living organ cactus.

A barefooted guard peered out, looked us over; there was
muttered conference; then the great gate swung open, to shut
behind us as we rolled into the adobe village of Jomulco.

"A senator and a deputy were killed at this gate," grinned
the man with gun at hip who sat beside me.

"Why?"

"Because they didn't like them."

"Was anybody prosecuted for the crime?"

"Pues no! It was the chief of police and the president of
the village who shot them."

The mud-brick houses lifted blank walls down a narrow
street. A small plaza opened out around a community house
decorated with Indian painting in sharp, geometrical designs.
Women with pottery jars on their shoulders walked erectly to
and from a fountain. A small, bare church pointed skyward a
whitewashed tower. One felt that here went on a life apart,
secret, and self-sufficient. Behind the cactus hedge and the
barred gate, these people held fast to an ancient heritage,
rifles under the low roofs kept oiled against any threat from
the great hostile world outside.

In a field beyond the gate, an ox was dragging a log, to
scratch the soil.

Jala was practically continuous with Jomulco, but subtly different—more pretentious, a Mexican rather than an Indian
town, more like a miniature copy of Ixtlán. Flowers bloomed
in the plaza; in a neglected garden behind it rose a mellow-
walled old church in whose cool, dim interior shawled women

were praying aloud beneath a copy of Murillo's "Assumption of the Virgin" and a lurid painting of Saint Sebastian pierced bloodily with arrows.

Everywhere were women; praying in the church, winding to and from the well. Were there no men in Jala?

"Later, when the rains come," replied one in the plaza, "the men will be here. They will plant corn, sugar, beans. Now they are all down near the coast, working in the tobacco fields."

On we lurched over rough tawny country to Ahuacatlán, that drowsed in noon heat around the dusty shrubbery of its plaza, where jacarandas dripped lavender bloom on scorched tiles.

Nothing stirred in the empty streets; the bandstand stood bathed in lonely sunlight; only under the arcades a few figures lounged. All these up-country towns were like that, but Ahuacatlán was even more so—silent, empty, as if in an enchanted trance.

In the deserted plaza, among flaming hibiscus and drowsy oleanders, a sign warned: "It is prohibited to cut flowers or shoot at birds."

Across the plaza a *cantina,* labeled "Foreign Club," was the only sign of life.

"No, we have no cold beer, only at room temperature. What do you expect? This isn't Guadalajara!... Points of interest? Only the volcano, Ceboruco"—and the barman indicated a scarred cone that thrust its tawny mass into the brilliant sky. "It's still more or less active; sulphur is mined in the crater. In 1870, it poured lava and scattered ashes all around."

That, I gathered, was the last time anything had happened in Ahuacatlán. There was little to see; at that hour, almost nobody with whom to talk. Weariness weighed heavy on me in the noon heat; I wandered into a cool, almost empty church, sank down on a wooden bench, and slept.

Nor was there much more to see, apart from the town's historical associations, at almost equally drowsy Compostela.

Moonlight in Ixtlán

From there, according to repute, started an expedition, in Colonial times, which penetrated as far north as the Columbia River. And the red stone church of Santiago is said to date from 1539.

"The king of the Nayaritos," revealed Don Aurelio, himself the perfect figure of a Colonial gentleman and as full of history and legend as his three mines were reputed to be of silver, "fled from the Spaniards into the sierra. Besieged there by fiercer tribes, he was killed. His followers hurled themselves into a barranca lest they be taken alive."

Thus began the story of the Lost Mine. For the seven officers of Francisco de Alvarado who married the seven daughters of the Nayarit king treated them badly and "destroyed the kingdom. So the guardians hid the royal mines.

"Don Antonio de Bazán y Caravantes, husband of a daughter of the last queen of Compostela, owned the hacienda Miravalles, four kilometers north of the town.

"Not content with his lands, Don Antonio sought gold, but God did not guide him to it. He lost his property in the futile search, fell ill and died. His widow and daughter were left poor.

"An old Indian woman, in rags, came to their door, asking food. They had little, but what they had they shared with her: a few tortillas, a handful of frijoles.

" 'I came,' she told them, 'to see whether the last descendants of my queen were charitable. Come, I will guide you to that which is yours.'

"She led them to a bent old man—Écatl, last guardian of the royal mines. They tramped into the sierra. With his staff he pried away a rock. He lighted a torch. The flame was reflected from a vein of gold three meters wide, its face shining like stars in the tunnel shaft.

" 'Touch with your hands,' he said, 'this treasure, which is yours—that it may bring you happiness and alleviate the misery of our brethren.'

71

"With the wealth from this mine, the family built the church and the city hall of Compostela. The pope, for such piety, made the place a bishopric; the king made the widow's daughter Countess of Miravalle."

"What became of the mine? Is it still worked?"

"Unfortunately, the vein ran out.... But we still have the church, and the city hall."

There was argument as we loaded to leave Ahuacatlán. A man with fierce mustachios, wearing white pajama *calzones,* was trying to enter the bus with a large pig. I gathered that there was no fundamental objection to transporting live pork by bus; it was only that on one ticket he wasn't entitled to so much "baggage."

The pig-owner appealed to me. I had no baggage. Would I take half of the pig on my ticket?

It would have been churlish to refuse so reasonable a request. I agreed; a murmur of approval sounded from the passengers, and the pig was loaded, protesting and dragging back with all his feet, into the *camión.*

"Ahuacatlán," apologized the youth who drove the bus, *"es triste."*

"No," I objected, loyally, "not sad; only *tranquilo."*

"It is a lonely town," he insisted. "It has no people."

But even Ahuacatlán, he admitted, as we bumped away toward Ixtlán, would awaken on the morrow into some semblance of life and gaiety.

"See, they have raised the crosses!" And he pointed where, on a barren hillside just out of town, the crude emblems stood like a leafless forest. It was a pity, he lamented, I could not stay for the fiesta. People would ride in on burros, or tramp the hot miles, from all over that region; from lost villages perched in the blue sierra. They would camp here, and ancient rites of Indian gods would mingle with adoration of a Christian saint.

Moonlight in Ixtlán

I grant freely that none of these towns is important. I mention them because they are typical of places in that region other than tourist centers, and because they were for me an instructive experience of the flavor of Mexico.

The plaza of Ixtlán was pleasant in the early evening—a plaza blessedly free of beggars. They go to the larger cities, such as Guadalajara.

"Here," a resident explained, "one is as poor as another. There is nobody from whom to beg."

Birds trilled from tall trees; children's voices tinkled like soft bells amid the hum of friendly conversation in the little park. The hill behind the church glowed a soft rose color in the fading light.

"Ixtlán," offered a man near me with a huge pistol at his side, as he waved an arm at the rampart of mountain that hedged the valley, "Ixtlán has strong defenses. If anybody comes"—and with a swift gesture he imitated the motion of firing a machine-gun.

Indeed, most Mexican towns seemed designed for defense —the buildings thick-walled and pierced with small, high windows like loopholes; the roofs parapeted. They are compact, these towns, as they were built to be in the adventurous Conquest days; the houses huddle together as if for protection against the vast, raw, wild New World.

In the patio, Doña María, more like a hostess in her home than an innkeeper, chatted brightly, striving to entertain her guests.

"I had Americans here once before," she confided. "A couple, not long married. They stayed three months. The wife could speak no Spanish, and when her husband was off in the mountains, among the mines, she ordered all her meals out of a book!"

Doña María brought out her little treasures: a tattered, discolored parchment bearing witness to the deeding to her family, in 1710, of the property where the hotel stood; a

73

medal of Our Lady of Guadalupe; a set of cracked porcelain, handed down through many generations.

"Have you seen the Tres Marías?" asked the engineer, at supper. "I have heard that they are more beautiful even than your Hawaii."

All I knew of the Tres Marías islands was that a penal colony was situated there, and this started a discussion of criminology.

"We have in Mexico," explained the lawyer, "no criminals by nature; only criminals by accident. Accident of social and economic forces, and of sudden passion."

"But no," objected Don Vicente. "It is also a question of principle. The man of strong character will not be affected by your social and economic forces; he will not give way to sudden passion." And the argument went on.

Later, the talk drifted to other subjects as we sat in the patio.

"I don't believe in ghosts," protested Don Manuel. "I merely tell you what happened. In my family's house in Morelia, a woman appears at midnight, wearing a long white gown. I have seen her many times. She doesn't speak; she only walks slowly through the room, and her face is sad.

"In a neighbor's house, an old man, night after night, would walk silently through the rooms. One of my friends, bolder than the others, followed him. The old man led him to a chimney and stood in front of it, slowly nodding his head—then vanished. Next morning my friend dug into the chimney, and behind the bricks he found thousands of pesos, where a former owner of the house had hidden them before he was killed by revolutionists.

"But I insist, I don't believe in ghosts."

Tale followed tale, as we sipped sweet, pungent almendrado provided out of a squat bottle by one of our company.

"You have heard," the purveyor of the liquor rejoined, "of the secret convent in Puebla. There were many such. My family owned a house in Mexico City, which opened into a hidden monastery. The skeleton was found there of a monk who had died in his cell.

"One night a young cousin and I went into the deserted chapel. It was a ghostly place, full of vague whisperings. We turned to run out—and the door closed before we could reach it. We tugged frantically at it. It wouldn't open. My cousin fainted. I tore an arm from a chair and battered on the door. My mother came; she worked at it from the outside, and still it wouldn't move. At last, when I was nearly out of my mind with terror—the door opened all by itself!"

"A friend of mine,"—a third man took up the thread—"was driving at night along old Lake Texcoco, near México. It was in the rainy season and several years ago, when there was more water in the lake than now. His headlamps lit up the figure of a man in *huaraches*, walking on the water."

Other anecdotes followed—stories of appearances of the Weeping Woman, ghost of Marina, the Indian companion of Cortés, who wanders at night through the streets of México, weeping in remorse for having betrayed her country, and in whose wake follows death; tales of the owl that is the hooting banshee of Indian towns in the sierra, and more than I can recall of mystery and sorcery and doom. After which, Don Manuel reiterated: "But I insist, I don't believe in ghosts."

One of the men brought out a little book of verses—delicate, fragile things like Japanese *haiku;* concise, thoughtful and full of sentimental overtones—exquisite, some of them, as a cameo carved from a peachstone. We passed the book from hand to hand, reading aloud in the dim light. The poems were his own; this copy was one of an edition of only six.

Music quivered in the open doorway—a band of *mariachis,* strumming frayed strings, singing in husky soaring voices out of the dark, strong, turbulent Mexican heart. Moonlight flowed in around the sarape-shrouded figures, around the soft, sentimental melody. We listened, while that sobbing, moon-drenched music fused with the mellow fire of the almendrado in our veins.

They ceased; we handed a few silver pieces to the blind leader and walked out into midnight Ixtlán—into streets smelling of pigpens and faulty drains but gilded with the full moon and romantic to the eye.

Singing, we stepped over the cobbles, avoiding by some sixth sense dark little heaps of manure and the nameless filth of the gutters. Don Manuel's rich voice struck up "Noche de Luna."

On we walked, street after street, song after song, in the spell of that haunted moonlight: "The Four Fields," "Adelita," "How far am I from the soil where I was born." Then "Borrachita," that marching song of the Revolution:

> "Little drunken girl, I go away to forget you.
> The general has called, and I must go.

> "Little drunken girl, I go to the capital.
> I would take you with me, but the boss said no."

We paused to admire the noble silhouette of the church tower against the moon, the severe classic line of an antique doorway, the chaste façade of an early Colonial house.

> "Now I go to the port from which shall sail
> the ship of gold that is to bear me hence..."

"Ixtlán," fulminated the man of soap, *"es un pueblo sucio, mugriente"*—a dirty, filthy town!

"For business, yes," amended Don Manuel, who sold German typewriters. "But for song and moonlight, no!"

Back in the patio, we let the last precious drops of the smooth, golden, pungent liquor trickle down our throats with slow, lingering enjoyment.

I do not remember all we discussed that night. These gentlemen of the road were cultured, charming, some of them

Moonlight in Ixtlán

with centuries of noble lineage running back to armored, besworded conquistadores. They were lovers of poetry and art, collectors of fine old things. Don Manuel inveigled from our hostess, next morning, for the equivalent of half a dollar, a cracked but, he maintained, priceless pitcher.

They spoke, not of sports and women and smoking-room anecdotes, but of the beauty of lost little Colonial towns like Ixtlán, of architectural jewels hidden away in obscure *pueblos,* of cherished works of great masters veiled in Indian churches —such as the Titian at Tzintzúntzan of the Hummingbirds, by the island-sown lake.

A glow of friendship spread through us, like the warmth of the almendrado that lingered so soothingly on the appreciative tongue. It was one of those rare nights of jest and talk, of laughter and song, that one remembers when "points of interest" are but blurred fragments in the mind.

We were all leaving in the morning. The handsome vendor of typewriters joked with Rosita as she leaned idle and smiling against the door-jamb, between sallies from the kitchen with fresh deals of hot breakfast tortillas; wheedling her, in the momentary absence of the *patrona,* to cut some of Doña María's hoarded private stock of special cheese.

They were all there in the patio to bid us good-by, and without a hand held out for tips: Pedro, the silent porter; Rosita, babbling of the infamous guest they once had who didn't pay his bill, but who "kissed Doña María"; the *patrona* herself, radiant with kindliness, in her spotless black; the aged blind mother, edging her rocker nearer the door to press our hands.

Doña María shook down a handful of little yellow *arrayanes,* dusted them with her finger-tips, and laid them in my hand. They were cool, fresh, delicately acid, the distinctive flavor of that country. The taste lingers on my tongue as I write—the slightly dusty, mingled sweet and bitter, faintly nostalgic taste of Ixtlán.

VIII · GUADALAJARA LIVES MERRILY

BETWEEN Ixtlán and Guadalajara the railway climbs
and twists and virtually leaps over a country so rugged
that, according to an early padre, it "took away the
courage of the conquerors." It is a region of dry, steep gorges,
criss-crossing and rocky, dotted with small trees and shrubs;
of precariously perched hillside villages and zigzag burro trails
—the "Barranca Country."

Along with the route from Gualalajara to Colima, the line
through the Michoacán lake country, and the Maltrata division between Mexico City and Vera Cruz, the Barranca region stands among the most impressive of readily accessible
scenic trips in the Republic.

At one place the track winds around a mountain ridge, with

Guadalajara Lives Merrily

steep cliffs rising a thousand feet above and dropping half as far again below, to a great wild valley. Again, the train glides over a desert of black, rough lava. It dives through long tunnels and deep rock cuts; it creeps along rims of chasms, where at one side, are still higher peaks, and at the other, an abrupt descent to the tropical foliage of the valley floor.

Over the Jalisco border, the way passes through miles of mezcal—a smaller relative of the giant maguey of the central highland. Its bluish, spiky leaves jab out of the soil all through this region. From this plant is distilled the fiery but smooth liquor called tequila, and nowhere more famously than in the town of that name—a rather bare collection of adobe houses dominated by the long bulk and tall chimneys of the distillery which is its only claim to distinction.

From the mezcal, comes tequila; from the maguey, pulque. Great quantities of both are consumed.

"En Guadalajara," said the man with the bullet-scarred cheek, *"se vive muy alegre."*

Just why one lives more "merrily" in Mexico's second city than elsewhere is one of those mysteries explained perhaps partly by such economic factors as fertile volcanic soil and mild semi-tropical climate. But since we saw so much poverty there, I suspect the merriment is largely a matter of tradition. West Coast folk are expected to be gay, and they try to live up to that reputation.

Guadalajara, Jalisco [the Mexican novelist Teodoro Torres has written], they are the undulating tapatía in the festal dance; the charro on his lively horse; serenades; smiling villages, fragrant of orange blossom, where girls have the color of ripe apples in their cheeks, eyes dark and dangerous, and where in mild nights, impregnated with perfume, guitar notes pierce the air, accompanying languorous songs full of promises of love and death.

Thus Mexico thinks of that city and its environs. And indeed, Guadalajara keeps much of its leisure and love of life from Colonial days when, according to a local historian, "people got up early in the morning, that they might have more time in which to do nothing."

Toward three in the morning of our first day in Guadalajara, we were awakened by music just around the corner— rich, lilting *mariachi* music that continued until well after four. Some young man was serenading his sweetheart before dawn on her saint's day, a custom abandoned in many cities but surviving in the conservative capital of Jalisco.

"I could have murdered them," gritted a North American woman tourist at breakfast.

"I hope the music didn't disturb you," the manager apologized to us.

"It's worth being waked up, for so beautiful a custom," replied Margaret, my wife.

Whatever the cause, and despite the beggars who blocked doorways of richly ornamented churches and exposed deformities from the curbstones, we felt here an atmosphere of joy-in-living that contrasted with the drab frontier region and the frost-bitten sierra towns.

There was laughter in the streets at any hour of day or night; the sidewalk merchants of toasted tortillas, deadly-looking fruit-juice beverages, and pyramids of roasted peanuts, did a brisk business among their sandalled clientele. Even the Indians from the country, sarape on shoulder and dusty, broken-nail toes thrusting out of worn sandals, showed little of the stolidity, not to say gloom, generally attributed to the peon. Their clear, dark faces lighted up in quick smiles, and their soft voices cracked simple jokes.

There have been occasions when Guadalajara could not escape serious moments. The conquest itself was no picnic, when, some four centuries ago, Cristóbal de Oñate founded the city in the valley of Atemajac, a few miles north of its present site. Within four months, the conquistador Oñate was dead

Guadalajara Lives Merrily

and his colonists fighting for their lives against the vengeful Indians whom they had dispossessed and enslaved.

From the port that is now Manzanillo, Pedro de Alvarado marched to the rescue and to his doom. The fighting was bitter in the dust of the barranca country, where battle surged back and forth around a hill. Fiercely rallying his men, Alvarado, as the tale is told in the city, saw Baltázar de Montoyo spur his horse to escape and hurried to call him back. The horse of Montoyo reared, crushing Alvarado, and the captain was hurled to earth.

"Don't let the Indians know of my misfortune," murmured Alvarado, as they lifted his broken body from the trail. They took him to Guadalajara—the old site—and he died there nine days later. So passed Tonatiuh of the Golden Hair, the right hand of Cortés.

Revolution after revolution battered the city, and its public buildings still look like forts, with walls in some cases twelve feet thick. Even in fairly recent years—

"I saw," said a man on a street-car, "men and women shot down in the streets in front of the churches" in the religious troubles of 1926.

"In this place," says an inscription at the market in the Hidalgo quarter, "was hanged, beheaded and quartered, on the twenty-third of May, 1812, by the Spanish despotism, the illustrious insurgent General Don José Antonio Torres, first chief of independence in Jalisco."

These and other currents of turmoil have surged over and past, leaving the "Tapatía" spirit of Jalisco little changed. In Guadalajara still, as the barber told me between unsuccessful efforts to sell me a dye, "life is contented."

"How you like?" asked the barber when he had finished. "O.K.?"

"Swell," I replied, in the vernacular.

"Swal?"" The barber was a bit doubtful. "Swal?"

81

"Yes, swell; that means *muy bueno.*"

"Ah, swal!" And he repeated it—a new *gringo* word for his vocabulary.

Especially in the evening, whether in the Plaza de Armas where plebeians sit on dilapidated benches munching toasted tortillas and listening to the dungaree-clad State Band, or in the smarter, less unkempt Park of the Revolution, frequented by residents of the better districts, there is a note of well-being that rises above the muttered plaint of the well-fed beggar on the side-street: "A charity, Señor, for the love of God!"

I took particular note of my favorite beggar, who occupied the same spot in the Calle Pedro Moreno every day. He was a benevolent-looking old mendicant, with Biblical beard and hair, for all the world like one of the saintly models of Rembrandt van Rijn. His dungarees were faded, but clean; from his neck hung a license, bearing a photograph of himself as he must have appeared wellnigh twenty years before, and official notice that Antonio ——— was entitled to beg for a living on the streets of Guadalajara. As I watched, he beckoned to a passing seller of soft drinks, chose a violently pink *refresco* and sipped it in leisurely enjoyment. He paid for the drink.

As in cities the world over, so here wealthy and poor live their separate lives. For the latter, the concerts in the plaza, the picnic in the Agua Azul Park, the local fiesta in the *barrio* on saints' days; for the diminishing privileged class, their social functions in private homes or at their clubs—more restricted to family, but otherwise not so very different from ours.

The cultured people of Guadalajara are smart, cosmopolitan. They speak English, French, or German, read world literature, dance to American popular tunes as well as to the folk melodies of Jalisco. Their homes may cling to Colonial type, or may be—and are increasingly—designed in imitation of the Germanic "modern" style. Occasionally some one tries to be "different"; a doctor in an exclusive district has a home in Japanese mode.

LOOKING ACROSS THE PLAZA TO THE CATHEDRAL, AT
GUADALAJARA

Guadalajara Lives Merrily

Life among the "better class" being, on the whole, so much like the life of that class elsewhere, the spectacle of the plaza and the market-place was more interesting—even with the continual annoyance of bootblacks inquiring *"Boleada?"* or *"Grasa?"* There is an army of them, and they seem not to realize—or perhaps they do realize, and make capital of it—that the most mirror-like shine is destroyed in three minutes by the dust that is prevalent at that time of year.

As the band plays, of evenings, in the plaza, one seeks an only moderately dilapidated bench, and sits looking across at the noble Plateresque façade of the Government Palace, at the oddly assorted architecture of the huge cathedral, or at the shop-populated arcades. The fashionable may be promenading in the green and neatly kept Park of the Revolution, where the benches aren't broken. But here in the Plaza de Armas, the humble of Guadalajara and the country roundabout gather in quiet contentment to enjoy the evening as they rest from the day's toil.

Simple people, living their lives in their own way, though looking much like the "bandits" in our movies.... "North Americans," said one of them who had been a laborer in the United States, "get their ideas of Mexico from the cinema. They think we are all bad men. I hope you'll tell your countrymen we are just poor, hard-working people trying to get along."

As we sat in the gathering dusk, a file of dark, wide-sombreroed figures, looking unusually tall in the dim light, with their sarapes swinging with the rhythm of their tread, marched in semi-military formation across the plaza toward the Government Palace. There was a purposefulness in their stride; I fancied the shadowed faces held a grim earnestness of expression.

"Agrarians," explained the sandalled man beside me. "Members of the Revolutionary Party, on their way to a meeting.

83

"People call them violent; say it was a mistake to arm them. But it was necessary. When the *hacendados* had arms and the people had none, there was no safety for a man's corn-field or his wife, no security for his life itself. An armed people is the only safeguard of liberty."

Only the girl in the book-and-magazine store was bitter. She had lived in the United States, and the relative abundance of the life she remembered north of the border had spoiled her for the poverty of her native town. When her parents' grocery store in a California city had failed in the depression, the family had returned to Mexico, and I gathered that they had looked forward to this repatriation. For her, at least, there had been disillusion. And now the restriction of immigration had been tightened. She couldn't go back to the United States, and she felt trapped.

"You should see where I live," she mourned, "on my wages" —and she named the equivalent of fifteen dollars a month. "What do the poor do? We starve!"

The man on the street-car to San Pedro confided that he, too, had found it difficult to become adjusted, after twelve years in the United States, to the slower pace of his native country. But he was more good-humored about it.

"In San Francisco I would pass, in the morning, foundations being laid; at noon the walls were up; here it takes six months to build a house. A handful of bricks are laid in a day.

"Make appointments with two or three businessmen in a day," he grumbled, "and you're lucky if you can see one. Everything comes before business."

Yes, he confirmed, Guadalajara people are poor; they count every centavo. Quite true, they charge tourists more. "You can't blame them; it's their only opportunity."

These two were the only people I met who would have their city different.

"Why is there so much blindness?" my wife asked a Mexican friend, who had lived all his life in Guadalajara. For it seemed there were more sightless people in that city than we had seen anywhere else.

"Are there many blind here?" was his reply. "I never noticed it."

They were so normal a part of the scene that their presence had never impinged upon his attention.

The state librarian, even as he mourned over the dusty heaps of worm-eaten ancient volumes—priceless, he contended —that lay in an upper room of his rambling old stone palace; even as he inveighed against the parsimony of a government that would not provide funds with which to save them, and as he supervised the making of a photographic record of this *"escándolo,"* confirmed:

"In Guadalajara, one lives joyfully."

IX · THE HAUNTED LAKE

THE road from Guadalajara wound between villages and ranchos walled with mud bricks, fields where oxen drew wooden plows, women washing clothes on smooth stones at the edges of streams or ditches—into a cup-shaped valley among haze-tinted mountains, and to Chapala by the long and lovely lake.

The shining motor-cars and buses from Guadalajara looked out of place in the simple village clustered around a tree-shaded plaza. Indeed, it is but a few years since an automobile was a rarity in Chapala, and the town itself is much as it was then. It is a famous resort for all the surrounding cities, and increasingly for all Mexico: a vacation retreat, a place of honeymoons.

The Haunted Lake

There, as in other towns, we saw life dividing itself sharply. Smartly dressed men and women strolled in the gardens of modern villas along the lake shore to right and left of the village, while the humbler crowd milled around the beer-booths and roast-corn stands fronting the public beach. The foreign tourists at the hotels—where a candle was set beside each bed at night for the hours when electric current was off—were, as in any land, a class apart from either.

The village, honestly and simply Mexican without the deliberately fostered "picturesqueness" of such places as Taxco, is scattered along the lake, around the tiny plaza, the small but clean market, the plain church. Apart from its rather recently developed tourist business, it is a fishing port, the waters off its beach forested with masts of boats, in a scene reminiscent of Oriental harbors. Nets hang drying in the sunshine; across the beautiful, shimmering lake gleam white church towers of the more remote villages, each with its special product —sombreros, sarapes, palm-leaf mats, and, always, fish. In these villages life retains the atmosphere of a world remote from the fevered haste of mechanized civilization.

Even in Chapala we found it largely the same. The motor-cars dashed in of Saturday afternoons, and out early on Mondays: the hotels filled with Mexican and foreign guests; Chapala went its way, paying little heed.

All day shawled women, with earthen jars on their shoulders and one arm curved up in classic pose, passed to and fro from the well, and professional water-carriers trotted under shoulder poles from each end of which hung a five-gallon tin.

Chapala was lovely in the morning, with the changing light on the wooded mountain and the broad lake; fishermen preparing their nets; the market-place astir with activity; the town tranquil, unhurried, looking out at the eternal mountains and legend-haunted water, absorbed in its own uneventful, placid life.

As day advanced, refreshment stands, musicians, vendors

of all kinds of knicknacks, picked up trade along the beach; vacationists from Guadalajara or the Capital sunned themselves on the broad sands or swam in the warm water; children pretended to angle, or teased parents for small coins with which to buy crisp-fried little *charal* fish, to be dipped in lime juice with pepper and salt.

By afternoon, haze curtained the mountains; they shimmered across the water like a mirage. And the sun dropped, red as a live coal, behind a scalloped sharp volcanic peak.

The man who had been selling ice water and little sweetmeats began to pack up his portable *refresquería* for the night. To watch him was an education in the amount of diverse freight a Mexican can carry. He hung his two buckets on a pole; folded a cloth over his tray, and raised the tray to his head; shouldered the pole; folded the stand and hung it on his other shoulder; then moved off, steadying the tray with one hand.

"Here is my country," said the ragged carrier on the bench in the plaza. "Chapala is a port"—waving a hand at the near-by lake. "It has, too, one of the handsomest railway stations in Mexico. It is true that no trains come here—since the company lost so much money that it gave up the service—but we have a very fine station.

"Chapala is very beautiful," he agreed, pointing to the great trees that domed over the plaza. "The branches interlace and make a canopy; in the spring the flowers fall and spread a many-colored carpet over the walks.

"In Chapala," he concluded with emphasis, reverting to the refrain I had heard throughout the State of Jalisco, "life is gay."

In the evening, young people trod the *paseo* over those flower-strewn paths; youths in clean dungarees or white cotton *calzones* and low-crowned sombreros with leather horseshoes worked into the straw; walking by twos and threes, clockwise

LAKE FRONT AT CHAPALA

The Haunted Lake

around the little square. Girls in their best dresses, in pairs or small groups, walking in the opposite direction. As they passed, one of them would hand a flower to one of the opposite sex, to accompaniment of subdued giggling; I noted, too, an occasional furtive pinch or pat.... On a bench at the far end sat a young couple, mildly and dispassionately "necking."

Chapala is frequented largely during week-ends, but I think one should stay longer and enjoy the charm of its daily life. Through the week, it is still a Mexican town rather than a foreign resort; the crush of crowds on the beach is thinned; one can rest or wander about the Old-World streets or sail on the lake to those other villages that know less contact with the world, or even hunt for the legendary secret gold-mine in the mountains, a gold-mine guarded by Indian ghosts.

For Chapala, residents told me, is haunted—all that valley, and the islands in the many-colored lake. "See that island?" said one. "It is the home of spirits of slain conquistadores."

Spanish ghosts, and Indian.... He told me, too, that the souls of the Aztecs lingered there when their god Méxitl bade the tribe move on in the migration that led them to the central valley of Mexico. "Those spirits glow by night in the form of fireflies in the marshes where the white egrets nest." Their sacred images, it is said, are still fished from the water of the lake.

All day the blind girl with the sweet sad face sat on the sand, unspeaking, clinking small pebbles in her hand. By their cooling, she knew when day was done.

X · "LITTLE MORNINGS OF JALISCO"

THE dungaree-uniformed conductor in Guadalajara seemed worried when we failed to get off his clanging, time-worn, but clean street-car at the end of the line. "Where did you want to go?" he asked.

"We're strangers," I explained. "We didn't want to go anywhere in particular. We just want to see your city."

"I am honored," he replied. "Make the round trip as our guests." And he refused the incredibly small fare for the return by a different route, winding through narrow streets with their Moorish-flavored houses whose open gateways yielded glimpses of flower-bright patios, cool with fountains, green with trees.

Guadalajara, like most Mexican cities, is compact, "small

for its size." One would scarcely credit that nearly two hundred thousand people live there, on the dusty plain between the low hills.

In the little plaza in front of the post-office, professional letter-writers, on battered Olivers, were reducing to typed lines the messages of the illiterate or the inarticulate. Until I saw them and their like elsewhere in Mexico, I had wondered what had become of all the Olivers, for the first typewriter I ever owned was one of those.

In the street behind the State Palace we marveled at the heaps of shoes. Shop after shop of them, overflowing into red and white and black piles on sidewalks; men and women trotting along under huge trays of footwear. In a country where so many of the people wear crude sandals, one wonders who buys the shoes. And let a visitor try to find one that fits a North American foot! All, apparently, are made to the same last: too short, a torture to wear.

The market in early morning is a lively place—its irregular streets, spotted with shade and sun, lined with booths dispensing stalks of sugar cane, fat green and yellow papayas, melons, grain, leather, cloth. Little outdoor kitchens serve hot food; strolling musicians wander over the cobbles; men with huge baskets on their heads trot between the stalls; dogs prospect among the trash underfoot; Indians sit silently around the monument in the flowered Paseo.

Pages have been written about the battered Murillo "Assumption of the Virgin" in the sacristy of the Cathedral, but little has been said of the eleven equally damaged and even more doubtful scenes from the life of Saint Francis, also attributed to Murillo, in the State Museum across the way, and the much better pictures, whether originals or copies, that hang there.

The museum is a venerable palace, of gracious Colonial architecture, housing not only paintings salvaged from Revolution-looted churches, but a haphazard collection of historical relics, natural curiosities, and freaks preserved in alcohol.

The director admitted that most of the works of art there were of doubtful origin, cast-offs from the great San Carlos galleries in Mexico City. But my wife halted before a painting dark with age: an angel with an arm about the shoulders of an old man—a work at once delicate and powerful, of infinite tenderness in the pose of the head, the weary droop of the sensitively modeled hand. It was obviously a painting worthy to hang in any of the world's finest galleries. Peering closer, she deciphered the almost obliterated signature of Francisco de Zurbarán.

As we admired the Spanish master's work and exulted in our "discovery"—for the local authority who was with us seemed as surprised as we—a young woman approached, without the shyness or the dignity of most "lower class" Mexicans. The click of high heels on too-small shoes betrayed the sojourn in the United States that had emboldened her and that impelled her to show off her knowledge of English by speaking to foreigners. But the half-Indian features, the rebozo folded around the baby in her arms, spoke of Mexico.

"Have you seen," she inquired, "the pig with eight feets?"

That, apparently, was the exhibit that had impressed her most.

Don Manuel, the polished Mexican salesman whom I had met in Ixtlán, had just been renewing the acquaintance, and was admiring the Zurbarán with us. As we answered civilly the remarks of this hybrid creature of vulgarity (for so he evidently considered her, this presumptuous peon girl), the aristocratic Don Manuel suddenly remembered another engagement.

We had read many pages about the Cathedral, that architectural crazy-quilt whose chief merit is its seldom mentioned but lovely stained-glass window-saints; but little apparently had been written about the authentic sixteenth-century church of

"Little Mornings of Jalisco"

San Sebastián de Analco, in a remote quarter of the city. The Asiatic-looking Indian angels, carved by converts in early Colonial times, are still in place on its stained façade. In posture and expression, in contour of limbs, they are startlingly like the prehistoric figurines that have been found in tombs.

There must be fifty or more churches in Guadalajara. We found them frequented mainly by women in black, heads piously veiled, on their pale faces a look of reverent rapture. Comforted, refreshed by that hour of quietness and beauty, they would pass into the street, dropping coins into the claws of the ever-present beggars at the doors.

The square-towered church of San Francisco, though fire-ravaged, was still beautiful. We never did see much of the interior of the dark and incense-fragrant Aranzazú, ponderously encrusted with gold, for a hideous leper always lay across its threshold. The doorway of Santa Mónica, with its twisted columns and straight-lined Plateresque façade, is famed throughout the Republic as one of the "jewels" of Mexico. It is dignified in its elaborateness, which contrasts effectively with the comparatively plain body of the building. At one corner projects a broken statue of Saint Christopher, in which it is said bandits once hid their loot, and to which girls pray for relief from loneliness.

"They pray to the saint for a sweetheart," wryly observed Don José, local connoisseur of Colonial architecture, "and by and by they pray to get rid of him."

Having so many churches, Guadalajara was building yet another, in the aristocratic quarter near the Parque de le Revolución. José Clemente Orozco was so interested in it that he took me, in a hot noon, to see it. Stone upon stone, a Gothic temple was rising, in that city of Colonial churches, to lift its delicate tracery against the sky. It was being built in the medieval way, by hand or with crude enginery—a work of dignity and beauty in subtly harmonizing old-rose and gray.

The huge, classic-columned Degollado theater was less impressive to us than to the citizenry, who look upon it with pride. But it has a certain overpowering heaviness of bulk.

A peasant stood gazing reverently up at Orozco's heroic historical and symbolic mural on the stairway of the Government Palace. All may enter there. But, in order to enter the rotunda of the University of Jalisco and study the modern allegory of the same master on its walls and flattened dome, we had to find the official who had the key. I shall discuss these works elsewhere.

An old woman guided us through long corridors and innumerable patios of the Orphanage to the chapel whose walls and dome bear still another powerful work of Orozco: his greatest, perhaps, in itself worth the trip to Guadalajara to see.

The five hundred orphans who troop through those arched corridors and flower-filled courts, the clean refectories and dormitories of the *hospicio* which Bishop Juan Ruíz Cabañas founded in 1803—they will scarcely know what these strange pictures are all about. The frescoes aren't for the orphans. The chapel services ceased when the government took over the institution. That domed and cruciform space is a sort of public exhibition hall, with a permanent one-man show, as Orozco commented with a smile.

As for the orphans, who sang for us more of those songs about *pasión* and *amor,* they are better off than they would be in their own homes, if they had homes. Little foundlings, picked up from streets and doorways, abandoned in some desperate hour of poverty or shame, all receive the name of Cabañas, after the Founder whose portrait looks down benevolently from the wall. After a century and a half, the good bishop must have rather a large family.

In the cavelike rooms of the glass factory in the Avenida Catalán, on the way to the suburb of San Pedro Tlaquepaque, quick little dark men were lifting molten stuff at the ends of long tubes, puffing it out with the breath until it looked like doughy soap-bubbles, and rolling it on a steel plate. Then they snipped off handles and slapped them on with tongs, tossing semi-finished articles into the sand-bed of a low-heat furnace to cool.

The sand, the manager said, was from Chapala; chemicals and coloring matter from Europe. The mixing and melting was a secret process. The effect of the famous Guadalajara "bubble glass," he said, was produced by a German chemical.

The workmen's skill was amazing, as they ran to and fro in that confined space, carrying balls of molten glass on the long tubes, without collision. Accidents, the manager said, were few.

"Oh, yes, our pottery is very strong," averred the young man at San Pedro Tlaquepaque, bouncing one of the stouter pieces, which I suspect is kept for that purpose, on a table-top. We had elbowed our way through a horde of snatching agents, each cajoling us to visit his particular pottery-factory, and had slipped into the cool patio of the one which does not employ these human mosquitoes. The young man admitted, as he bounced the "very strong" piece, that seven are packed to the half dozen, to allow for breakage in transit. From our experience, I am inclined to think even that is hardly enough. Tlaquepaque pottery is brittle.

Indians were mixing and kneading dark clay, then shaping it with clever fingers on a rude wheel kicked irregularly with the feet. "They have to fit the speed of the wheel to what they are doing, so a power wheel wouldn't do," the manager explained.

This foot-turned wheel, a rag, and a piece of metal to smooth the pot—there were no other tools. The piece must dry three or four days in shade, one day in sunlight, he said.

Other Indians sat on mats, painting with dog's-hair brushes dipped in colors mixed by themselves from earth. The brushes were held between thumb and forefinger and drawn away from the body rather than toward it—deliberately, surely, with never a false motion. A cactus, a man with a burden, took form: first the hat, then the load, then limbs and torso, all free-hand and from the inner vision, without model.

"This man," said the guide, "avoids faces, paints only figures. He designs his own; they are similar, but never alike. The men have never had any formal education; some can't write their own names. They are trained from father to son. There are few at work to-day, because it is Monday. Most of them get drunk on Sunday. They work when and how they please; they are 'temperamental.' They make designs more or less to order, but when there is no definite order they just do what they feel like.

"This man paints the outline, another colors it.

"The goods are baked once before glazing, and once afterward. That makes them strong.

"The Indians prefer to paint animals, such as deer, or vegetable forms, and also conventional designs. But our customers like the pictures of men with big sombreros, under cactus plants."

They worked without speech, without song, eyes on the craft, intent. We felt that they enjoyed it with an artist's consciousness of creation. The designs, debased though many of them are by trade demands, are good; these men seemed to have a natural sense of proportion and composition.

Outside, in the sun-filled plaza between the arcades of outdoor shops and an odorous and fly-spotted market, musicians were strumming, singing a merry song. From a booth a man offered us pulque. Across the way, one was "washing" lettuce in a tub of dirty water. Papayas, bananas, mangoes, vegetables stood in heaps of blending or contrasting colors. Meats, unidentifiable as to cut, hung, fly-covered, like fantastic draperies. At the corner stood the dilapidated bus that plies to the once far more famous potters' town of Tonalá. Pottery is still made there—mostly kitchen ware—but the best ceramic "sculptors," I was told, have been brought to San Pedro.

In a rear patio of a fine old house in a scented Guadalajara garden, men and women were operating hand and foot looms, weaving of violently colored wool and cotton—and alas! in these commercialized days, cellophane—curtains, rugs, shopping bags, neckties that sell for much higher prices in the tourist shops of the Capital than at their place of origin.

"The yarn," explained the young woman who admitted us, "is Mexican. At first we used vegetable dyes, but in late years, when we could get them, we have used German dyes, because they are more permanent."

The looms were of wood, the shuttles worked by cords with handles. Part of the web was lowered, part raised, alternately, as the thread was shot through. Some of the more complicated designs were woven in, thread by thread, with the hand.

"At San Andrés," she said, "they make blankets the same way, without a preconceived pattern, just creating the design as they go along."

The Colonia Penal of the State of Jalisco, in the outskirts of the suburb of San Andrés, looked sufficiently prison-like outside: its gray walls and squat guard-towers rose grimly from the dusty plain where a lone but optimistic organ grinder was trundling out, for no visible audience, the notes of the "Jarabe Tapatía." Once past the barred gate and bepistoled guards, however, we might have thought we were in a public park.

In a great fountained patio, with flowers all about, men were lounging, strumming guitars.

"It isn't their turn to work," explained the soft-voiced, gentle-eyed convict who was assigned to guide us. "We take turns working, by number, so many a day. There isn't work enough for all."

With pride he showed us the bakery where machines were

stamping out tortillas for eight hundred prisoners; the kitchen, with steaming vats of stew; mess halls, library, school, manufacturing shops, decorated with murals by resident artists. We went through the garden, where vegetables and fruits were grown for the mess; the foundry where convicts were forging their own cell-bars (a temptation, one would think, but our guide said the armed guards in the towers effectively discouraged escape.) There were cell blocks of varying comfort for various classes of inmates.

Outside, men with long strands of bright-colored yarn were weaving shopping bags and purses; others, with hand drills, were making cheap jewelry for sale to visitors. One trusty, who spoke a little English, followed us persistently with a rug he had made in his spare time, and a sad story about wanting to send the money to his wife and family in the United States.

"I got in a jam," he told us. "I hit a man—too hard."

Over the door of the theater and social hall, a placard read: "We can not announce the title of the film, as we have not received it, but we expect some advertising very soon."

"Every week we have movies, and on feast days a dance," the guide explained. "Our friends and relatives come—and our sweethearts."

"Not a bad life," I commented.

"It's very nice," he admitted. "But I like it better outside."

"What was your crime?"

The big brown eyes looked frankly from the open brown face; the white teeth showed in an unembarrassed smile.

"I killed a man," he answered, with evident pride. "I shot him here . . . and here . . . and here."

At Juanacatlán, the Río Santiago leaped in a wide horseshoe fall over the rocks, turning the wheels that generated light and power for Guadalajara. When the rains came, people said, the torrent would hurl great clumps of uprooted blue water-flowers to the pools below, to the delight of wading pigs. Little terraced truck farms clung to the steep sides of the

ALONG THE RIVER AT CÓRDOBA

"Little Mornings of Jalisco"

Barranca de Oblatos, a wild gorge of ferns and flowers. . . .
The tram jolted over uneven rails, past the "futbol" field and
the brick kilns, to Zapópan, with its monastery from whose
eaves projected rainspouts shaped like guns and its seventeenth-century tile-domed church with rich façade and the doorway that the director of the state library had described, with
a connoisseur's appreciation of the Colonial, as *"preciosa."*

Back in Guadalajara the leper still sprawled across the
threshold of the Chapel of Our Lady of Aranzazú. The para-
lytic still moaned unintelligibly under the orange trees in the
atrium of Jesús María. The girl with the open wound gaping
in her side still lay on the sidewalk in the Street of the Sixteenth of September, and the blind one, who never spoke,
waved a soiled hand before her useless eyes. The dust of the
last weeks of the half-year dry season swirled up and smote
us, laying us low with the influenza from which our physician
said ninety per cent of Guadalajara had suffered that winter
and spring, and the old plague of visitors in the southern Republic, the embarrassing intestinal malady described euphe-
mistically as "Mexican toothache," fastened its fangs in our
viscera.

("Have you had the great Mexican ailment?" inquired the
bureau chief of the Associated Press, later, in the Capital.
"Yes, several times." "Then you're qualified; you can write
about Mexico.")

We struggled up, relapsed. It seemed we would never gather
enough energy to leave Guadalajara. At last, by sheer force
of will, we staggered to the train, to awaken next morning in
the cleaner air of Mexico City.

But these mishaps are not the things one remembers oftenest
of Guadalajara. One remembers cool soft evenings in the
plaza; the humble folk nursing their simple pleasures while
the band plays unrecognizable, undistinguished tunes; sweet

Pattern of Mexico

serious faces of little girls walking with black-shawled mothers in the Jardín de San Francisco, and the lovely light on the soft-tinted venerable stones of the church across. One remembers the street-stands with cucumbers cut in fancy shapes and sprinkled with red chile; the markets with tropical fruits; the water-men carrying covered pails like slop-jars, vending ice water tinctured with a trace of lime juice, and dousing the one glass in another pail, to the soaring cry, *"Agua helada!";* the *tostada*-vendor dropping the crisped corn-pancake on the sidewalk and quickly restoring it to its place on his tray; the bright shopping-bags carried by many of the men; chime of bells in early morning; musical cries of street merchants; the *refresco* cart with its sign: *"Toda persona decente..."*—"every decent person will drink *tejuino* to relieve the heat."

Above all, one remembers the unfailing courtesy of that gracious city where, whether in relative opulence, genteel poverty, or frank rags, "one lives merrily."

Lights bloom softly in the great square; shadows under the *portales* merge with evening; Guadalajara comes out to stroll in the quiet coolness, and from some side-street *cantina* drifts a *mariachi* song:

> The little mornings
> that I spent with you,
> while God gives me life
> I shan't forget...

XI · THE NORTH GATE

THE gates of the north, too, open upon desert, whether one goes by rail from El Paso through the scenes of Pancho Villa's battles, or by motor or rail from Laredo, through Monterrey, up the hunched shoulder of mountain and down into the tropical valleys of the northeast, and thence to the hub of all roads, the Capital.

Monterrey, the first considerable city on the way from Laredo to México, D. F. (Distrito Federal), is a brisk, bustling town of clean wide streets and modern buildings against a background of steep serrate mountains. Fresh arrivals from across the border were exclaiming over it as "so typically Mexican," and others who had seen more of Mexico were hailing it as "so American." It is a city of air-conditioned restaurants serving "typically American" food drowned in nondescript gravy; of liquor stores that are literally "sample rooms," where one sips cocktails "on the house" until, in a pleasant haze, one walks out with an armful of purchased ingredients which the proprietor asserts are imported from Europe, though bottled in Mexico, and sold, he insists, at one-fifth what they would cost north of the border.

Industry hums in foundries, smelters, glassworks, and an impressive brewery, vine-clad and huge in its vast park: all controlled, we were informed, by the "ten families" who virtually own the town and surrounding country.

As we drove along broad boulevards fringed with magnificent trees, past large, neat parks, to opulent residential "colonies," house after house was pointed out to us as "the home of one of the brewers."

Rivaling the brewery as a show-place, however, was the military post established by General Juan Andreu Almazán when he was zone commander in that area and had an eye on the presidency. The Campo Militar is a city of neat stuccoed homes where soldiers who formerly, as the guide reported, "lived like pigs," reside with wives and families, surrounded by flower gardens and luxuriating in such conveniences as running water, electricity, and artificial refrigeration. Officers and enlisted men have separate club-houses; both classes share an ample swimming pool. The whole place is a huge park. No wonder that, as one man told us, "every soldier thinks Almazán is his father and grandfather."

The shot-scarred ruin of the old episcopal palace stands, crumbling, on a dusty hill facing the Saddle Mountain which recalled the reputed remark of a hard-riding revolutionary general, on entering for the first time the National Palace in the Capital, that he had always supposed the "presidential seat" (*silla*) was a saddle.

We found Monterrey aggressive, modern. It glittered at night. Girls dressed smartly as in many a North American city promenaded in the plaza; there was not a recognizable Indian in sight. Fox-trot music throbbed from night clubs, into some of which, our driver informed us, "one can't go without a coat and necktie."

Although Monterrey seemed more motorized than any other Mexican city except the Capital; there were still horse-drawn *calesas,* whose drivers wanted the same rate as the autos. When I told one of them of the prices one-quarter to one-half as high in Guadalajara and Mérida, he replied scornfully:

"Monterrey is the richest city in Mexico. Don't talk to us about Mérida and Guadalajara. We are not hungry, as they are."

Yellow- and blue-tiled domes, great bells green with the weathering of centuries, rose above curving streets where Querétaro, farther down toward the Capital, nestled among the hills. Vendors thronged the station platform with opals drilled out of the surrounding mountains, and little round boxes of sweets.

Upon the city, with its crumbling relics of Colonial architecture, the weight of history rests like a heavy hand.

"When the Spaniards came here in 1531," said a resident, "the Otomíes thought their chances with bow and arrow against guns were not so good. So they proposed a fist fight. With fists, then, they fought all day, and the Spaniards won."

The dignified façade of the city hall bears an inscription that from this building the Corregidora Josefa Órtiz de Domínguez sent the warning to Ignacio Allende and Padre Hidalgo that touched off the revolution of 1810. On the floor of her room she tapped a signal to the alcalde Ignacio Pérez, listening in the dark below. A crystal casket in the Moorish-arched monastery, that has since become a government building, holds the lock through which she murmured instructions to the messenger.

On the Hill of the Bells, just outside the city, a brownstone chapel encloses three stone pillars that mark the spot where the Emperor Maximilian and his loyal generals Mejía and Miramón fell before the firing-squad of Benito Juárez. A melancholy spot, yet peaceful: the little chapel, the rocky hill, the clouds sailing over.

The streets of Guanajuato, ancient city off the main line from El Paso to Mexico, are narrow and steep, climbing in acute inclines and worn stairways the sides of a gorge. All about lie deep-chiseled cañons and tunneled mountains, whose silver built Colonial wealth. The richest mine is commemorated in the church of San Cayetano, every stone of which is said to have been blessed by the Holy Father, and the mortar mixed with precious wines. Every miner contributed weekly the value of a piece of ore as big as his hand. Silver and gold and carved stone run riot in its Arabesque and Churrigueresque interior.

Indeed, as the sacristan said, a vein of ore runs under the very church—and the Conde de Rul refused an offer to remove the church stone by stone and rebuild elsewhere that the vein might be mined.

Guanajuato seems to be most widely known, among foreigners, for its cemetery, where mummified corpses of those whose relatives could not pay for permanent interment stand in ghastly rows, more numerous but not more interesting than those to be seen elsewhere in Mexico.

A heroic story clings to the Moorish-windowed Alhóndiga de Granaditas, once a grain market, then a fort, and later a prison. When Hidalgo's rebels stormed the city in 1810, the Spanish royalists held out in the Alhóndiga. Without artillery, the rebels could make no impression on the thick walls and could not batter down the wooden door.

Then arose José Barrajas, nicknamed Pípila, a stout peasant who worked in one of the mines. Heaving up a paving stone or tile, he hoisted it to his back to shield himself from bullets pouring from roof and windows of the fort. Under it, he crept

A STREET IN QUERÉTARO

to the great door, set the door afire. The rebels rushed into
the patio. Up the stairway to the roof the fighting raged, and
when it was over, local tradition avers, not one royalist was
left alive. But from the corners of the Alhóndiga project iron
hooks from which hung for ten years the heads of the rebel
leaders Hidalgo, Allende, Jiménez and Aldama, until independence was achieved in 1821.

Celaya, not far from Guanajuato and Querétaro, is famed
for two things: the boxes of milk-and-sugar candy, *cajetas de
Celaya,* that are sold on the streets, and the memory of Francisco Eduardo Tresguerras, born there in 1765, whose genius
left its mark on the architecture of his own and neighboring
cities.

Architect, painter and etcher, sculptor, musician, poet,
Tresguerras designed and decorated here, among other buildings, the graceful church of Our Lady of Carmen, considered
one of the most beautiful in Mexico. It is simpler in style, more
integrated in design, than most Mexican churches, and its green
and gold tiled dome is a happy union of delicacy and strength.

Tresguerras, it is said, used to walk in the fields or sit under
a tree, playing a flute or talking with passing peasants. The
vagaries of an artist were forgiven: he was pardoned for having joined Hidalgo in the fight for independence. After that
movement had triumphed, he designed the monument in the
plaza of his native city which commemorates the event. This
is a column in front of the impressively ugly City Hall (the
latter not of Tresguerras' design), bearing an eagle whose
head is turned sharply away from that edifice. Sylvester Baxter, authority on Mexican church architecture, confirms the
local anecdote that when asked why he had designed the eagle
so, the artist replied: "That he may not see the barbarities
perpetrated by the municipal authorities."

XII · SAN MIGUEL THE "PRECIOUS"

Y OU must see San Miguel de Allende," advised the
director of the State Library of Jalisco. "It is
precioso."

"By all means don't miss San Miguel," echoed one after
another of the Mexican admirers of their country's Colonial
splendors.

We found the little town, between Querétaro and Monterrey, interesting mainly because it was as yet largely "un-
spoiled"; perhaps by the time this appears in print, tourists
will have discovered the place and made it another Taxco.

Its natural setting is less advantageous scenically: it is situated in a gentle valley, rather than among spectacular mountains; its streets, though cobbled and running up and down

hill, are less steep and winding. But it has the tiled roofs, the spires and domes, the authentic Colonial mansions tastefully restored in the spirit of the originals by modern artists and others who make their homes in the town.

"Few visitors come, as yet," said our host, Don Leofino, "because we are not well known. But San Miguel is better than Taxco: more Colonial architecture, fewer dogs, fewer drunken North Americans making noise...."

He indicated a sober plain-walled house in a descending street.

"That is where the Revolution of Independence started. The revolutionists had a 'ball'; the women danced together on the upper floor, and made noise, while the men went below to conspire."

For San Miguel claims a share with neighboring Dolores Hidalgo in the "cradleship" of the Revolution, as birthplace of General Ignacio Allende. It was also the post where he was stationed with his regiment when the Corregidora sent her warning from Querétaro in September, 1810, that the plan for the December rising had been discovered.

"The Corregidora's messenger couldn't find Allende, so he gave the news to Don Juan Aldama, whose house still stands here. Don Juan rode to Dolores and woke up Padre Hidalgo before dawn of September sixteenth. Hidalgo called all his friends together, and as soon as it was light they imprisoned all the Spaniards in town. Then he rang the bell, gathered the Indians in his church, and they marched to San Miguel to pick up Allende's soldiers.

"The man who carried the flagstone on his back and set fire to the door of the Alhóndiga at Guanajuato was also from San Miguel. Our city has been the home of many heroes. General Montés was born here.... And now we have José Mojica the singer, Pepe Ortiz the bull-fighter, and many, many artists...."

He showed us through his father's house, which was being

restored to its original Colonial beauty: disfiguring plaster was being scraped from walls of dull red stone. We admired the graceful arches, balconies, the fountain in the patio, the lamp in its wrought-iron frame.

"Tresguerras, architect of Celaya," boasted Carlos Mérida, "was inspired by the Colonial wonders of San Miguel."

The streets were neat: crews of men swept them early each morning. The running water in the open gutters was clean, though it made a trap for unwary feet.

The market was small but genuine, with its roofed platform opposite the hollow half-dome of a graceful old church; outside, crude umbrellas shaded merchants who had walked in over hot, dusty miles. Here were pottery from San Felipe and Dolores; heavy sandals of a peculiar local type, for walking on cobbles; woven fabrics of excellent quality in tasteful combinations of bright hues.

Early in the morning, bells sounded from the numerous churches: San Francisco, the floridness of whose façade is softened by the quality of the old-rose stone; the Chapel of the Holy House, with lanterned domes and intricately splendid interior; the delicate though elaborate baroque Oratorio; the graceful two-storied dome of La Concepción.

The pride of San Miguel, however, is the quaint psuedo-Gothic mask of its parochial church, one of few attempts in all Mexico to adapt that style.

Facing the plaza, the needle spires dominate the town from every point of view. Behind the many-pointed façade sprawls the original building, of familiar Colonial style: a typical Mexican church masquerading behind a false front that is reminiscent of the Rhineland.

"About a hundred years ago," related Don Leofino, "the people decided they wanted a new front on their church. An Indian stonemason, Ceferino Gutiérrez, took the job. A friend had sent him a picture postcard of a Gothic cathedral in Germany, and he liked the style.

San Miguel the "Precious"

"He drew the design in the sand with a pointed stick, adapting and cutting down the proportions to fit the job, and the workmen built it as you see."

Quite out of place, of course, but locally much admired. "The unknown artist," wrote Carlos Mérida, "without any wider knowledge of architecture than that inspired by his own genius, erected a votive monument full of the grace and elegance characteristic of medieval construction."

For sheer architectural beauty, the most harmonious structure in town is the old convent known informally as "Las Monjas," in recent years the home of a school of art.

The dome, on its two-story base, has been stripped of its gilding, but its beautiful proportions—also, I was told, the work of Gutiérrez—defy time. Below, stately cypresses shade cloistered patios; across multiple roofs rises a curiously shaped tower, surmounted by a bulbous dome.

A liberal portion of the convent had been given by the government—on the initiative of the Peruvian Aprista refugee Don Felipe Cossío del Pomar, who was abetted by Mexican and foreign artists—for the School of Fine Arts. Part of the building was still occupied as a military barracks, and in another corner a few of the "expelled" nuns could be seen, at times, from the roofs, strolling in their patios, as in official "secrecy" they continued their vocation. Soldiers, artists, and nuns, I was told, never interfered with one another, and the existence of the last group was considerately ignored—a pleasing evidence of humane amelioration of the letter of the law.

"An old lady," related Stirling Dickinson, "came to San Miguel looking for a thrill among the 'art colony.' Apparently she was expecting to see something wicked. She was disappointed; there were no orgies. The nearest she got to a thrill was when we boosted her, with some difficulty, up on the roof and showed her the nuns' quarters."

Dickinson took me to a tiny ruined church, on an eroded hilltop, that bore signs of current repairs.

"Indians," he explained, "come here after the day's work and lay stone by lantern light. I like that devotion."

A "Society of Friends of San Miguel," under patronage of the State of Guanajuato, has undertaken to "watch over the preservation of the physiognomy of the city so that none of its charm may be lost and its innermost aspect be not destroyed through the introduction of spurious construction."

For the sake of that innermost aspect, I hope they will preserve the *posada,* or lodging-house for pack animals and their drivers, near the market-place, with the handsome tiled sign in the entrance to its patio:

This establishment opens at five A.M. and closes at ten P.M. The management will not be responsible for any objects not left in care of the person in charge. Payment of the conventional prices must be made in advance. The management will not be responsible for confusion of mules or horses due to similarity of color. Entrance of public women and persons having no business in the establishment is prohibited.

XIII · RICH CITY OF THE TRUE CROSS

L A Villa Rica de la Vera Cruz," as Cortés named it when he planted the settlement on the sands in 1519, is of interest to-day chiefly as the Gulf Coast gateway to Mexico—a landing-place from which to go elsewhere—and, to the history-minded, as a place full of relics of the past.

A horde of officious *cargadores* descends upon one at the dock, to carry one's bags whether one wants them carried or not. Their business and their rates are protected by law: I read in the press, while there, of the arrest of a defiant tourist who insisted upon carrying his own luggage.

It is hot in Vera Cruz. A good share of the population seems to spend much of its time drinking beer and chatting in side-walk cafés under the arcades of the Hotel Diligencias and ad-

joining structures that front on the flower-and-croton-bright
Plaza de la Constitución. The visitor, unless he is unusually
energetic or a confirmed calophile, feels the impulse to do
likewise.

Indeed, the life of the *portales* is perhaps the most attractive
feature of Vera Cruz. The massive stonework shields one
from the sun, while the long rows of arches, aided by electric
fans over the tables, admit whatever breeze may wander in
off the Gulf.

Vendors saunter from table to table, offering combs and
other objects of tortoise-shell which they insist are hand-made,
despite the factory stamp plainly imprinted thereon; purses,
cigarette cases, and belts of alligator, snake, or iguana hide;
panama hats, cigars, objects of doubtful use constructed of
seashells, and many another knickknack presumably dear to the
tourist heart. Beggars, sellers of lottery tickets, blind musicians
behind dark glasses, boot-blacks, sailors from ships of many
nations, a few Indians, some of them showing traces of Negro
mixture—the whole life of the city drifts past.

It is gay and noisy with the mercurial atmosphere of the hot
country. Across the way, vultures blacken the roof of the
lamentably "renovated" white parochial church, with its tiled
dome: the church is uninteresting by day, but at night the cement coating fades and the noble proportions of the old edifice,
with its bold flying buttresses, stand out.

Little open-faced tram-cars, with the lowest fares I found
in Mexico, rumble through humble residential streets of
wooden houses painted blue, green, pink, or striped, and set
in riotous tropical gardens behind picket fences; their windows
are barred with turned wood instead of iron as at most places
in Mexico. Among the blazing bougainvillea, the hibiscus and
oleander, the fanning fronds of bananas, they recall the back
streets of Papeete.

It was fun to stroll down the Paseo de los Cocos, a favorite
promenade of evenings when the moon silvers its palms, and to

WATERFRONT SCENE

Rich City of the True Cross

look into the Juárez library which occupies the old Church of San Francisco. From a sense of duty I stepped into the Tourist Bureau in a corner of the Municipal Palace—and, characteristically enough, found nobody there.

Launches take one to the thick-walled ruin of the fort and prison of San Juan de Ulua, on an island off the port. The cells—including those below water level which were the death of many a political offender in the old days—were empty; the place was being cleaned and renovated for other uses.

The water-front, like that of all active harbors, was interesting. Foreign liners and freighters bulked along the piers; small schooners like those of the South Seas were loading goods for ports in Tabasco, or discharging cargoes of bananas and chicle. Sailors of a dozen nations went to and fro.

A youth approached, with a mien of mingled diffidence and candor. A difference in his appearance, a suggestion of distinction, attracted us sympathetically at once. To us, there seemed a haunting memory of Polynesia in the open brown face, under sunburnt wavy hair, the frank gaze of the large dark eyes, the full-lipped, disarming smile. Something of all this favorably predisposed us to his appeal.

"Pardon me for mentioning it," he began, "but I'm hungry. I haven't eaten for three days."

He looked well nourished; his skin and clothes were clean. There was nothing in his appearance to indicate lack of care. And yet—he seemed interesting.

Such an appeal is not unusual in Mexico, but few offer so circumstantial or so novel a story as did he when I gave him the opportunity. I led him to a noisy little café near the wharves, where a radio blared forth North American and Mexican popular tunes.

Over a small cup of *café con leche* and a plate of scrambled eggs-and-beans, of which he ate but sparingly, he told his tale. "My father was from the island of Bali. He died when I was five years old; my mother died when I was ten, so I don't know how he came to Mexico. A sailor, perhaps.

"I'm a machinist; my brothers in Mexico and in Chihuahua, who are married, also are machinists. I'm good at the trade. But I lost my union papers; they made politics on me, and I was out of work.

"I came here from Puebla; six days on the way, sleeping in the fields by day and walking at night, because of the cold. I thought surely in this busy city I could find work. But there was none.

"I am grateful to you, Señor, and I wish you from my heart much good fortune."

With the same low-voiced, smiling dignity he accepted the coin I pressed into his brown hand.

Months later, I sat in a hotel lobby in a northern city with a writer who travels about the country for the publication called Hoy, a Mexican adaptation of our picture-magazines and news weeklies. He was speaking of the *"sablistas"* or genteel spongers who haunt the Tupinamba café on the Calle Bolívar in the Capital.

"One of them will come up to you at a table," he related, with a *Buenas tardes,* and start talking politics, which leads naturally to a hard-luck story. His estate, he will tell you, has been expropriated. More haciendas have been thus 'seized' than ever existed in Mexico. Or perhaps he expects money from property that is in probate or litigation, or he holds a winning lottery ticket on which he hasn't had time to collect. By the time he's through talking, he has 'borrowed' five or ten pesos."

I told him of the "Balinese" boy in Vera Cruz.

"I know him," the journalist replied. "He's been making a good living by that story for five years."

XIV · IN LOFTY LIGHT

THE morning train out of Vera Cruz on the Ferro-
carril Mexicano curves along the dunes and bird-busy
marshes of the shore into flowering, bristle-topped
jungles beneath far hazy hills; then climbs steeply toward the
plateau.

Topographically, the route is a cross-section of Mexico:
from the hot country to the heights in a few hours. One should
travel between Mexico City and Vera Cruz at least one way
by daylight.

The train passes through thickly lined tunnels and across
arched bridges, past the tumbling Falls of Atoyac; it rumbles
over caverns; it goes through rainy Córdoba and flowery Fortín, thence into the deep and steep Metlac Gorge: slowly over

a long, curving bridge, looking straight down almost a hundred feet to the river, and along a height overlooking valleys of forests and fields and thatched villages, to Orizaba.

Beyond, the rails plunge into another deep and precipitous cañon, called picturesquely El Infiernillo, the Little Hell. Then climbing, among pines and scrub oaks, the train loops and spirals and zigzags, coiling up and up; circling, like an airplane, for altitude. We found that from the observation platform at the rear we could see at one time five or six loops of track, one above another, over which the wheels had rolled to gain height.

From the cloudy ridge-crest at Alta Luz, a broad valley lay spread out in checkered fields and woods; two thousand feet below, the tiled roofs of Maltrata, toylike with distance, glowed in apparent low-relief among their gardens and around the red-domed church.

More bridges, more lofty escarpments, more tremendous chasms: Boca del Monte, a mile and a half above the sea; Esperanza, with its fine view of the Peak of Orizaba; thence across the maguey fields—bargaining, if one wishes, on the platform at Apizaco for the carved and painted canes distinctive of the place—to the Capital.

SCENE BETWEEN VERA CRUZ AND ORIZABA

XV · MOUNT OF THE STAR

THE mountain," wrote Mme. Calderón de la Barca, "has what mortals rarely possess united, a warm heart, with a clear, cold head."

It was the Peak of Orizaba that she thus anthropomorphically described: that eighteen thousand-foot cone that the Indians call the Mountain of the Star, whence the spirit of the Feathered Serpent flew to heaven. Its pyramidal outline climbs from friendly subtropical forest and field to point a snow-wrapped summit into wind-washed sky.

From almost any spot for miles around, the "Pico" is visible, serene and white above the undulant green.

All about it rise lesser mountains, steep and wooded to the top, bannered with cloud. Nestled in their circling clasp lies the neat, tile-roofed city of Orizaba, in the vale called of old "The Joyful Waters."

It is a place of trees and flowers and birds, an oasis in the vast sear dustiness of Mexico. More prosperous, too, it seems, than many sections of that country so ill served by nature and by history.

"The land here has not been redistributed," explained Alfredo, as we drove through coffee groves shaded by tall fan-leaved banana plants that obscured the little houses bedded in flowers. "Each Indito has his own little farm, as you see here, and his house in the midst of it. Half the year he works on the sugar haciendas; the other six months he plants and harvests his own crops.

"The Indians here," he added, "are not poor—but they are not progressive. They are very backward. They don't think. Perhaps that is why they are happy."

We drove down through forests where wild orchids hung, to a cañon where water leaped, singing a murmuring baritone, almost veiled in foliage. Beyond, the tiered amphitheater of the mountains rose in a great terrace of green to where the "Pico" hung its white tent in the sky.

One could have no doubts of Orizaba's water supply. For in another such cañon, Alfredo showed me the springs, gushing from the living rock, that feed the city's mains. "There can be no contamination," he said, pointing up at the steep rocky slope. "There is nobody above here."

We approached still another tremendous gash in the land, healed over with tropical green. From a powerhouse on the rim, a pair of sleek rails plunged down a startlingly acute grade toward a village on the valley floor.

A metal cable was coiled about a huge drum, hauling a car up that precipitous valley wall, to be released later and, restrained only by the cable, hurtle back into the abyss.

An Indian on his way home from market showed calm independence of such mechanized luxury. Picking up a stone and

a handful of leaves and smearing them with the thick grease
in the cable-groove, he laid the improvised seat upon one rail,
sat on it, and with feet raised, both arms clutching his bundles,
with still another parcel balanced on his head, he slid at dizzy
speed down into the valley.

The car carried us less rapidly, straining at the cable. The
green hillside moved past; roofs and trees surged toward us.
Looking back from the bottom, we found we were in a great
box. The walls looked steeper than ever; a little way off, the
Cascade of Tuxpango veiled a mossy cliff with sounding water.

Orizaba is a busy town, as Mexican cities go. The power-
plant at Tuxpango kindles lights and turns wheels not only of
Orizaba but of Puebla and Vera Cruz as well. The tobacco
whose broad leaves lift from fields round about, as well as
that brought from other parts of the Republic, is rolled into
cigars by bright-faced girls in a large factory in the city. The
cotton mills near-by are said to be the largest in Mexico.

Those mills, in the suburbs of Nogales and Río Blanco, are
modern-looking plants, surrounded by neat homes for the
workers, with a large recreation park for them, and their club-
house, provided with all manner of comforts and means of
relaxation. The cotton spinners of Orizaba seemed to fare
rather well, although there had just been a prolonged strike.

We noticed that Orizaba's streets were clean, clustered
around a laureled plaza. The market was a place of abundance,
not only for grains and meats, the usual pottery, and products
of the mills, but for richness of tropical and subtropical fruits
—oranges and limes; deep orange-fleshed mamey under thick
brown rind; zapotes, and many another sort—and for color
and size and variety of flowers. Iron-grilled residences pushed
projecting eaves out over sidewalks, shielding from sun and
rain, among bird-murmuring trees.

The principal church had suffered, like that at Vera Cruz,
from "renovation," but Santa Gertrudis, in the outskirts, still

kept its ornate but authentic Churrigueresque yellow plaster façade.

Among the statues and monuments which infest the plaza, no better or worse than most municipal art, was one with a story: the figure of a priest, kindly featured, poor of habit, looking down at a little Indian girl, whose hand grasps a small box.

"It is the beloved curate, Don Nicolás de Llano," related Alfredo. "A hundred years or more ago, he served here, and rich and poor loved him. Some wealthy citizens, as a testimonial, gave him a jeweled cigarette case. After that, when a needy person came to him, he would take out the case, saying 'Sell this to Don So-and-so' (naming some wealthy man).

"Then the wealthy man would buy the case back and give it to Don Nicolás again. Hundreds of times that cigarette case was sold."

Over the Spanish road on which the Empress Carlota, we were told, had traveled, and across a carved bridge said to date from Aztec times, we drove from Orizaba through a beautiful valley to El Fortín and history-robed Córdoba.

In a roadside café along the way, the proprietress was arguing with an official. She had already paid her tax, she protested. "Nevertheless," he insisted, "pay me so many pesos, or I will close your place." It was local extortions such as this, we reflected, that caused discontent in Mexico.

Orchids hung from trees in the plaza of El Fortín. Indian women vended giant gardenias in tubes of bamboo. The old Hacienda Las Ánimas dreamed in the sunlight: its manorial dwelling, still well kept; the private chapel with its chimes, among gardens of oranges, grapefruit, and rubber trees; its bananas and its cane.

Córdoba is older-looking, quainter than Orizaba, full of memories of Colonial times. Venerable arcades surround the great plaza on which fronts the Hotel Zeballos, looking as if

PLAZA AT CÓRDOBA, WHERE MEXICO'S INDEPENDENCE WAS
RECOGNIZED BY A SPANISH VICEROY IN 1821

it had remained unchanged since Iturbide and O'Donojú signed the treaty of independence there in 1821. Indian women come in from the village of Amatlán, a few miles away in the mountains, robed in embroidered white cotton and strung with silver ornaments, to sell needlework in the market which perhaps outdoes even that of Orizaba—at least in bananas, of which I have seldom seen such profusion or such quality.

In the medieval atmosphere of Córdoba, one might almost credit the city's most picturesque legend, that of the sorceress La Mulata.

She was addicted to good works, the story runs, a woman of many charities. But she fell under suspicion, not only because of her convenient habit of flying over housetops and her even more confusing custom of appearing in several places at the same time, but above all because, though her life was reasonably long, she never grew old.

Young men of Córdoba were infatuated with her, almost unanimously. But she spurned them all. Satan, it was whispered, visited her every night, so she had no need of mortal men.

To some of these rejected suitors, or to envious women, perhaps, may be attributed the complaint that led to her arrest by officers of the Inquisition. She was taken to the Capital, tried, and condemned. The day was set for her burning.

A jailer, entering her cell with food, found her drawing on the wall a picture of a galleon under full sail.

"How do you like it?" she asked him.

"It's fair enough," he replied without enthusiasm.

"Well, what does it lack?"

"It can't sail anywhere."

"If you like, I'll make it sail."

"Let's see you do it," returned the incredulous jailer.

"Like this!" and she leaped aboard the pictured ship, which sailed away before the eyes of the astonished turnkey.

Pattern of Mexico

Of Orizaba, I treasure most the memory of the excursion to the mountain-shadowed village of San Andrés Tebejápan, at the end of what must have been one of the worst roads in Mexico, and hence little altered from its rustic state.

That road was populous with Indians bearing big packs of produce, walking into market, stopping here and there to rest or to refresh their dusty weariness with drink, each with his smile and murmured *"Buenas días"* to the traveler. Many hours some of them had tramped, from beyond the end of the road, where steep foot-trails zigzag down out of the mountain. But just try to buy any of their load from them midway! No Indian is willing to be cheated out of the fun of going to market. The market, the church, the fiesta—these are the distractions that lighten the monotony of his life.

Where the road, which had grown steadily narrower and more rutted, gave up in despair between encroaching ranges, a handful of adobe houses blended into the landscape around a big bare plaza. School was in session in the old mission: a neat, bright school of clean-faced, intelligent-eyed Indian children in the costume of the region. The little girls made an especially attractive picture, in dark wool pleated skirts and embroidered blouses in contrasting gay colors, each with her black hair in two glossy braids tied together at the back.

They were so neat, so dressed-up, that one suspected they had already realized that they were an "exhibit." For all that, they were a charming sight.

The teacher welcomed us to the school-room. The children arose and sang a greeting, then filed up, one by one, to show their written exercises in amazingly neat penmanship and correct Spanish; their handicrafts in cotton and in wood.

Tiny and lost in the brooding mountains, this village, too, was being brought into the integrating program of the Republic: its children were learning the language of the country and, with it, perfecting their own simple crafts.

They rose to sing again, and called softly, *"Buenas días"* as we left to join the stream of countryfolk flowing toward Orizaba.

"The cemetery here," said Alfredo, injecting the somber note that we had learned to expect in bright pictures of Mexico, "is full of children who died from eating unripe fruit."

III · "La Capital"

México, D.F., is considered in this section: first, scenes in the city proper, then some of its suburbs and near-by points.

XVI · "LITTLE STREETS OF GOD"

THE City of Mexico lifts a mélange of carved red stone Colonial palaces, precariously leaning church towers, and modern step-pyramid business structures, from the ruins of the Indian city that Cortés destroyed, stone by stone, in 1521.

Many of those stones went into the Colonial churches and palaces. The Capital, like other Mexican cities, is a closely intertwined structure of old and new—in architecture, in atmosphere, in language and customs.

Here extremes meet: poverty and wealth; natural nobility and the depravity of all great cities; Mexican and foreign, European and Indian; from all corners of the Republic the tribes flow in to the center, as they did when Moctézuma ruled from his palace on the great plaza, and the pyramid temples pointed, stained with sacrifice, to sun and stars.

Native markets display neat cubes and cones of fruits and vegetables as did the Aztec *tianguis* before the Conquest; luxuries of America and Europe glitter from windows of expensive shops; perhaps before their doors an Indian from the stark mountain country offers his load of hand-loomed sarapes.

Its streets flow with a varied current of people, from the broad Paseo de la Reforma, tree-lined and islanded with statue-bearing *glorietas,* to narrow, miry alleys where squalor simmers in a ferment of the slum.

It is a city of sound and movement and color, of ebullient human life. A radio blares a *mariachi* tune or an Argentine tango—and past the banks and stores and money-changing shops of the street of Isabel la Católica trots an Indian burden-bearer almost hidden by a great bale of paper or rags, or a roomful of furniture, strapped upon his back; a boy rides past on a bicycle, balancing upon his head a wide tray of rolls. I saw a man being carried through a downtown street and into his bank on the shoulders of a human taxicab, a *cargador*.

Street vendors utter unintelligible musical calls; at almost every corner a little sidewalk stand offers cigarettes, chewing-gum and cheap candy, or temperate-zone and tropical fruits. We could scarcely walk a block without being importuned to buy tickets in the National Lottery: "Only one left, Señor; a lucky number, a precious number. See, it has the same termination as the ticket that won the grand prize in the last drawing. Thank you, *Patrón,* and good luck!"

Furtive beggars sidle up to ask an alms "for the love of God." Past them, tram-cars and omnibuses clang and grind; motor-cars dash in apparent recklessness through narrow, one-way streets; the sun that shone on Moctézuma and on Quetzalcóatl casts pyramid-shadows from the Sagrario, or the rain for which they prayed to Tlaloc slants through thinned air from the mountain-framed sky.

"Little Streets of God"

At first sight, México appears a European city; there are thoroughfares that might be those of France or Italy, as well as Spain. But I walked one day by chance into the puddled passageway that bore, evidently for some historical reason, the name of Street of the Tobacconists. The narrow, uneven pavement was packed with tiny outdoor kitchens, whence arose a stench of entrails frying in rancid grease. Around them squatted dark, lank-haired figures. It was a bit of Indian Mexico, only a few squares from the heart of the city.

There are streets of *mesones*—inns where horses and mules are lodged, primarily, and their owners incidentally. There are pulque shops, garishly decorated with tassels of colored paper across their fronts and naïve murals on their inner walls. There are moldy tenements that house hundreds, a family to a room, with a communal water fountain in the patio and a short row of noisome toilets in the rear.

There are, too, sections of model homes for workers, great functionally designed schools, and rows of opulent mansions in more or less questionable architectural taste.

In the heart of the downtown area, the tower of La Profesa leans as if about to fall into the pavement of Isabel la Católica; a bank occupies the carven palace of a Colonial count; the tall, modern, stepped-back La Nacional building looks across at the House of Tiles and the remains of the once vast establishment of the Franciscans. In the same street, the palace of the emperor Agustín Iturbide houses twentieth-century businesses.

Foreign life, the life of tourists, centers thereabout, converging from the scattered pretentious hotels. As the summer deepened, we heard at times almost as much English as Spanish on the Avenida Francisco I. Madero and the Cinco de Mayo. Lunch tables in the House of Tiles were thronged, the side-lines packed with standing North Americans waiting their turn. A double line filed from the street doors to the twin mail-windows of the Wells Fargo Express. These blocks in Madero are the tourist capital of Mexico.

Pattern of Mexico

But for Mexico itself, if all roads lead to the Capital, within the Capital most roads lead to the Plaza de la Constitución, known less officially as the Zócalo. At least ten streets converge upon the parked rectangle, with its shrubs, its statues, its diagonal crosswalks—that was the hub of the city of Moctézuma's time just as it is now. At that time the three causeways met here that linked the island city with the mainland of the valley, and canals from the floating gardens in the south came to the very edge of the square, where the arches bear still the name of Portal of the Merchants.

The canal is filled, now, to a point far behind its old quay; the causeways are buried under pavements; the lake is a shrunken remnant of itself in the plain to the northeast, over which stalk whirling pillars of dust.

Old prints and photographs show the Zócalo full of noble trees. They were cut down in Carranza's time, they say—but almost every one gives a different reason. To avoid obscuring traffic at those busy corners, say the most practical. But the other explanations are interesting, and perhaps more in character: the trees were cut, some say, so that revolutionists couldn't hide behind them to snipe at the National Palace; others say that it was done so that the rebels could bombard the palace more effectively. And still another version is that they were sold for graft.

The squat, massive National Palace, with broad, guarded gates and iron-grilled balconies, fills one whole side of the rectangle. Opposite it, beside a row of shops, stands the red-brown Colonial palace that houses the National Pawnshop, the Mount of Piety. At the south, the City Hall guards its archives behind a portal flanked by the Arcade of the Merchants. This looks across at the huge bulk of the Cathedral and the smaller, rose-tinted Sagrario.

Those temples stand nearly on the spot where the tall oratories of the Aztecs defied with sullen drums the Spaniards besieged in the palace on or near the site of the present Mount

130

of Piety. Just beyond the northeast corner of the square, excavation has laid bare the foundations of a part of that complex of temples, priests' quarters and attendant structures:
bases of slanting walls, to which adhere bits of plaster; a stone
stairway, a carved snake's head, a pavement—ten feet or more
beneath the present level of the street.

Down steps like these, here or near-by, bodies rolled, when
the obsidian knife had slashed the chest, and the priest held
up the heart of the victim to the god who was nourished by
its blood. Blood had flowed in Mexico for ages before; it has
flowed since; the Smoking Mirror and the Child of the Hummingbird still thirst, it seems.

Where the Calle de Tacuba runs west out of the Zócalo,
Cortés, his mailed Spaniards, and his Indian allies fled on
that night of rain and death in 1520: creeping along the causeway, clutched from beneath, dragged down into dark water,
while from above and from all sides sang sling-stones, arrows,
spears.

A few blocks farther, the Church of San Hipólito marks a
spot "where many Spaniards died." In the great stone at the
corner of its atrium is carved the fabled Indian, borne aloft in
the claws of an eagle, to whom the gods revealed the Aztec
empire's doom.

Beyond, where the little balls that determine the fates in
the National Lottery click in their hollow spheres, the name
"Alvarado's Bridge" still clings to the street. For there, according to legend, Pedro de Alvarado, cut off from his companions in that disastrous retreat, vaulted the gap in the causeway to rejoin Cortés.

The western end of the park called the Alameda, fronting
on the street that covers the ancient causeway, was the scene
of the pious burnings with which the "Holy Office" replaced
the blood-sacrifices of the Aztec faith. Here, between his
guards, came in 1649, Don Tomás Treviño y Sobremonte,
saying to his executioners, as the flames licked about him:

"Throw on more wood! I paid for it with my own money."

Or take another direction: west on Guatemala to Carmen, formerly the Street of the Sad Indian. Mme. Calderón de la Barca relayed its story; Luís González Obregón investigated it almost a century later. An Indian noble, in the mid-sixteenth century, took money from the viceroy to spy on his compatriots or other possible subversive elements. He became so busy spending his wealth in pleasures that he failed to detect a plot, whereupon the viceroy seized his property. The spy sat in the street, weeping and refusing food, until he died, and the viceroy had a statue of a seated Indian carved and set up at that point, as a warning to other spies.

It is sad that so touching a story should be of doubtful authenticity. But any one can look at the statue, which has been removed to the National Museum, not far from the spot. The Indian doesn't look particularly sad. He is pretty clearly an Aztec banner-stone, such as upheld, from a ring where the hands meet, an emblem in front of the temple. The sculpture became known as the Sad Indian, and it has been conjectured that the story was invented to account for the name.

"No recommendation is needed for entry into this hospital," says an inscription at the entrance to the venerable Hospital de Jesús, in the Avenida República de Salvador. Founded by Cortés in 1527 on the site where he is said to have first met Moctézuma, it is still operating to-day. The building is low and arched, the courts well kept up, with flowers and fountains; its old chapel, rich with age-darkened ceiling of mosaic wood.

South on Bolívar, and a little west, near the San Juan market, we came upon the Street of the Vizcainas. It is a quarter of the poor; the street is ill paved, but among the little shops, tenements, and small factories bulks the huge baroque Colegio de San Ignacio. It is a magnificent ruin, still occupied although its heavy dark-red walls have sunk, and the noble façade is sadly out of repair.

"Little Streets of God"

Founded in 1732 by Vizcayan merchants for widows and children of Spaniards, "Las Vizcainas," as it is popularly called, still functions as a school, though parts of the building have been given over to tenements and small workshops. A beautiful patio, large and cloistered, is lit by red blossoms of pomegranate trees, and a magnificent stairway rises to the upper floors.

In a corner of the block-shaped pile, beyond a row of cell-like dwelling-rooms of the poor, we came upon Indian workmen singing as their small hammers tinkled upon bits of silver. In response to their call came Don Valentín, the master, who had diverted his talent from painting to the designing of jewelry after ancient models from the tombs.

Across the way, we took refuge from rain in the patio of another old building converted into a tenement. A carved stone figure looked down from over the gate. Within, living quarters fronted on the courtyard, where washings hung from balcony to balcony, caged birds sang, and children played among pots of flowers. The apartments were very small, and there was evidence of faulty drains, but the residents did not seem depressed by their environment.

The Lagunilla, north on Bolívar, has succeeded the old "Thieves' Market" of the Volador. Street after street, on Sundays, is blocked with booths and people. All manner of merchandise is spread on the pavement: tools, pottery, blankets, jewels, cameras, brushes, Aztec images, arrowheads, bits of obsidian, paintings, frames, a box of serum, a badge reading "Texas—Delegate," old coins, a medal of the four hundredth anniversary of the Virgin of Guadalupe, silver miracle tokens, old books—some rare; anything, everything, most of it of doubtful origin and much of it useless. But collectors were prowling from booth to booth, prospecting for treasure.

Don Mario stood treat with *tacos de gusanos:* fat maguey-grubs fried crisp and rolled in a tortilla. Hollow and crunchy with frying, they had a delicate, not unpleasant flavor.

133

Pattern of Mexico

"After all," commented Don Mario, with more poetry than entomology, "they are only butterflies."

It was a marvel to me how the buses penetrated the length of the crowded, obstructed streets in the vicinity of the Merced market. Merchandise was heaped and piled and hung there in as great quantity and almost as much variety as in the Lagunilla—as Frances Toor said of another market, the Tepito, even to "second-hand toothbrushes."

Threading those streets, I came upon a medicine vendor extolling his wares by ventriloquism through a carved and painted dummy. Farther on, another was exhorting his audience over a platform occupied by live snakes. He would slap the boards, and the snakes, disturbed by the vibration, would move about. Then he would pour a few drops of his medicine under their noses, and as the snakes quieted down: "See, they are tranquil—because their nerves are sound. This medicine is good for nerves, kidneys, heart, stomach, liver; for rheumatism" (and he named an alarming series of ailments) "and it costs only a few miserable centavos." Distributing samples: "See how good it tastes." One after another, customers brought forth their coins.

Such, full of life, are "the little streets of God."

XVII · HALLS OF STATE AND CHURCH

AS a visitor enters, through its broad gateway, the main patio of the National Palace, a dapper young man with an ingratiating manner is likely to step up and offer to lead him to the portions of the building that are of interest. Those trusting tourists who assume he is a government employee appointed for that purpose as a courtesy to the nation's guests are often surprised when, as they are about to leave, he displays his license from the Department of Tourism and states that under the rules of his union the fee is two pesos and a half.

One tourist, after cannily declining such a guide's attentions in another public building, later asked the same guide, on some hasty impulse, in what year the structure had been built. Just why she wanted to know does not appear; it is one of those things tourists are told in every such place and promptly forget.

But he wouldn't tell her. "That," he said haughtily, "is what the two pesos fifty is for."

Of course the guides have to make a living, but a competent guidebook will furnish one as much of the same information as one may want, without forcing upon one other facts, dates and dimensions in which one may not be interested and which may distract one from contemplation of the scene.

It does not seem necessary here to describe or enumerate the corridors, offices, ceremonial halls, and government departments that cluster around the dozen or more courtyards of the National Palace, or the historical objects which they contain. They mean nothing unless one sees them.

We ourselves came back often to the main stairway, whose walls Diego Rivera had covered with a crowded pageant of Mexican legend and history. The Sun-God and the Feathered Serpent, the Conquest, the Colonial period, the French and North American invasions, stand forth in bright color. Revolutionary heroes march across the upper center. At the left the Sun of Science flares above a representation of Our Lady of Guadalupe, symbolizing religion; a pipe-line leads from the wealth of the Church to the military and executive departments. There sits a president of Mexico, at the mouth of a money-chute from Wall Street, signing a bill; here stands the fat general whom Santa Anna made a dignitary of the Church. Here is pictured the legend of Porfirio Díaz and the poisoned mangoes: he burned his tongue with hot metal to draw out the poison, a Mexican told me. Above, the giant figure of Karl Marx holds a scroll proclaiming: "All the history of human society is the history of the class struggle."

Propaganda, of course; but expressed in plastic terms that must command admiration, whatever one may think of the doctrine.

Halls of State and Church

We noticed that a splotch of acid-stain marred the section symbolizing the Church. These and other historical and sociological murals of the period were and are controversial.

At the foot of the stairway, in the quiet of noon, squatted a soldier, eating the lunch brought by his wife, who squatted beside him.

If a male tourist misses his wife, one of the likely places to look for her is the National Mount of Piety, the government pawn shop, which occupies a Colonial palace on the site of an Aztec palace, across the square from the Palacio Nacional.

Founded in 1775 as a private charity to rescue the poor from loan sharks, the Monte de Piedad, or Monte Pió as Mexicans more often call it, has since become a government institution and a magnet for feminine visitors as well as the bargain-hunters of Mexico itself.

Almost anything can be found there, from fountain pens and dilapidated coffee urns to grand pianos and sets of furniture. There are whole rooms of jewelry, tables and shelves of books. I saw everything imaginable except the silver-mounted pistols a friend at home had asked me to find for him. I could find there no firearms of any sort. Possibly they are the one article not accepted, but I suspect a Mexican will pawn everything else before he will give up his gun.

An official's explanation of the operation of Monte Pió may be of interest, as it was to us. Experts, he said, appraise the objects, which are pawned at one-third their appraised value. The owner has six months to repay the loan, after which time two per cent interest begins. The article is sold only if the owner defaults the interest. Proceeds of the sale, minus principal and interest of the loan, go to the owner. If the article fails to sell at the monthly auction, it is placed on sale as in a shop, at its appraised value. If it fails to sell and the owner still can't redeem it, the appraiser must buy it himself—a precaution against overvaluing.

Objects for sale are labeled with apparent exactness: "genuine antique," "copy," "imitation," "damaged." Most of them are in good condition. The official told me that watches, for example, are not accepted unless in running order.

Even those who have little zest for bargain-chasing or for shopping of any kind often succumb to the fascinations of the Monte Pió. Like its twin, the National Lottery, it is insidious.

The powerful and bitter modern murals of José Clemente Orozco in the courts of the National Preparatory School were scratched, eaten with acid, scrawled with names, initials, and scurrilous comments. A group of society women once demanded that the artist remove the frescoes, which, they complained, would be an inappropriate background for a charity bazaar they had planned. When he refused, they covered the paintings with green branches. And that, no doubt, is why Orozco later painted on these walls high-heeled, sharp-nosed society women marching over the prostrate bodies of the poor.

Among the most interesting paintings there, I thought, were Fernando Leal's encaustic of the Chalma fiesta and Jean Charlot's fresco of the Cholula massacre, at the top of the main stairway.

In contrast to their modernity, the ancient carved wood choir-stalls from the monastery and church of Saint Augustine lent a rich beauty to the dark, close salon, "El Generalito," beneath the stained walls.

Shouting students trooped in and out; basketball hoops projected from worn pillars of a broad, mid-eighteenth century courtyard.

We returned often to the three floors around the two great patios of the Secretariat of Public Education. Here was another tremendous panorama of Mexico—historical, geographic, economic, social—the work of an artists' syndicate and mainly of Rivera. At close view, the paintings were obscured and their composition cut through by the heavy arches in front of them, but seen from across the patio, the arrangement cohered and the color pattern stood out in its full richness.

These walls are a library in paint: a detailed description of them would require a book to itself. Roughly, they present occupations, festivals, amusements of various parts of the country; scenes from the Revolution, socialistic doctrines of its aims, and a picture of its shortcomings, together with an imaginary portrayal of the more thorough revolution that the artist expected to come, scrolled with couplets from a proletarian ballad.

We went back again and again to enjoy the tender beauty of the scene portraying "the sleep of the poor," and the one inscribed: "The fruits of the earth are better than hard pesos."

"It reminds me," Don Mario ventured, looking up at the cream-colored dome, ribbed with brown, of the Palacio de las Bellas Artes, "of a chocolate soda at Sanborn's."

The Bellas Artes indeed seems out of harmony, in its smug neo-classic lines, with either the Colonial or the modern architecture near-by. But it deserves perhaps to be classified as a national monument to the taste of the Díaz period.

The interior is overpowering in its heavy magnificence of marble and metal, but there is a strong lift from the floor to the dome, two hundred feet above, that relieves the ponderousness of the surrounding design.

In the foyer, clever use has been made, in the metal pilaster capitals, of themes from ancient structures.

The National Theater, one of several auditoriums in the building, seats three thousand. The Mexican who accompanied me on my first visit said that Porfirio Díaz had had it constructed "to entertain his friends." Whereupon another companion replied: "From all I hear of him, I didn't think he had so many."

The theater itself is heavy but magnificent—rich and somber with velvet. But the seats are cramped, the aisles narrow. The famous Tiffany glass curtain, I was told each time I entered the building as a tourist, was "out of repair," but I saw it used at several performances: it is an expensive *tour de force* (said to have cost $47,000) depicting the volcanoes Popocatépetl and Ixtaccíhuatl under changing lights.

Above, there are halls of paintings, most of them of more historical than artistic interest (the real old masters are in the San Carlos galleries), and exhibitions of native arts: pottery from Tlaquepaque, Puebla, Oaxaca; sarapes from Saltillo, Guadalajara, Sonora; chicle sculpture; glass figurines from Guadalajara; Uruápan lacquer-ware; quaint painted chests of the fragrant wood of Olinalá. There are masks of wood and of metal: deer masks of the Yaqui dancers, lion masks of Acapulco and Colima: grotesque, a cry out of Mexico's past into the uncomprehending present. All these things are another pageant of Mexico: of the hot country and the highland; the Mexico that loves flowers and song and that looks upon death with Indian calm; the soul of Mexico whose history is a succession of slain Messiahs and whose saints and Virgins and Christs are fused with the gods of fire and wind, the goddesses of water and of the corn.

In one of the salons, a government archæologist showed me objects from the more recent of the explorations in the Valley of Oaxaca: fantastic funeral urns, pottery of bewilderingly varied periods, models of excavated temples.

Two large murals at the ends of the second floor hall contrast strongly with the tame prettiness of many of the more formal works of art. One is by Orozco. It is higher in color than much of his work, and contains themes traceable in his later frescoes at Guadalajara: war and revolution; parts of machinery blending with or growing out of human bodies;

scenes of orgy and of slaughter. Constructive and destructive forces, one might interpret them, in the turmoil of revolution.

Opposite is Rivera's reproduction of his rejected fresco painted originally for Rockefeller Center in New York City. Here is Leon Trotsky, white hair streaming defiantly. A hammer proclaims the Internationale. Nikolai Lenin clasps the hands of worker, peasant, soldier. There is a great telescope, in its wheel, with far constellations whirling; a microscope above biological specimens; revelers contrasted with a mob that clamors in the street for jobs and bread—an obvious reference to economic depression. No wonder Rockefeller balked at paying for a lampoon on his class—though a livelier sense of humor might have impelled him to accept it.

The drawing room of the National Lottery was like a theater. In one of many curving rows of seats we waited among a tense audience of Mexicans and foreigners of all classes, most of them holding sheaves of tickets. On the stage sat public officials; in the foreground stood two large hollow globes formed of metal bands, each containing hundreds of little balls. The balls in one container bore numbers; those opposite, the amounts of prizes.

Rapidly the *sorto* went forward. Uniformed officials turned cranks operating the two globes. A numbered ball rolled down a chute from the left, and a blue-uniformed boy from one of the orphanages supported by the lottery sang out the number. At the same time another ball rolled from the other globe, and another orphan chanted the amount of the prize.

"Veinte-cinco pesos" ... over and over in rapid sing-song chant, broken here and there by larger amounts, the sums and numbers uttered at amazing speed, with scarcely a pause and almost never an error. A radio blared the announcements to Mexico outside, and an official marked on a blackboard the winning numbers, while another functionary placed the released balls, in pairs, in a frame like an abacus. An official an-

nounced where the larger winning tickets had been sold—the grand prize in Chihuahua, the second in Vera Cruz, and so on.

The government dignitaries on the stage watched every move.

Thus is the National Lottery, on its three nights a week, conducted. Under the Cárdenas administration it was the only form of gambling permitted in the Republic. The proceeds support a number of institutions, and advertisements urge citizens of that country that loves to take a chance to combine charity with possible profit by investing in the tickets that are sold on every street in the Capital and in every town of consequence throughout the Republic.

Public confidence reflects the elaborate precautions taken to insure an equitable drawing. Lists of all winning numbers are published in daily newspapers and posted in lottery agencies—even to the *reintegros,* whereby tickets whose numbers end with the same digit as the major winner carry a return of the price paid. The agencies, I was told, get a ten per cent commission on sales; street vendors of tickets, eight or nine per cent out of this. The rest, after prizes are paid, goes to charity.

When gambling in general was abolished, the once tremendously popular Basque ball or jai alai, known in Mexico as pelota or frontón, was abandoned. "For," explained my host in the Capital, "without gambling, what is frontón?"

There are two signs in almost every church in Mexico. One reads, "Beware of pickpockets"; the other, "Don't spit on the floor." The former, at least, is conspicuous in the Cathedral, where it is probably as applicable as it is in any place frequented by crowds.

There, too, one may have "guide trouble." We declined, on many visits, to be guided, but at last, in a moment of weakness or sympathy, capitulated. As we were midway through the great church, heads buzzing with a confusing accumulation of names, dates, dimensions, and miscellaneous statistics, a service started: high clear voices of choir boys, tinkle of hand-turned bells, solemn priestly chanting. It was beautiful; we wanted to listen. But the guide, conscientiously earning his fee, droned on: "This picture is twenty-two feet by sixteen in size; it was painted by So-and-So in the year Umpty-such-and-such, and cost fifty thousand pesos...."

The Cathedral is of noble proportions, though the sweep of its interior is broken by the altar and choir in the center. It is so vast and high and smoky and dim that, save for a couple of hours in late morning, we could scarcely discern the details of the big Colonial paintings by Cabrera, Correa, Villalpando and the rest, the measurements of which the guide considered so important.

It was two and a half centuries in construction, we were told, by "Indian slave labor," and all by hand. It contains no nails, no iron, save the hinges on the thick doors, the spikes studding those doors, and the plates on the worn sills. The building was modeled, in hand-fitted stone, after the Cathedral of Seville.

The varied architecture reflects the periods through which the Cathedral advanced to completion: the plain style of the sixteenth century, the flamboyance of the seventeenth, the pseudo-classicism of the eighteenth, and the eagles on the front, added since it became government property.

Within, up and down the sides are ranged numerous barred chapels, each with its gilded altar, its sacred images, its florid painting. At the far end stands the heavy gold-encrusted Altar of the Kings, said to be the finest example of Churrigueresque art in the Republic: Mexico ran away with the originally comparatively chaste style attributed to Churriguera—the Indian love of ornament, of closely packed space, rioted in luscious carving and in heaped-up gold. The green-columned neo-classic High Altar, opposite that of the Kings, seems severe by contrast.

I heard a quaint story about the silver-framed square por-

trait of Our Lady, in the Altar of Pardons, facing the main
door. The Flemish artist Simon Pereyns, or Perinés, was confined on a charge of heresy, because he had said he liked to
paint portraits of beautiful women better than sacred images.
The artist occupied his time, while awaiting trial, by painting
this Virgin on the door of his cell. The Grand Inquisitor held
that it cleared Perinés of the charges, since no heretic could
paint so obviously holy a picture. Luís González Obregón, who
has debunked many a delightful myth of his city, traced down
the original proceedings: Perinés "was sentenced to paint a
retablo of Our Lady of Mercy, on August 22, 1744."

Large and magnificent as it is, the Cathedral, we were told,
falls short of its intended splendor. "There were to have been
seven naves," the guide said, "but only five were built. They
never got the money."

The silver balustrade of the choir was melted down for coin-
age by a revolutionary general and replaced by bronze. But
the stone crosses flanking the font are said to have stood in the
first church the Franciscans built on or near this site in 1525.
Tombs of archbishops and other dignitaries line the walls between the chapels. There are more tombs, it is said, beneath
the uneven, creaking wooden floor that contrasts so strangely
with the magnificence above: an aristocratic cemetery locked
up by the government.

On St. John the Baptist's Day the Cathedral was full of
mothers holding protesting babies and filing up to the rail of
the High Altar to have their children baptized by a gorgeously
robed archbishop and his attendants. Some were content with
similar ministrations at other altars.

But we liked best the services in which only a few were in the
great dim space: the rich-robed priests, the marching choir in
bright colors, with the hand-pumped organ sounding and the
cylinder of bells tinkling in the loft.

The adjoining Sagrario, badly cracked by earthquakes, shadows forth in the form of its rose and white stone the shapes

that stood long ago on this ground: the pyramid of the Aztec gods seems to issue, ghost-like, through the squared and scalloped outline of the church.

The holy places of the Capital are many, and I must confess to what Herbert Spinden characterized in his own case, at San Augustín Acolman, as "only a diluted interest in churches." The remnant of monastic San Francisco appalled us with its tasteless interior, but we used to take shelter—from rain or from the weariness of the siesta hour which too often we did not use sensibly for its ordained purpose—in neat, aristocratic, Byzantine-tinctured San Felipe de Jesús, next door. I stepped oftenest, however, into shattered, leaning La Profesa, whose closed garden dreams behind tall iron gates in the heart of the business section.

The interior was dim and lofty: dark red velvet hung over heavy stone columns; the white-and-gold altar was set off with rich marble carving; above it, stained murals spread across the cracked ceiling. An engineer was sighting his transit, often, in the nave; a plumb-line hung from the ceiling; outside, a buttress of cement braced the tottering wall.

Even the normally irreligious must feel a sense of spiritual repose, of soothing calm, in these quiet interiors—when they are not filled with people. There are always a few—silent, reverent, with serious, adoring faces under the rebozo and the straight black hair.

XVIII · OLD STONES AND NEW

WE never could be quite sure of finding either the
National Museum or the San Carlos art gallery
open. They had their official hours, but—

"Not open to-day. This is a holiday. It will be open
Monday."

On Monday: "Yes, the building is officially open to-day, but
you can't come in. It is under repair. Come next week at the
same hour."

And next week, the hours had been changed.

The official name of the academy and art museum that
nearly everybody still calls "San Carlos" had been changed so
frequently that even our host, Señor Forte, who seldom failed
to provide information on any subject, didn't know where to

Old Stones and New

look for it in either of the two telephone directories. At last, by calling a series of government offices, he ran it down.

"The San Carlos will be open at eleven o'clock."

But on arrival, there was likely to be some other reason why the public was not admitted that day.

One gets used to those things; or one gives up and goes home.

After some persistence, however, we spent many hours in the San Carlos, which is said to house the largest collection of old masters in the Western Hemisphere. At least, much of the best of the older European art now in Mexico is assembled there. Church and Crown were fabulously wealthy in Colonial times. Kings and emperors rewarded cities and churches and monasteries of New Spain with works from their private collections, or had them painted to order for the purpose. When revolution raged, some prized paintings were hidden away deep in walls or in crypts. Some disappeared completely, but many became government property.

Like most galleries, the San Carlos presents a confusing array of good, bad, and mediocre. But we found many master works that repaid prolonged study: a powerful El Greco saint; a severe Adam and Eve by Cranach the Elder; the rich texture of a Titian Suzanna in interesting contrast to two treatments of the same theme by Rubens; a marvelous Salome of Tintoretto. Some less widely celebrated masters intrigued us: the glowing texture of Delilah's robes and jewels, the detail of the hands, as portrayed by Francisco de Zurbarán; a stark "Piedad" of Luís de Morales, foreshadowing some of the German moderns. It would be tedious to catalogue them; it is enough to say that the San Carlos is well worth the trouble of visiting it many times.

All over Mexico, the story of a race is written in stone. Nearly every city, every archæological site of consequence, has its local collection. But the greatest of them all is in the National Museum.

Many things are housed in the halls around its stone-flagged patio: historical relics; art objects and paintings, good and bad; specimens of the industrial arts. I enjoyed studying case after case of prehistoric pottery and figurines. But the most spectacular objects are the ancient sculptures in the Hall of Monoliths, where the larger objects from all parts of the Republic have been brought together.

There was always a crowd of visitors before the Sun Stone of the Aztecs—known throughout the world as the Calendar Stone, and the only Mexican archæological object of which many laymen seem to have heard. At least, more questions have been asked me about it than of any other. Always a guide, with pointer in hand, was explaining its meaning in detail—and each guide had a different interpretation.

The huge carved disk is a book in stone: roughly, as authorities told me, the days, weeks, months of the year circle around the flaming face of the Sun; beyond and bounding them, coil the twin fire-serpents of the universe. Here are the four cardinal directions, the four past ages, the four destructions and rebirths of the world, the Fifth Sun that is to end in shattering upheaval on the day Four Earthquake. The stone is man's record of the seasons and of human life: a record of struggle, the overcoming of Nature by man, who is only to be overcome by Nature in the end—for "all the roundness of the earth," sang Nezahualcóyotl, "is a tomb; there is no thing which endures, no thing which with title of piety is not hidden in the earth."

The victories of the Aztec emperor Tizoc march around the rim of another great disk, known popularly as the Stone of Sacrifice. Guides are fond of describing in sanguinary detail the Aztec ceremony which tore out the beating heart. They even point to a trench cut along one radius of the disk as a channel to carry away the blood. I was told on good authority, however, that the trench is the mark of the ignorant vandalism of workmen who tried to cut through the stone when their tools struck it as they were digging a ditch, and that the disk is really a historical memorial of the emperor's conquests. The known sacrificial stones are smaller and convex on the upper surface, to facilitate bending the victim back into the required position for the rite.

Less widely known abroad, but deserving almost as much attention for the curious "prophecy" connected with it, is the National Stone: a miniature platform and stairway, suggesting a temple, with a copy of the Sun Stone at the summit. When it was found in the course of repairs in the National Palace in 1926, as the Revolution was beginning to consolidate its gains, some one remembered the ancient words:

"When the principal temple of the Aztecs appears in the main plaza of Tenochtitlán" (Mexico City) "bearing upon it the sun, then the ancient people shall regain their ancient rights."

Row after row, the "monoliths" are ranged down the hall: portraits of the gods; the seated banner-bearer dubbed the Sad Indian; conical coiled serpents; a powerful ocelot; a strikingly "modern" and lifelike *ixcuintli*—the dog that guided souls to the world of the gods.

Art value they have, heavy as most of them are in their stern finality; but they are more significant, perhaps, in their record of the beliefs and aspirations of a people, and their record of that people's adjustments to the forces of the Nature under whose dominion they lived.

Mexico is not all Colonial monuments, moldering churches, ruined Indian temples. Far out toward the northwest corner of the city, the National Polytechnic Institute lifts its promise of the new Mexico. It is probably one of the most constructive developments that have grown out of the Revolution.

From the Villa Rosa car-line, we approached the Institute

by a muddy, irregularly paved street, crossed a narrow wooden bridge over a ditch, and passed through an iron gate into a large campus, bristling with big, ugly, but efficient buildings of functional architecture in white concrete. Machine shops, foundries, electrical and electroplating shops; woodturning and carpentry halls; laboratories; a commercial school for girls; needlework class-rooms; dormitories, a stadium.

The Instituto Nacional Polytécnico was founded, I was told, about 1935, with thirty-four regional branches. It claims some 17,000 students. It is distinct from the National University and does not compete with it. "It is much more orderly and free of politics," said Professor Maldonado, who showed us through the plant.

Promising boys, who have had six years in the lower schools, have four years' training here in preparation for entering vocational schools in the same institution. Most of them, the professor said, are workers' sons, chosen for proficiency from schools throughout the Republic, and brought here on government scholarships to become the future engineers, architects, technicians of all kinds, surgeons, and biological research workers—all the various highly skilled professional men that Mexico needs so much.

Each student had his "problem"; here a boy was wiring a miniature room for electricity; another was setting up a motor. Boys in the forge shop were making spikes and angle irons, from patterns on the wall. "They begin at the bottom," said the professor.

"Bartered from Germany with Mexican oil," he explained, as he exhibited beautiful precision machinery: stamps, drills, cutters, filers, each powered by its own motor rather than by belt transmission from a central source. "But this one"—indicating a particularly intricate microphotography unit—"is made only to order. We had to pay cash for it. They wouldn't take oil. It's the most advanced instrument of its kind in the world."

Old Stones and New

There was a bewildering array of laboratories, in a state of precise order and neatness; cages of rats and guinea pigs; a dog with an artificial fistula for a study of gastric juice (he didn't seem to mind). The genial German entomologist, into whose precincts we wandered, would have spent the rest of the afternoon, if he could have held us, showing us in detail what he said was the most comprehensive collection of butter-flies in Mexico.

Here an earnest youth was studying fruit flies; there stood a row of inoculated animals; here a stall in which horses were bled to make serums; there a tank for experimental turtles and frogs. A medical dissecting laboratory adjoined a modern clinical class-room, with tiers of seats in an ascending **U** around an operating theater. "Even at Johns Hopkins," exclaimed Don Mario, "we had nothing more advanced."

There was even an anthropology department, recalling the saying of Manuel Gamio that the key to progress in Mexico is ethnological study. "We can't help the Indian," was his argument, "until we know how the Indian thinks."

The lifelong resident of Mexico who accompanied us said he had not realized before that there was in his country an institution of this kind so well organized and equipped. "It is the answer," he declared, "to the complaints of the conserva-tives about the 'futility' of the government program."

For contrast, we walked out through a street clangorous with tram-cars to Popotla, to sit a while beneath the venerable branches of the Tree of the Sad Night, guarded behind an iron fence said to have been forged from instruments of the In-quisition.

Here, according to tradition, Cortés sat down and wept, at the first halt on the retreat from the Capital, when he saw how few of his men were still alive, all the survivors sorely wounded, and the guns and treasure lost in the waters of the lake.

Pattern of Mexico

The Tree, though not very high, is of tremendous girth, obviously very old, of the kind called by the Aztecs *ahuehuete,* usually translated "cypress." It is split and scarred with time and riot, mended skilfully with concrete; but the top, that June day, was still green as it must have been in that other June when it looked upon desperate battle and the sorrow of defeat.

The Tree, I felt, should not be viewed hastily; it is a place for meditation on the events that have occurred in this valley since the Arcáicos first planted the life-giving maize. It is a symbol, one might fancy, of Mexico: old, scarred with war and revolution, patched with alien materials, but still vital, still green, still rooted in the enduring strength of the American soil.

One should take time to see other bits of modern Mexico as, in a sense, a corrective for the heavy dose of churches, monasteries, and ruins. There is the Centro Escolar, for example: a huge modern school on the former site of the notoriously filthy and disease-ridden Belén prison. It is a vast complex of functional buildings in brick, reinforced concrete, and steel, around spacious courts and playgrounds, with accommodations for five thousand students to avail themselves of its comprehensive and advanced curriculum. Here, too, are spirited murals by various artists: scenes of the brutality associated with the old prison, and, in the library, stained glass windows reputed to have been designed by Rivera.

Farther out, near the entrance to Chapultepec Park, the Department of Public Health is a massive institution in gray stone, its modern laboratories arranged around a beautiful garden. Its Hall of Acts is decorated with bold Rivera frescoes.

Eastward from the center of town, on the way to the Valbuena airport, the Venustiano Carranza workers' park spreads over many acres, with its gray stone concert hall, gymnasium,

Old Stones and New

library, and open-air theater; its day nursery; its athletic grounds and swimming pools—and the sign on the gate which seems rather odd in a public park, but which is, no doubt, in the interests of neatness, forbidding the bringing of food into the precincts.

Beyond are model homes built by the government of the Federal District. They are for sale to workers at reasonable prices and on easy terms. There is little to describe about them; they are of interest as an antidote to the inevitable emphasis, in writing or speaking of a country from a "travel" viewpoint, on the "picturesque" and the "quaint."

These constructive developments may have less romantic appeal, they may not be tourist attractions, but they reveal what has been going on in Mexico—the practical phases which are too often overlooked. Such developments, up and down the country, are still comparatively few, but they are an encouraging beginning. Viewing them, one realizes that the new Mexico is not a land of *"mañana"* and stagnation; some one has had a vision.

XIX · THE "LITTLE HORSE"

LIFE in the Capital is many-faceted; one can but suggest bits here and there. "Eating around the city" is an occupation in itself: specific places change, but the types go on in infinite variety. Of the places we visited, a French restaurant in the Calle Luís Moya was a satisfaction for epicures; an overdecorated but friendly place in República de Chile delighted the palate with tasty Mexican dishes; North American food was available to the less adventurous in the Avenida Francisco I. Madero; German food in the Calle Génova and in an obscure little place in Isabel la Católica; Hungarian in the Calle de Motolinia; Italian in the Calle Gante.

On a balcony in the Calle Uruguay, innumerable Spanish

courses were served in almost stupefying profusion, at the somewhat puzzling rate of "one peso seventy-five with beer; without beer, two pesos." What they were trying to say was that you paid for the beer whether you drank it or not. In the Avenida República de Colombia, we entered a kitchen from the street, to find ourselves among huge pots of steaming Mexican food and the strains of a *mariachi* orchestra. A tour conductor reported that one of a party whom she conducted thither remarked, "It's very interesting—but surely you don't expect us to eat here!"

And there was that street of food shops, Sixteenth of September, where, when tired of hotel or restaurant fare, one might pick up bread and wine, cheese and fruit, with a whole roast chicken or turkey hot off the spit, from a delicatessen in the Calle Motolinia.

There were Spanish theaters where one paid separately for as many acts resembling vaudeville as one cared to see; night clubs, some of them luxurious and expensive, with floor shows featuring brilliant dancing and throaty, impassioned "Flamenco" song. And there were any number of bars, of course, and cinemas where, in addition to North American and Mexican films, highly interesting European screen dramas were shown.

In the summer months, the curiously carved House of the Masks, beyond a bulging outdoor market on the Ribera de San Cosme, was gay and busy with students—a few Mexicans, some Europeans, and many North Americans—who attended the Summer School of the National University of Mexico. Class-rooms in the old Colonial mansion hummed with activity; on certain afternoons, between showers, the patio resounded to folk music and the thud of feet beating out regional dances in school fiestas. Teachers on vacation from the States, Mexicans making up requirements for the winter sessions, Cubans, Germans—Dean Pablo Martínez del Río welcomed them all with kindly graciousness and helpful advice.

155

Pattern of Mexico

The streets of Mexico have an intriguing custom, which may be somewhat confusing to new-comers until they get used to it, of changing their names every few blocks. This uses up more names, but there are so many national heroes and so many historical dates that the authorities seem never to run short of material, though duplication occurs from city to city.

The Avenida Francisco I. Madero, where it crosses San Juan Letrán, abruptly becomes the Avenida Juárez, at the same time broadening to boulevard proportions along the tree-green Alameda. It is a street of smart shops, the site of the city's most elaborate cinema, and a scene of color and gaiety by day or evening.

Where the streets of Juárez and Bucareli meet, a bronze man bestrides a bronze horse. The man is Charles IV of Spain, but it is a commentary on the relative importance of royalty that the statue is identified by Mexicans as *"El Caballito,"* the Little Horse. Set up in the Zócalo in 1803, it was hidden away in time of revolution and placed here after feeling had subsided. Designed by the eminent sculptor Manuel Tolsá, it has been declared a national Colonial monument, as—the directory of such monuments carefully adds—"a notable work of art which Mexico preserves solely as such."

The Little Horse and, a bit farther on, the tall structure like a dome on stilts, which commemorates the revolution of 1910, are landmarks and meeting-places by which people orientate themselves in that part of the city and identify directions to other destinations.

The "Little Horse" marks the entrance to the Paseo de la Reforma, one of the famous boulevards of the world. Maximilian laid it out in 1866 to provide a direct route to his castle at Chapultepec, but it was not he who named it after the "Reform" fostered by his arch-foe, Benito Juárez. The eucalyptus trees that Carlota planted along it died from lack of water, as the empire itself died from lack of support. But other trees have replaced them, and a succession of heroic monuments

MÉXICO, D. F.—AVENIDA JUÁREZ LOOKING TOWARD THE
REVOLUTION MONUMENT

The "Little Horse"

adorns the half-dozen 400-foot circular *glorietas* that break the straight sweep of the thoroughfare. Most interesting of them, to me, was the one in the second circle, commemorating the last Aztec emperor, Cuauhtémoc, and his desperate resistance to the conquering Spaniards.

A monument of a different sort is the remnants of the nine hundred arches that formerly led water from Chapultepec. They stand somewhat forlornly in a not quite parallel street opposite the modern Revolutionary School.

The Paseo de la Reforma and some adjacent streets are among the most European-looking in the Capital, many of the buildings showing the influence of the French period of Mexican culture, though the precincts are being invaded by structures of more modern type.

At the end of the boulevard, the park and castle of Chapultepec are another bit of ancient and Colonial Mexico entwined. The Hill of the Grasshopper was an Aztec fort and a summer residence of Moctézuma, who is reputed to have planted some of the giant ahuehuete trees that stand, wreathed with vines, on the tangled slopes. Moctézuma's bath, however, seems to be a less popular resort than the more recent Don Quijote fountain, with its tile insets depicting scenes in Cervantes' satirical romance.

Around the hill stretch the many acres of the park: here almost impenetrable forest, there formal garden; lakes, playgrounds, shaded walks and drives, riding paths. They are frequented, especially on Sunday, by Mexicans of all classes, from humble picnickers to equestrian *charros* in wide, silver-ornamented hats, tight trousers, and striped sarapes.

As we wandered through the showy interior of the castle, we understood why recent presidents have preferred not to live in it; it would be like inhabiting a museum. A Spanish viceroy built it, Maximilian renovated and redecorated it, and Carlota laid out the garden at the top of the hill; they and succeeding rulers filled it with cabinet work and art objects from Mexico,

157

Europe, and the Orient. The place is full of memories: Maximilian's clock, Carlota's boudoir, room after room of French furniture, carved or inlaid Chinese chests and cabinets, miscellaneous bric-à-brac—in a total effect bewilderingly ornate.

A monument in the park commemorates the Mexican cadets who fell when the castle was shelled and stormed by North American troops in the invasion of 1847.

My grandfather, who fought there, used to tell of the charge through the grove: how the shells crashed through the huge, moss-hung branches, hurling showers of splinters among the vines; how the attacking sharpshooters took shelter among the rocks, picking off gunners with deadly accuracy; how they swarmed up the scaling-ladders for a hand-to-hand fight on the terraces. And how the last of the cadets—the *Niños Héroës* for whom streets are named—wrapping his country's flag around him, hurled himself from the battlement rather than surrender.

It was not surprising to hear that the place was haunted: the woods by the spirit of Cortés' Indian mistress Doña Marina, the stairway by the ghost of a young zouave of Marshal Bazaine's French army—an admirer of Carlota's who, according to a somewhat malicious Mexican legend, was assassinated there in her absence by Herzfeld and Pilimentz, intimates of the emperor.

No less an authority than President Díaz himself is said to have encountered the ghost at close range and put it to flight with revolver shots. But the caretakers told of ghostly footfalls, voices, laughter, sounding in the luxurious salons: because of those noises, they said, they would pass through the halls only in pairs, never alone.

From the terraces the view sweeps over the valley.

"The whole Valley of Mexico lies stretched out, as in a map" [wrote Mme. Calderón de la Barca]. "The city itself, with its innumerable churches and convents; the two great aqueducts which cross the plain; the avenues of elms and poplars which lead to the city; the villages,

The "Little Horse"

lakes and plains which surround it. To the north the magnificent cathedral of Our Lady of Guadalupe; to the south, the villages of San Augustín, San Angel and Tacubaya, which seem embosomed in trees and look like an immense garden. And if in the plains below there are many uncultivated fields and many buildings falling to ruin, yet with its mighty enclosure of mountains, above which tower the two mighty volcanoes Popocatépetl and Ixtaccíhuatl, the Gog and Magog of the valley, off whose giant sides great volumes of misty smoke were rolling, and with its turquoise sky forever smiling on the scene, the whole landscape, as viewed from this height, is one of nearly unparalleled beauty."

Though the scene has changed somewhat in detail, the general effect remains much the same. Mme. Calderón saw it, however (in the early 1840's), before the colossal sign "Euzcadi," advertising a brand of tires, was emblazoned upon the horizon of the valley.

XX · BLOOD ON SAND

SUNLIGHT floods the circular expanse of sand. Around
rise, tier on tier, strung solidly on spidery steelwork,
the twenty thousand seats of what is said to be the
world's largest bullring. There are ringside places for invet-
erate fans—called, here, *aficionados*—expensive seats on the
so-called shady side (shady only in part and for a time), and
less aristocratic positions in the "sun."

The presiding officer enters his box. Plumed and mounted
marshals dash from the gates beneath, ride in opposite directions around the ring, meet, and dash back to salute the *presidente*. The band plays, but, to the possible surprise of North
American visitors, not selections from *Carmen*.

Like the "grand entry" of an old-fashioned circus performance, the participants march in: behind the marshals the richly clad *matadores* (literally "killers") on foot, with brilliant capes over their left arms; dart-planters; mounted lancers; the attendant "wise monkeys" who are the deckhands of the ring; the mules which will drag away the carcasses.

All is formal, ceremonious. If indeed the bull-fight was introduced into Spain by Moors or Romans as a martial exercise, it may still have originated, in the mists of antiquity, as a sacrificial rite. It has the manner and atmosphere of one.

The head marshal bows to the presiding officer; the fighters lift their capes. All is done with courtly gesture, with graceful dignity. The marshals and the mule teams depart; the lancers (*picadores*) take their places; the fighters toss their showy capes to friends in the ringside seats and await the bull with stained red and yellow cloths.

The *presidente* signals; drums and bugles sound; the bull enters. As he moves down the narrow corridor into the arena, an attendant plunges between his shoulders a small sharp instrument beribboned with the colors of his owner.

The animal rushes wildly about. A fighter provokes him with the cape. He charges; the man, feet perhaps unmoving, swings the cloak, deflecting the charge, and passes the fabric lightly over the lowered horns. Again and again this basic manœuver is repeated, with variations, each of which has its technical name, until this, the first act of the drama, is completed according to rule.

The fighter, having exhibited his skill, walks away. A lancer rides at the bull. The animal charges; the lowered horns strive for a hold through or under the matlike armor of the horse. The horse falls; another *picador* canters up to distract the bull while the overturned horse regains his feet and the unhorsed lancer hobbles to safety.

Bugles cry out over the sand: the second act begins.

Gravely, deliberately, a *banderillero* approaches the bull, two ribboned darts in his hands. His movement is like a dance:

slow, graceful, coördinated: every gesture, apparently, prescribed by some law of the ring. Like a dance, that slow but smooth, catlike step, poised with rear foot lifted on toe, darts held perpendicularly at end of outstretched arms—casting patterned shadows on the sand.

He throws his hat, perhaps, to attract the bull. The animal charges down like a locomotive: then the swift, deft half-turn of avoidance, and the darts, close together and parallel, drive into the thick hide.

Another *banderillero* takes his turn; the first plants two more darts. The crowd, it may be, stirred by the show of skill, clamors, "Another pair!" and the feat is repeated.

The bugle note quivers again in the shimmering air. The *matador* walks to the *presidente's* box, speaks briefly in salutation, then advances for the kill.

He waves away the assistants: this is his individual moment. But first they pour water on the scarlet cloth he carries, drag it in the sand—to give it weight for manipulation, I was told. But may not the action be a vestige of forgotten sacrifice? Water and earth, the vital elements under the sun—and soon blood, which nourishes the earth.

Deliberately, holding the red cloth on a slight pointed support, he moves toward the bull: cool, but watchful, circling warily.

He is very near. . . . Suddenly he thrusts out the scarlet lure. The bull rushes forward. Feet motionless, the man sweeps the cloth back; the bull, intent upon the bright rag, brushes past him; the cloth trails over the deadly horns.

Again and again the movement is repeated, with variations that only a connoisseur knows or cares to describe. The *matador* is manœuvering the animal into position for the slaughter.

At last, the climactic moment. The bull's head is down; the way to the vital spot is exposed. Swiftly, gracefully, the man thrusts the sword, at the same time draping the scarlet cloth over the bull's face to draw the bull aside while he himself deftly steps past the animal.

The blade plunges, behind the great armed head, deep, to the heart. The bull stands, bewildered; the rich blood wells up around the hilt. The killer resumes his play with the scarlet cloth. The bull rushes briefly to this side, to that; then stands still, wonderingly. He sinks to his knees, crumples, lies still.

A quick stroke sinks to the base of the brain. The mules drag the body out of the arena—and it draws a graceful curve in the sand.

Shouts roll down from the tiers of seats. Straw hats fly, thickly sowing the ring like monstrous marigolds—the flowers of death. The *matador* struts about the circle, tossing them back. Admirers rush out, lift him to their shoulders, parade him around the circuit in triumph.

Uniformed attendants shovel the blood-wet sand into wheelbarrows and smooth the arena for the next victim.

For a detailed description, one must consult Ernest Hemingway or some other connoisseur. This is merely how the proceeding looked to us. At first it seems to many an unaccustomed observer a stupid performance—as stupid, probably, as some of our sports must appear to foreigners. But as one watches, the barbaric beauty of the rite comes over one. It is a little like a game, yet with a deadly seriousness beneath the bright surface. Death is there in the arena. Death for the bull, of course; perhaps for some of the horses, although, armored as they are, this occurs less frequently than it did. It may be death for the man.

That combat in the circle of sand is in its way symbolic of humanity's unending battle with Nature. Here the advantage would seem to be with man, in numbers, intelligence, and weapons—but he must be superbly quick and light of foot; if he miscalculates, he will be caught. Stupid as the bull is in attacking the cape instead of the man, and bewildered as he must be by the whole business, he is still a formidable animal. I saw a fighter thrown to earth, wounded, to lie motionless for a tense moment, until his companions rushed to distract the bull. Thereupon the man rose painfully and limped away.

Many people consider it cruel. I have no wish either to attack or to defend it. I only seek to explore the reasons for the people's interest in it—its skill, its processional and dramatic quality, its color and movement and composition.

From one point of view, the bull-fight is merely an execution attended by certain barbarous and somewhat tedious formalities. But if it were only that, the millions of Spaniards and Spanish Americans who throng the rings would not have so deep a passion for it. And, indeed, many foreign visitors do not regard it so. It is a spectacle which one may view as an art form, a stately drama in pantomime, fulfilling the classic formula of purging through pity and terror; and a marvel of pageantry, a bright-colored pattern on the sunlit sand.

Here man's struggle with the wild forces of the earth is brought down to a point, concentrated in the duel between the intelligence and skill of man and the stark power of the beast. Man normally conquers, because he must. In the long history of evolution, has not man always conquered? There is a hint here of ancient, heroic things, when man went forth with sharpened stake or stone-tipped spear to wrest the meat of life from forest and swamp and plain; a memory, too, of the blood sacrifice that purged man of the errors of living and inclined the hearts of the gods to favor him with rain and sun.

Looking upon that bright pattern of movement and color and death, I remembered the great charging bulls painted, these thousands of years agone, on the living stone in the darkness of the caves.

XXI · GARDENS, CELLS, AND TEMPLES

SHALLOW waterways, between low banks bristling with tall slender trees like Lombardy poplars, are all that is left of one of the five ancient lakes of the Valley of Mexico. The region (southeast of the city) is called, in the Nahua tongue, Xochimilco, Place of Flowers.

Chichimeca tribes, according to tradition, finding themselves overcrowded on the islands in the lake, established *chinampas* or floating gardens. They wove a foundation of twigs covered with earth, large enough to bear thatched huts as well as crops. The gardens no longer float. In time, roots pierced the bottom and thrust into the mud, or the owners purposely anchored the *chinampas* with poles. I have heard this account of their origin doubted, but there is ancient authority for it, and a record that on one occasion a *chinampa* broke loose in a storm and blocked the canal of San José. Only recently Luís Marden reported them actually floating, at Mixquic.

Cortés came this way, crossing the great causeway northward to his conquest of the Capital, and his soldiers marveled at the white "palaces" erected among the groves by vassals of the Aztec emperor. In the direction of the city stood the strong Xoloc fortress which Cortés used as a base from which to operate during the siege. In the maze of canals of Xochimilco he came near ending his career, according to his companion the chronicler Bernal Díaz: his horse sank in the mud, and only an intrepid sally by one of his Indian allies saved him.

The town, like others in Mexico, has its Colonial churches, two of which are listed as "national monuments," but the chief attraction of Xochimilco is its embowered waterways winding among the flowers. Narrow, and flecked with floating strands of vegetation, they run between low banks of dark earth planted not only with flowers but with corn, cabbage, and all manner of small crops. Flat-bottomed boats, canvas-shaded like "covered wagons," are poled by Indian boatmen along these watery streets. Each bears, over the bow end of the canopy, its name, in flowers: *Conchita, Adelita, Concepción*.

Canoes pass, heaped with glowing cargoes of carnations, violets, and giant pansies. Others vend food, soft drinks, and beer. Still others draw alongside, bearing small volunteer orchestras: a marimba, a violin, a bass. They have their own ideas of tourist taste. "La Paloma" and "Rancho Grande" are almost invariable selections, but the most frequent is likely to be some popular North American tune, regardless of its age, such as "Alexander's Ragtime Band." After two or three compositions are played, one of the musicians boards the tourist boat to collect.

I have heard travelers describe Xochimilco as the most beautiful place in Mexico. It can be very attractive, on its less crowded days: there is a pervading sense of greenness and quiet, a dreaminess of clouds reflected in the calm water. The gentle gliding of the boat, the slow rhythmic motion of the pole-wielding gondolier, the flower-bright margins slipping past, induce a mood of repose. On Sundays and feast days, however, it is a Mexican Coney Island. As Dr. Jorge Enciso, authority on Colonial art and architecture, remarked when some one in our party praised it as a beautiful spot—"Yes, when without music and without photographers."

Villa Obregón is the official name since Alvaro Obregón fell before an assassin's bullets there, but to most Mexicans the neat southern suburb, around its two pleasant plazas, is still San Ángel.

The old Carmelite monastery, in its character of government museum, seemed to be nearly in its ancient state when the clanging tram deposited us in San Ángel. Soldiers of the Revolution had whitewashed over the mural frescoes, taken some of the vestments, and beheaded one of the dismal saints. But the Indian-laid stonework, the refectory basins lined with the first Puebla tiles, the three-tiled domes, each of a different color, remained intact, as did the cells, with narrow barred windows, those of the novices having a narrow wooden shelf on which to sleep, with a wooden pillow.

Below were penitential cells, dark and airless, with a small opening through which to thrust bread and water. The watchman, having his choice of two hundred and more rooms, had chosen, with the Mexican dread of fresh air, one of these unventilated dungeons as his sleeping quarters.

We admired the ceilings in the white-and-gold chapel and in a room near it, colored by Indian artists with vegetable pigments; the lace work in maguey fiber by Indian sisters; the intricate beadcraft, the wool embroidery, immeasurably patient and fine.

The rude litter on which dead monks, of old, were carried to their tombs stood in a corridor outside the burial crypt. In adjoining rooms, the caretaker displayed rows of mummified bodies. Soldiers in 1914, he said, seeking treasure, dug up the floor and found only these pitiful remains. They stood before us, in crumbling coffins—preserved, even to remnants of clothing, by "gases in the volcanic soil," as he explained. Spanish nobles, the cut and material of their garments still discernible, one with petrified beard; monks, nuns—one with tongue outthrust and arms raised as if in struggle ("buried alive, I think," suggested the caretaker). The rich noble, the poor monk, here and there an Indian convert—all alike at the end went down to God's impartial darkness; the earth that had borne them received them, and one is as handsome as another in the festooned fantastic jewelry of petrified worms.

The caretaker thrust his hand into a hole in the wall, a repository for bones when removed from the crypts to make room for new burials. He drew forth a skull on which some one, with mordant Mexican humor, had lettered prematurely, "Lázaro Cárdenas."

The garden outside had fallen to neglect: prisoners were lounging in an adjoining patio; in another courtyard, boys of the village were playing handball against the seventeenth-century walls.

The adjacent church, still in use, was packed with Indians when we made another of our visits. It was July 16th, the day of Our Lady of Carmen. Arriving from mountain villages, they had camped all night in the stone Portal of the Pilgrims, and as we entered they were dancing in the church before the image of Our Lady.

Men, women, children, in buckskin ornamented with glittering beads and round bits of glass or mica, with round painted and tasseled shields on their arms, and high head-dresses of colored plumes, made a barbaric picture. Marching out, they danced again, company after company, around tall banners in the patio. Mandolin-like instruments of armadillo shell strummed a simple melody of a few chords over and over; it

STREET IN SAN ÁNGEL, FROM LOWER PLAZA

was a little like the crooning of a wind-harp—a gentle but persistent sylvan sound. Small bells tinkled on leggings as the dancers lifted their feet with the balancing movement characteristic of the Indian rite.

As the leader gave the word, all wheeled and bowed, plumes swaying like waves of grain; one thought of Archibald Mac-Leish's graphic image: "The armies of Mexico marching, the leaning wind in their garments." It was pure Indian, this, in music, in costume, in movement and feeling: here was a man in the mask of an Aztec Eagle Knight; here a Wolf Warrior in dogskin with a toothed mask, and a wooden Aztec war-sword hanging from his wrist.

Hour after hour it continued: a moving scene of color and life, psychologically affecting with almost hypnotic rhythm of movement and repetition of tinkling sound.

Thence the way led past the monastery walls and between rows of wealthy residences to the Pedregal, the ancient lava flow that covered the prehistoric cemetery of Copilco.

Rude shacks stood near the quarry mouth; women were washing clothes on stones beside a trickle of water; ragged children swarmed to beg *centavitos* from the visitors. Beyond, a government guard watched the entrance to the tunnels that housed the remains of central Mexico's earliest known people.

Madame Calderón de la Barca, writing in 1841, told of an Indian tradition of a "buried population" under the Pedregal. The tradition was confirmed in 1917, when government archæologists drove tunnels under the thirty-foot cap of lava at the back of the Copilco quarry.

There they lie, those ancient people, just as they were found: tall folk, by the length of the bones, stretched out in burial, each with his bowl beside him for food or water, and his stone for grinding corn, shaped much like those in use to-day. The archæologists had not disturbed them, but had enclosed them in glass cases, to preserve them and to prevent visitors from carrying away bones as souvenirs.

In other cases there were more pottery and an amazing variety of hand-modeled clay figurines from which, more than from any other source, the life of these people—called "Archaic" for want of a more exact name—has been traced. These clever statuettes are believed to be portraits, they are so varied in feature and expression. They show styles of clothing and ornament, even to tattooing, display varieties of weapons and tools, and suggest the physical type. There is no mystery about this last. The bones indicate that they were American Indians.

On another occasion I stood at Copilco while half a dozen eminent archæologists argued over the composition of the soil under the lava: over whether it was a lake deposit or volcanic, and over the age of the site. There is probably no way of determining just how long ago these early Mexicans lived. All that is known certainly is that they had been buried before the lava poured out of Xictli, the crater on the slope of giant Ajusco, and that the lava is estimated to be at least two thousand years old.

Already, in that dim period uncounted years ago, they had a civilization of a sort: a notion of a future life, agriculture, domestic animals—for there are statuettes of dogs of a peculiar breed. The people grew corn and ground it with implements like those used to-day. Perhaps they were the first to do so: the fathers of Mexican civilization.

A few miles away, behind the Peña Pobre paper-mill at Tlalpan, is an elliptical temple-mound where these people worshiped. It was overwhelmed by the same lava flow, but the upper part projects above the congealed sea of rock. It is a crude structure, compared with those of later times, but it shows the same exaltation of worship by placing it on a physical height. It suggests the development of the truncated and terraced pyramidal form from the features of the surrounding landscape.

We could distinguish four terraces, built of earth and

Gardens, Cells, and Temples

rubble and faced with a layer of boulders. Our feet pressed the stones of a ruined stair to the red-painted clay altars that must have seen ceremonies to the gods of Rain and Sun.

"The oldest building in the Americas," said an enthusiastic archæologist. But, as some of his colleagues pointed out, that is taking in a great deal of territory.

The gardens of Churubusco looked green and tranquil between the powerful arches; as summer rain slanted past the cloister walks, the church and monastery were scented with the fragrance of roses.

We found it a delightful place, better preserved than the near-by San Ángel, with lovely patios, beautiful tile work, rich gold altars; in the loft a fine old illuminated choir book, with large enough letters so that the monks might read them from any distance within the room. The library with its window-seats and their hollowed footrests, was a place in which to linger over venerable parchment volumes—though many visitors seemed to prefer the relics of the battle with the North Americans, and the collection of historic carriages, including those of Iturbide, Maximilian, and Santa Anna. For this, too, is a government museum.

The light dimmed. It was closing time. The caretakers peered out at the thickening rain and invited us, in gracious abrogation of the rules, to remain.

Out of the low lands of the valley north of the Capital rises a tall, fortress-like bulk of wall, surmounted by the pointed ornaments that mark sixteenth-century Mexican architecture. From the great plain tower, with its intricately ornamented entrance, the cloistered arches of the monastery extend along a sunken court.

San Agustín Acolman was founded by Augustinian friars on an island in 1539. It was flooded four times, abandoned, and

171

then excavated by the government in the early 1930's as a national monument.

Traces of the water and mud that had filled its lower rooms and corridors were still apparent as we entered. Even above the flood line, the frescoed plaster had peeled from the discolored walls; about the place hung a musty odor of dampness and decay.

The cells are small but neat, each with its window-seat looking out on the green valley, and a hollowed niche for the feet. Below are a great bare refectory, a kitchen with a huge arched primitive fireplace, a maze of corridors and rooms. The library, with its moldering ancient volumes, and the empty church are on a higher level; both are hung with fine paintings by Nicolás Rodríguez Juárez and other Colonial painters. In the church, remnants of early frescoes cling to the walls. They represent, so a guide said, a friar's memory of those in the Sistine chapel.

Birds nest high in the dilapidated altar; where human beings no longer worship, their voices chant in Nature's choir.

On Fridays, motor caravans climb out of the Capital to Toluca, which stands on the height with two snowy volcanoes towering beyond. Here, in the market that sprawls for blocks through the Colonial town, tourists come to bargain for sarapes and needlework, for pottery and baskets and toys, and for the local liquor that is said to come in four strengths: "for children, women, old folk, and men."

Under the impact of this weekly visitation, Toluca has, I fear, become tourist-conscious: Nahuas. Otomíes and Matlazincas have begun to share the notion of the Capital that all North Americans are of fabulous wealth. Nor do the residents, apparently, limit themselves always to legitimate trade. A friend of mine, admiring sarapes in the market, inadvertently allowed himself to be caught in a jostling crowd—and emerged with every pocket slashed and the contents deftly withdrawn. The police were sympathetic but scarcely encourag-

CHURCHES WITH ELABORATELY CARVED FAÇADES STAND OUT
IN RELIEF AGAINST A BACKGROUND OF MOUNTAINS

ing, as they pointed out the difficulty of finding or identifying the thieves in that throng.

"After all," they added consolingly, "the poor must live."

The temple pyramid of Tenayuca stands in its enclosure behind the adobe village of San Bártolo in the tawny plain north of the Capital. It is guarded round about by the fifty-two snakes of the year sculptured in stone, and more snake heads jut out from the slanting walls. On either side of the temple a great coiled reptile with a carven crest points to the position of the sun or planets at certain seasons.

Smaller and ruder than some of the other sacred structures of Mexico, Tenayuca is impressive for its steep pitch, which gives an illusion of greater height.

Before the grand stairway, the interior of a boxlike receptacle still holds traces of fresco: a skull, crossed thighbones, richly colored ornamentation.

Tunnels dive into the walls, cutting across five periods of construction—for this temple was rebuilt and enlarged again and again: at the beginning of each fifty-two-year cycle, in the general opinion of archæologists with whom I traced those tunnels. But the glyphs on the exposed walls of the buried structures within may, when fully interpreted, give a different answer.

Government investigators had cut away the outer structure at the front, exposing the steep stairway of an earlier time, and our feet trod the stones of centuries past, ascending to the broken summit, whence we had a view of the wide plain of the Chichimeca tribes who laid these stones.

"Spaniards superintended, but Indians did the work," said the Indian boy with pride as he guided us through the "House of Probation of San Martín Tepotzotlán, 1670-82; façade of church, 1760-62," and its attendant buildings, some of them even older than this.

Pattern of Mexico

"It's beautiful! It's beautiful!" he repeated, pointing out this or that detail of gold leaf on profusely carved wood; the frescoes on the ceiling, still fresh and bright; delicate colors on the vestments of carved and painted Virgins and saints; painted benches three centuries old.

"A degenerate form of baroque," pronounced the Chief of the Division of Colonial Monuments, on another occasion as we stood before the bewilderingly carved façade.

The interior is very elaborate, but in reasonably good taste, in view of the style of the period, and in better condition than many of its kind. The richness and brightness of the decoration are amazingly preserved. In the course of the Revolution soldiers had stripped the gold away as high as they could reach, but had not troubled to find ladders in order to attain the rest; no doubt they reasoned that there were more churches to loot, farther on.

The main altar is overpowering with its heavy intricacy of glittering Churrigueresque adornment. But the chapels are the glory of Tepotzotlán: the replica of Bethlehem, with its carved benches and gold altar; the one with exquisitely tiled floor, its doorway barred to preserve the delicately tinted ceramic from destroying feet; the bizarre octagonal chapel in five styles of architecture, pointing up into a tower windowed with alabaster, in whose gracious light the dove of the Holy Spirit hangs poised. The doors and walls are gorgeously carved and painted; among Moorish, Florentine, Baroque, Churrigueresque and Plateresque motifs are scattered Indian symbols of the sun, moon, and stars.

The Indian boy was all but overcome with wonder when, through the opera glasses my wife handed him, the upper windows were brought close to his eyes, for the first time. "It's beautiful! It's beautiful!" was all he could say, but his tone and the expression of his face told of a reverent rapture exquisitely touching.

Thronged with delegates to the Congress of Americanists,

174

XXII · AT THE HILL OF THE STAR

THE bus rumbled south out of Mexico City, past the
Viga Canal, green and slimy and full of weeds but
still navigated by flat-bottomed boats, one man pol-
ing, another dragging by a rope the clumsy craft loaded with
vegetables and flowers. Occasionally one of the gardeners
would dip a bunch of carrots or lettuce in the sewer-like water,
to keep it fresh and "clean" for the market.

Past Santa Anita of the flower festivals and east across
low fields—vegetables, corn, flowers—between rows of somber
trees, to Ixtapalápa.

For a vegetable peddler had told a cousin of Don Mario
that on this Sunday pilgrims returning from Chalma would
dance at Ixtapalápa in honor of Our Lord of the Caves.

Pattern of Mexico

Even as we entered the adobe town that has replaced the white palaces of Cortés' time, we could see home-made rockets soaring from the hill behind the church, filling the air with puffs of smoke and a prodigious clatter of explosions. In front of the church a band was playing. Pilgrims were arriving, carrying ceremonial canes, wearing sacred images in small bags slung from their necks. From all parts of Mexico they journey, mostly on foot, to dance before the shrine of mountain-cupped Chalma.

At Ixtapalápa, the local Lord of the Caves, whose history is similar to that of the Lord of Chalma, had been taken from his niche in the cavern and installed on the altar. The church was hung with long cables of zacate herb and flowers, and so full of people and more flowers that it was almost impossible for us to see the image, or even to get inside.

But the greatest activity was without. Vendors of food and drinks swarmed over the church grounds and the roadway beyond. Prominent among their wares were the local bread, mixed with maguey juice and baked in round loaves, and *alegría,* a confection, said to be of Aztec origin, of small seeds stuck together with honey and covered with a purple-pink paste.

There was a puppet show, and a showman of trained birds which rang tiny bells, danced, picked fortunes out of a toy hat: "You will meet a handsome young man...." A ballad seller recited his wares with dramatic feeling, through his white beard. In the churchyard, a photographer had set up his gaudy background, and pilgrims were flocking to have their portraits made.

The ground was littered with the reed sticks of spent rockets; boys went about, gathering them into bundles and looking remarkably like the pictures in ancient codices of youths with bundles of reeds at the fire ceremony held of old on the Hill of the Star near-by. Crude little crosses—two sticks tied together with grass—were stuck into the roof of the cave.

At the Hill of the Star

Some of them were easily identified as having previously borne that confection known in this country as "popsicle."

"The Indians," explained Don Mario, "worshiped an image in the cave, and the friars, with all their preaching, couldn't get them to give up that worship.

"One day when the Indians came to the cave, the image wasn't there. They went to the mission, and found that the friars were gone, too. But a little later the friars were back and a new image—a crucifix—was in the cave. Clearly a miracle, the Indians thought. The friars agreed with them. And that miraculous image is Our Lord of the Caves."

The dancers hadn't arrived, we were told. When would they come? Who knew? Perhaps at noon, perhaps at evening, perhaps next day.... There is no pinning down a fiesta to hours of the clock.

We bought food in the marketplace—maguey bread, bright sweet *alegría,* small avocados, oranges, bananas, zapotes, and a tiny paper-twist of salt—and set off through fields of young corn toward the hill, where groups of pilgrims were already scattered under the infrequent trees.

Beneath our feet crunched shards of ancient pottery that almost paved the countryside, mingled with bits of more modern ware easily identified by its glaze. For the Hill of the Star was a pilgrimage place of old. There, at the end of the fifty-two year cycle, the sacred fire was kindled anew, and the new cycle of years was born. The world had been destroyed four times, each time at the end of such a cycle. Four suns had perished. And the fifth sun was fated to end in a great earthquake at the close of one of those cycles. Therefore there was anxiety as the end of the period approached. On the eve of the new year, all fires were quenched, pottery and utensils were broken, and priests led the people in solemn procession to the Hill of the Star. There they waited for Aldebaran to cross the center of the sky. If it should fail to do so, the stars and planets, in the form of wild beasts, would devour men, and the earthquake would swallow the sun. A captive was stretched upon an altar at the summit. When Aldebaran crossed the meridian, the captive was slain and a new fire kindled on his body. Runners lighted fagots at the new fire and hurried to all the temples in the Valley of Mexico. There was rejoicing. For the fifth sun was not yet to perish: mankind had still fifty-two years, at least, of life.

A metal cylinder sunk into the ground to hold a flagpole on holidays marks the site of that altar, said the forest guard posted there.

From that height, the valley lay spread out before us like a great flat-bottomed bowl. Dust-whirls marched over the dry bed of Lake Texcoco; above the cloud strata, the peaks of Popocatépetl and Ixtaccíhuatl gleamed white with snow, as if floating on the sea of cloud.

Picnickers were trooping down the hill, singing, as we returned, pausing to pick up a glassy dark bit of obsidian knife, or a little clay head, or a wedge of curiously decorated potsherd. As we neared the church we heard the mutter of drums and the thin wail of Indian flutes. The dancers had arrived.

The crowd was denser than ever around the cleared place before the church where the pilgrims were paying their respects to Our Lord of the Caves.

The dance was "The Moors and Christians," said to be an early Spanish introduction based on Charlemagne's victory over the Saracens, but interpreted by the Indians in their own way and doubtless incorporating older rites of their own—perhaps the battles of the gods in the legendary destruction of the suns.

Both "Moors" and "Christians" were extravagantly garbed in what the Indians supposed those worthies would wear: one party in a fancy-dress-ball version of medieval Spanish costume, the other in fantastic robes and turbans—a barbaric clash of colors, though most of them were shod with tennis shoes and several looked through dark sun-glasses.

At the Hill of the Star

The dance was simple and monotonous—a few steps from side to side, weaving in and out, then a brief clash of swords, preceded by dialogue in which the leaders of the two "armies" defied each other in reasonably clear Spanish. "I will defend the true faith with my own blood," I heard the King of the Christians mutter sternly as I approached.

Hour after hour, with slight variations, the dance was repeated, to the thud of drums and whine of flutes, with pauses in which the combatants took time out to munch a miniature ice-cream cone or puff a cigarette.

The King of the Christians—a spare, dark-brown man with black glasses and bristling mustache—warned me sternly not to photograph the festivities. But the King of the Moors—in private life plain Domingo Ibáñez—looking, behind his beard of combed-out rope, like a fantastically robed Santa Claus, posed willingly, scepter in one hand, cigarette in the other, on my pledge to send him a print of the result.

A masked clown, inescapable feature of most fiestas, swaggered about, indulging in horseplay, mimicking the dancers, and performing all manner of antics at which the spectators looked without a smile. His practical function apparently was that of a sergeant-at-arms, keeping the crowd back with the flat of his sword so as to leave space for the dancers.

The affair would go on all afternoon, perhaps all night, with little change, and Don Mario wanted to pay his respects to the friend who had sent him word of the fiesta.

The house of Don Juan Morales was like most of the houses in Ixtapalápa—a quadrangle of adobe and volcanic rock around an earth-floored patio, upon which opened small dark rooms. It was somewhat like a Polynesian home in its simplicity: mats on the earth floors, and no other furniture; a roll of blanket on a shelf, a few pottery jars, a saint on the wall.

Pattern of Mexico

In a corner of the patio was a pit of water, beside which lay a flat stone on which to wash clothes.

All was plain, bare, and poor—but with Mexican and Indian courtesy members of the family brought a jug of clear fresh water and slices of field-ripened pineapple, and pressed us to share the remains of their earlier feast of fiery brown turkey *mole*.

We showed them the broken clay statuettes we had found on the lower slopes of the Hill of the Star. Don Mario had heard that the family of Don Juan had a stone image. No, they had none, our host replied. But later, as we sat in the tawny light of late afternoon, he brought out a small terra-cotta head, in almost perfect preservation, which he gave me: a portrait, said the Cuban archæological student who was with us, of one dead, for the eyes were closed and the tongue thrust out: thus, she said, the Aztecs buried their dead.

A neighbor, Don Juan remembered, had a stone *idolo*. Small boys were sent to summon the bent old woman. The image was brought: a foot-high seated female figure in soft gray volcanic stone, crude but unmistakably genuine. No steel tool had carved these features; they bore the marks of the stone chisel. From the sculptured earrings, the necklace, the shape of the head-dress, we identified the figure as the Jade-Skirted One, Chalchictlícue of the Flowing Water, bride of Tlaloc of the Rains.

The owner could tell nothing of its meaning and little of its history. This *"idolito"* had belonged to her grandfather, yet she was willing to part with this heirloom, on persuasion, for an insignificant sum.

The small pottery head, it appeared, had been found near a spring in a near-by field. The old woman who met us at the indicated gateway said there was nothing to be found; she had had some pieces, but the children had played with them and destroyed or lost them. Nor should we enter the field, she warned us grumblingly, for there were fierce dogs and half-

At the Hill of the Star

wild cattle. Nevertheless, guided by a pair of plump, quiet children, we explored the margins of the muddy water-hole in a corner of a pasture. Scratching the dry, pebbly earth under its sparse shrubbery, we turned up in a few minutes obsidian arrowheads, tiny clay masks, figurines.

The Hill of the Star, it is said, was the appointed rallying place for an attack on the Capital in the revolution set for November 20, 1910. But President Porfirio Díaz learned of the plans and frustrated the attempt, for the time. As he sat studying the plot, his minister of war, General González Cosío, said contemptuously, "Those aren't plans. They're just nothing."

"It's like this," Díaz is said to have replied. "If you order a pair of trousers for Saturday, and you go to look at them on Thursday, what do you see? Only some pieces of cloth. If you wait until Saturday, they're trousers. Well, you're right; these aren't plans—but only because we arrived on Thursday."

The dictator's humor, did not, however, prevent his overthrow before another year had passed—the end of another "sun."

XXIII · DARK MADONNA

SUCH was not done for any other nation," said Benedict XIV when Fray Francisco López showed him a copy
of the painting enshrined at Guadalupe as the portrait
of Our Lady of Guadalupe, the Dark Madonna of Mexico.
(Guadalupe, a suburb just north of the Capital, is known officially as Villa Gustavo A. Madero.)

Every Mexican knows the story, and many Americans. On
a Saturday morning (December 9th, for the tale is precise) in
1531, Juan Diego Quauhtlatohua was passing the hill of Tepeyac on his way to Mass. He heard mysterious music, saw a
rainbow arc that tinted with prismatic color the rocks and cacti
of the hill. From a luminous cloud appeared a divine face and
form; a voice spoke in the Nahua language, bidding him tell

Dark Madonna

Bishop Zumárraga that Our Lady wished a church built at that spot.

The Ylustrísimo don Fray Juan de Zumárraga (the same who, to the undying wrath of modern archæologists, burned most of the Aztec books) was inclined at first to regard Juan Diego's vision as proceeding from too much pulque.

A second time the Blessed Virgin appeared, and Juan Diego repeated her message to the bishop. If the Indian had indeed seen Our Lady, she would have given him a sign to prove his statements, the bishop declared.

Very well, the apparition in effect told Juan, return to-morrow for the sign. But Juan Diego's uncle was ill of a fever, and he did not keep the appointment. On the following day, which was Tuesday, the twelfth, the old man appeared to be dying. Juan Diego hurried to find a priest, taking another path around the hill. But the divine apparition rose up in his way, and at her feet flowed a spring of water. His uncle had already recovered, she told him. As for the sign: pluck roses on the hill and take them to the bishop.

Juan gathered the roses—the first that ever grew there, and the last, likely enough, for it is an arid place. When he opened his cloak and let the roses fall before the bishop, there was the portrait of Our Lady, as he had seen her, on the fabric.

Just how much Fray Juan de Zumárraga may have had to do with the performance of the miracle does not appear in the record. I am not concerned with crediting or discrediting the story. It was accepted, and is accepted to-day, throughout Mexico, and Our Lady of Guadalupe was officially recognized by Pope Benedict XIV as patroness of that country. The event of Tepeyac was followed by numerous similar and not very original miracles elsewhere, but she of Guadalupe remains preëminent, the Indians' own Divine Mother. It is a beautiful story, and a beautiful faith.

It is typical of Mexico, of the intertwining of the old belief with the new, the reappearance of Indian deities under Christian names. For anciently, this hill was sacred to that other Virgin Mother, Coacíhuatl the Snake Woman, also called Tonantzin, "Our Lady." The day of her feast fell at about the season when Juan Diego experienced his vision.

"This appears to be," wrote Fray Bernardino de Sahagún, "a satanic invention, in order to palliate idolatry under the equivocation of this name Tonantzin, and they come now from very far, as before, to visit this Tonantzin, which devotion also is suspicious, because in all parts there are many churches of Our Lady, and they do not go to them, but come from far lands to this Tonantzin, as of old."

Guadalupe is a quaint and fairly neat village, swarming with street vendors, its market-place piled with pottery and Indian wares. It is a busy place at any time, for there are always pilgrims; on feast days, the crowd is so dense that a stranger can scarcely get about. In the big plaza, Indians were sitting on fountain-ledges—types out of murals, they looked, with clear brown skin, smooth black hair, lustrous large eyes—smiling, laughing. We saw no "sad Indian" in Guadalupe. On a bench near us sat a couple, holding hands.

The big church at the foot of the hill is relatively new, undistinguished in its exterior, and surrounded by a tall iron fence which keeps the innumerable vendors at a respectful distance. The interior is ornate but subdued, in better taste than many —though the gold, we were assured, is "a quarter of an inch thick."

The *tilma* of Juan Diego, bearing the miraculous painting, is enshrined behind thick glass over the main altar, at a distance from the observer. It is difficult to approach near enough to examine it in detail, but the colors are softer, the execution better, than in the numerous copies in every church and almost every home in Mexico.

Our Lady stands enveloped in an aura of gold and red. Her head is slightly bowed, the black Indian hair parted in the center, the eyes downcast. She wears a rose-colored tunic flecked with gold, over which falls a cloak of the blue-green color of the robe of the goddess of flowing waters, spangled with golden stars. The face, it has often been remarked, resembles that of a typical Aztec noblewoman at the time of the Conquest. She is known affectionately as La Morena, the Dark One.

Here, on feast days, come Indian *concheros,* in tinkling belled sandals and leggings, fringed buckskin garments and beaded head-dresses, with clicking tassels of shells; strumming armadillo-shell guitars in a plaintive, monotonous, reiterated melody; lifting their feet in a solemn ritual dance that must have been centuries old when Juan Diego spoke with Divinity beneath this hill. They raise their voices in a hymn in the Nahua tongue: do they themselves know to which "Our Lady" it is addressed?

They are sure, at least, that she is a lady of many miracles. The walls of the right-hand chapel at the rear are covered with small votive paintings on tin, in naïve but effective style: here a motor-car careers wildly down a Mexican street, here a train is derailed, there a sufferer lies on a sick-bed or kneels on the floor of a prison cell. Always in an upper corner appears Our Lady in her luminous cloud, and below, an inscription setting forth in detail the place, date, and circumstance, and the gratitude of the worshiper for his deliverance.

Another room is decorated in stars and crosses formed of little silver replicas of parts of the body, for whose healing credit is given to the Dark Madonna. There is a preponderance of arms and legs, whence one might conclude that injuries to these members are more frequent, or that Our Lady is more attentive to their particular afflictions.

In the heavily gilded Chapel of the Sacred Heart, a glass case contains a warped cross. An attempt, said the sacristan, was made to blow up Our Lady, but the sacred picture resisted the explosion: not even the glass was broken. Only the cross near it was bent, and it is preserved as evidence of the miracle.

A cobbled way winds up the hill of Tepeyac to the humbler

chapel to which, on days of pilgrimage, the devout climb painfully on their knees ("I walked all the way from the city to the Guadalupe on my knees," said the young man who climbed with me the many-staired Estribo at Pátzcuaro), and to the stone-hollowed tombs of Mexico's most aristocratic mausoleum.

Almost every house along the path is a photographic studio. Everywhere against the adobe walls are spread gaudy backgrounds, are hung bright, spangled *china poblana* costumes; before crude backdrops stand toy horses, unconvincing airplanes, here and there a live pony—accessories of the memorial photograph that seems to be an essential feature of the pilgrimage.

An entire family was sitting for one of these portraits as I mounted the hill. "Favor to remove the hat," requested the photographer. The head of the family hesitated, took off his wide sombrero, then, with a decisive sweep, put it on again. "I don't want to take off my hat," he announced with finality —and, amid laughter, the picture was taken. Below, a group of girls, one at a time, posed in borrowed finery.

The Chapel of the Hill is shabby and primitive but much venerated. Its votive paintings are cruder and more interesting, recording an impressive number of divinely aided escapes from prison or from firing-squads. It is a church of the humble.

From the summit, there is a view over the valley, where dust clouds swirl across dry beds of ancient lakes; in the distance, snow lies on the volcanic peaks.

Below, the three blue, white, and yellow tiled domes of the Chapel of the Well make a vivid spot of color among adobe-walled streets. Here, according to the legend, the spring gushed forth when Our Lady told Juan Diego to gather the roses. The brackish, somewhat ill-smelling water is reputed to have miraculous curative virtues. Bottles in which to carry it home are for sale, along with amulets and medals, small re-

CHAPELS CLIMB THE HILLS

Dark Madonna

productions of the sacred painting, bits of "holy plaster," and many another souvenir.

Indian women were reclining on the steps of the well, which was built up in a high curb and covered with a wooden lid pierced by a square opening through which to dip up water. The visitor who drinks of the well will surely return to Mexico, says a tradition.

The chapel itself is circular, adorned with crude paintings of the apparition of Our Lady, a carved figure reputed to be a portrait of Juan Diego, and other decorations in a mixture of Spanish and Indian taste.

The streets outside were full of sandal-shod Indians from the country, with hair hanging free or in long dark braids. In a street near the Chapel of the Well, vendors were frying intestines on open griddles and wrapping them in tortillas for numerous customers. They offered us some, recommending them as "very savory." An old woman held up a great forkful of garbage-like greens: "Mud," she defined it, to the accompaniment of laughter from the crowd. More satisfactory to foreign taste were the *gorditos* (little fat ones)—small, round, rich cookies associated particularly with Guadalupe but common at fiestas everywhere in the Valley.

> Out of the deep strong steadfast Indian heart
> this pure and sweet embodiment of prayer:
> these downcast eyes, serene as evening air,
> and generous lips as if about to part
> in words of healing for whatever smart;
> calm face beneath the fluent Indian hair.
> Witness of Juan Diego's humble trust,
> the miracle roses on the barren hill
> impressed this image (fresh it lingers still)
> upon his mantle, doubt it if you must!
> Even we strangers, from a world thrust
> deep into greed and hate—with reverent thrill
> we pause to ask, for all hearts wrung and torn,
> your blessing, Little Mother of the Corn.

XXIV · CITY OF THE GODS

TEOTIHUACAN stands in the plain northeast of the
Capital—a sacred city, pointing toward the stars.
Tier upon tier its stones rise, gray and clear-cut in
the lofty light. The full name of the near-by village, in pious
Castilian and equally reverent Nahua, bears the impress of
Mexico's mingled cultures: "Saint John Dwelling of the Gods."

The Toltecs built it; how long ago is a matter of dispute,
but clearly no later than the ninth century A.D., which—despite
calculations of guides who impress visitors by relating the city
to a time before the Christian era—is quite old enough.

Like most ancient Mexican structures, these temples were
rebuilt many times, or rather were enlarged by burying the old
structure beneath the new.

City of the Gods

In those days, the Place of the Gods was probably near the edge of the lake that covered a large part of the valley floor. Parts of it may have been on islands. Here, apparently, was the capital of the Toltec "empire": its religious and political center, its stronghold in war, which did not fall until the eleventh century before the tribes from the north.

"The Aztecs," said a guide at Teotihuacan, "conquered the Toltecs by arms, but the Toltecs conquered them in turn by culture."

The site is miles in area, arranged according to a masterly plan revolving about the great axis known as the Road of the Dead, with the various groups of structures about subordinate axes related to this, and all orientated seventeen degrees from the true points of the compass.

This orientation is responsible for extreme estimates of the age of the temples. Some investigators assumed that the structures were arranged according to the cardinal directions. One went so far as to calculate on a basis of their having originally faced the North Star. As they now face nearly west, he figured the time it would have taken for the North Star to move from west to north.

It appears now, according to the eminent Mexican archæologist Don Enrique Juan Palacios, who has made a special study of the Toltec remains, that the points of the compass, as such, were not so important to that people. The temples, his studies have led him to conclude, face the setting sun on the days when it passes the local zenith for that latitude. The priests, as they marched up the grand stairway, climbed toward the rising sun.

The Road of the Dead runs nearly north and south, between rows of mounds which the Aztecs took for tombs, though later study has shown that the Toltecs cremated their dead. At the northern end is the Pyramid of the Moon; to the south, the quadrangle of the Feathered Serpent (Quetzalcóatl); between them, the Pyramid of the Sun.

Other structures situated near these have been identified as the temple of Tlaloc the rain god, the temple of agriculture, houses of priests, and so on. Frescoes in the farmers' temple, now much worn away, show scenes of labor and of ceremony: cremation of the dead, homage to the corn, the kindling of the sacred fire.

This temple was built no fewer than three times, one structure upon another. But all can be identified as characteristic Toltec architecture.

The priests' quarters, excavated and roofed over by the government for their preservation, are a maze of neat rooms, with fine stairways, channels for water supply, even a water-worn chute from a ceiling, which the guides display as a "shower bath."

The quadrangle of Quetzalcóatl, sometimes called the Citadel, is a sunken court, more than four hundred yards on a side, flanked by symmetrical pyramidal structures facing a central platform on which, each fifty-two years in Toltec times, it is believed, was kindled the sacred fire.

At the rear, investigators have cut away a rough pyramid of later construction to expose the more ornate temple-base beneath. It has been conjectured that the newer structure may have been piled upon this to hide the earlier work from vandals.

Though the narrow artificial corridor does not permit an adequate view in perspective, the façade of the ancient temple of Quetzalcóatl is one of the most impressive sights in Mexico. The Plumed Serpent undulates along the base. Rows of feathered serpent heads project from the paneled faces of six ascending masses of masonry, alternating with a motif identified variously as the sacred obsidian butterfly of Heaven, a sun symbol, and the goggled face of the god of rain. Up the western face slants a ruined stairway, flanked by still other colossal snake heads, which loses itself in the ruined masonry that merges with the mound.

City of the Gods

This structure alone of all those at Teotihuacan, I was told, is of solid stone, cut to fit without mortar (although some cement has been used in restoration). The others are of adobe and rubble faced with cut stone, to which adhere traces of an outer coating of stucco and flecks of paint. The Pyramid of the Moon, I was informed, originally gleamed moon-white, and in the court before it was found the colossal statue of the moon goddess which is exhibited in the National Museum.

The greater Pyramid of the Sun was formerly painted, it appears, a blood red. The temple for which it served as foundation has long since disappeared, but the great western stairway has been preserved, or restored, almost intact. At its summit stood, in Cortés' time, it is said, a huge statue of Tonatiuh the sun god, on his breast a plaque of gold which reflected the sun to a great distance. The first archbishop of Mexico ordered the image destroyed; it is easy to guess what happened to the gold.

The structures, of course, are not properly pyramids, but the term is used for convenience. They are simply four-sided terraces, composed of a number of "bodies" with slanting sides, each set back some distance from the one beneath, and culminating in a flat top which originally bore the temple. Thus they resemble the Assyrian and Babylonian zikkurat rather than the Egyptian pyramid, with which they have almost nothing in common. The Mexican "pyramids" are solid masses, having no rooms inside; they are stepped, rather than sloped in an unbroken, inclined plane surface; they do not rise to a point, and their orientation is, apparently, not to the points of the compass. They are not buildings, but bases for buildings.

A museum on the grounds houses case after case of pottery and figurines from the Archaic and Toltec periods, along with primitive jewelry, images, and models of the structures without. At the entrance to the little park where visitors picnic,

Indians sell the black pottery of the region, and sometimes older bowls, unglazed, tawny in color, with red wavy stripes, from the transition period at the end of the Toltec ascendancy. They offer also small, delicately carved jadeite heads, fragments of obsidian blades, terra-cotta figurines among which only an expert can distinguish those dug out of the earth from those made yesterday. For the Toltecs cast these statuettes in molds; some of the molds have been recovered and are used to turn out replicas of the ancient ware.

Hence the reply of one of my archaeologist friends when a visitor brought him a handful of figurines and asked his opinion of their authenticity.

"Madame," he answered, "they were made by genuine Indians, of genuine clay, in genuine molds. What more could you ask?"

Of my visits to Teotihuacan, the most precious in retrospect is one that was almost a ceremony. It was on the twenty-sixth of July, reputed to be the day of the Toltec New Year. With Professor Palacios, a group of us went to the ancient sacred place to test the theory, to which I have referred above, of its orientation. On that day, if the professor was right, the rays of the setting sun would fall exactly in the middle of the great stairway of the Pyramid of the Sun.

The hour approached. We set off up the four great tiers of stairs. First the rectangular bare platform of Quetzalcóatl (not to be confused with the quadrangle and carved temple of that god at some distance to the south); thence up the broad and the narrow stairways that are set off one from the other in an architectural design of stupendous scale. At the first level, for a preliminary test, we set up a cane as a sundial. On the worn adobe beside it lay a fragment of an obsidian knife, among scattered shards.

The shadow still lacked a little of falling exactly in the center. On we climbed to the partly reconstructed platform at the top, where the temple once stood.

City of the Gods

There we remained until sunset. All around, the Valley of Mexico was dark with clouds and striped with rain; lightning flashed over the city. Only at Teotihuacan the sun shone—its level rays full on the great stair. We set up the cane again and waited. Seven o'clock. The last rays. Very nearly, but not quite centered. The professor was tremendously excited. They must have centered when the temple was built. From the slight deviation, it might be possible to compute the structure's true age. He would come back on another twenty-sixth of July to confirm the deviation with accurate instruments and measure it exactly. Or was it only, perhaps, that the reconstruction was not quite true? From where we stood, the smaller rectangular structure at the base was apparently not quite in line with the main body of the pyramid. That might be the simpler answer. Which one was right, we might never know.

Tonatiuh the Sun dropped in splendor behind the mountains; a pale moon appeared, and the clouds in the north glowed with afterlight—the streaked clouds, the piled clouds, the painted pottery of heaven.

On the crumbled summit we gathered the little wild flower, like a small yellow daisy with a brown center, that the Mexicans call *girasol* because all day it turns its face, following the course of the sun. And its face repeats the Toltec symbol of the sun.

Standing upon that worn threshold of a vanished sanctuary, we spoke among ourselves of its departed glory, repeating the prophecy that Hueman uttered when Teotihuacan was a city mighty in the land:

"A lord shall rule with the will of some and against the will of others, and he will bear certain signs in his body, the most principal of which will be that he will have curling hair, of which Nature will form a crown upon his head. . . .

"The empire of the Toltecs shall be destroyed by wars and these signs will arise: the rabbit shall grow horns like the

195

deer; the hummingbird spurs like the cock, and the rocks shall bear fruit.

"There shall be abundance of lightning and of hail, of snow and of hunger, many vermin, and incredible rise of prices, and one day animals shall climb the pedestals on which once sat enthroned the gods."

IV · The Face of the Land

In this section we journey from the Capital to various regions, in most cases returning from each of these to the Capital and starting out again in a fresh direction.

IV · The Face of the Land

XXV · THE ROAD TO TAXCO

THE road to Cuernavaca and Taxco makes a breath-taking ascent out of the bowl of the Valley of Mexico, and then plunges down again: up and up to the dizzy ten thousand-foot rim, curving on through valleys and over mountain ridges curtained with mist. Where it winds along the parapet, the whole vale of Anáhuac is spread below: shrunken lakes, broad dusty plains, forests, the streets of Mexico like white ribbons streaming out of lavender haze.

Drivers on this route are so skilful or so reckless that they proceed with astonishing nonchalance: tilting around curves on dizzying grades, shaving past oncoming vehicles with a minimum of space, and seemingly disdaining to sound their horns even when approaching a corner.

Mountains pile range on range, wooded or bare, in myriad shades of color. Streams, sinuously bordered with trees, wind through valleys below. The earth-brown walls and roofs of villages merge with the landscape as if they had been rooted there by Nature rather than intruded by the hand of man. On some bare hillsides near-by, rocks and vegetation seem to be startling caricatures of human forms.

Beyond Cuernavaca, marching file upon ragged file, the tile roofs of Taxco mount green and tawny slopes. Curving, turning sharp angles, climbing steep, narrow streets—as pigs and chickens scurry from beneath the wheels, and heavily loaded burros edge to the walls—one enters the town that silver built: Taxco de Alarcon.

"Taxco, so peculiarly Mexican," wrote a Mexican commentator, "appears to-day to be a reproduction made in Hollywood."

The town did appear, at first sight, a little too deliberately "quaint." It was like a stage setting: one could scarcely believe, at first, that people actually lived and worked there. And its residents, increasingly tourist-conscious and abetted by tour-promoting interests, did their utmost to make capital of the naturally picturesque qualities of the setting.

Streets paved with small cobbles wind up the steep mountainside. We observed that they were clean: Taxco is neatly kept. Its maintenance as an exhibit ensures that. For the municipal authorities, encouraged by a group of residents of the Capital known as "Friends of Taxco," have taken pains—not without an eye to tourist business—to preserve it as a type of Spanish Colonial town.

Sunlight on Taxco has a gracious quality. Clouds drift in fleecy masses above the piled mountains, patterning the valleys in dark and light; between them the rays fall on faded cream-color, pink, and blue walls and on red-tiled roofs—not a uniform red, but mottled with brown and gray and black. Almost anywhere one looks, the prospect falls into a design of ascending angles and parallelograms, of lights and shadows cast by tile awnings, and delicate patterns of sub-tropical leaves.

Although the silver mine occupies a more imposing situation on a hill and new tourist hotels flaunt their arches and verandas on opposite and adjoining slopes, Taxco still is dominated by the cathedral of Saints Sebastian and Prisca: by its time-stained pinkish walls, tawny-pink twin towers, and blue and yellow dome starred with white—and the gray cloisters of an old convent moldering beneath.

The interior, like that of many Mexican churches, is confusingly ornate: wood elaborately carved, gold piled in fantastically labored masses—but beneath it all lies the good honest stone, laid, block upon block, by the hands of stout Indian builders.

The small plaza, in the shade of its noble laurels, is a favorite haunt of townspeople and, in festival times, of Indians from all the countryside. It is surrounded, in these latter days, by silversmithies and curio shops, and is infested by small boys speaking a little English, whose occupation is to disturb the peace by importuning visitors, with indefatigable persistence, to buy picture postcards, hire a "guide," or have their shoes shined.

For Taxco is tourist-ridden and tourist-pursuing. The attendant in the church shuffled up to us with a collection plate. Near the plaza almost every door opened into a curio shop: one sign spelled it "Curious."

Sarapes hung from doorways; colored baskets were piled high; the odor of ill-cured leather announced shops that made *huaraches*: but, appropriately enough, the main industry is silver.

On the hill where the road turns toward Cuernavaca and the Capital, clanking chains were hauling up buckets of ore and dumping it into hoppers. Men wearing squat metal helmets streamed out of the shaft at noon to eat lunch in the open air.

And down in the village sounded the tap, tap of hammers pounding out silver trays, mirror frames, tea sets, ash trays, jewelry, and miniature sombreros of silver which so many tourists seem to consider an indispensable souvenir.

Silver articles have been made in Taxco for a long time, but it was William Spratling, an American, who organized the industry, setting up a sort of model workshop (with, it is said, higher wages) and introducing new designs, either original or adapted from those of sarapes, pottery, and other crafts.

Tin and copper, too, are worked into useful and ornamental objects: hand looms turn out wool fabrics dyed in vibrant colors.

Through Spratling's studio, the "Taller de las Delicias," wandered a tame deer, nuzzling the visitors curiously, while a parrot squawked in a window. "The deer licks people, and they break out in chestnut blight," said a cynical tourist. "That's why Spratling keeps it."

Taxco has let the world into its gates since it was "discovered" in 1928, with the opening of the motor road that replaced the burro trail down which silver used to travel. Taxco was there long before that—an Indian town, and the source, according to local tradition, of the first silver Cortés sent to Spain.

But the chief story of Taxco is that of José de la Borda, hero of a success-tale that fits the spacious days when the riches of a new country were unlocked.

Early in the eighteenth century he came from France, a youth of sixteen. At first, prospecting brought him little success, but the legend relates that as he was returning in discouragement to the Capital, his mule stumbled over the Taxco mine that was the beginning of a fortune of millions.

In gratitude for this favor of Providence, as he interpreted it, he built the church at Taxco and inscribed at the base of its dome: "Glory to God in the highest."

The Road to Taxco

"God gives to Borda, Borda gives to God," was his highly equitable motto.

The church, like nearly every other one in Mexico, has its own legends, the most spectacular of which is commemorated in an oil painting within the building. The story is that when the church was being built, a violent thunderstorm burst upon the town; terrified builders and villagers feared their work would be destroyed. At the height of the storm, it is related, Saint Prisca appeared above the church, grasping the lightning shafts with one hand, while with the other she held forth a palm leaf, blessing church and village.

The lavishness of gold in the interior leads one to credit the tale that when the church was dedicated, Borda strewed with gold dust the path by which the prelates approached, and left it for the poor to glean when the ceremonies were over.

Nor, when we remember the many other legends of his munificence, along with the amount that must have been lavished on his home and gardens at Cuernavaca and the millions for the church, is it difficult for us to believe the further tradition that he died poor.

Even if Taxco has "gone Hollywood," as the Mexican writer suggested, and even if it is true, as I was told, that no Mexican, but the North American writer John Dos Passos, invented the "typically Mexican" combination of tequila and lime juice that refreshes thirsty visitors at Doña Berta's *cantina,* still Taxco has its charm. The climbing cobbles and the age-stained houses are genuine, as is the fountain whither women come with earthen jars—or, in these modern days, with galvanized pails and converted oil tins—for water; so also are the outdoor community laundry pools, confined in white curbing, where they do their washing.

It was a deep pleasure to climb those streets, pausing to look back on ever new angles of the view over the town and the green valley, or just to sit on the cool veranda of the comfortable Rancho Telva and let the peace and contentment of the scene flood the spirit.

This, even though one could not go near the plaza without being besieged by boys who wanted to "guide" one to the market—which no one with his normal senses could miss—or to sell those eternal postcards; despite the demands of "picturesque" little girls for a tip in consideration of their being photographed—girls who laughed derisively as they turned their backs to the camera, or, clutching the coin in brown little hands, whipped concealing rebozos over their faces.

I suspect this attitude has developed from the presence of so many artists—many of them North Americans—who constitute virtually a permanent colony. Rambling up one of those winding hill streets, I came upon the studio of a Mexican artist, whose window framed perfectly the towers of the church. Taxco was a good place for an artist, he said. Surroundings pleasant, material abundant, and tourist visitors a ready market. One could be content here. As he turned from his easel, a small banded pet snake slithered under a couch, his scales making a dry rustling sound on the mat that covered the floor.

Once away from the plaza and the market, Taxco is a place in which to linger contemplatively. Aside from the town itself, as such, there are few "sights"; yet even in Taxco one can meet adventure. As I sat in the sunny garden of the Rancho—while from the balcony Pancho the parrot, who knew the tune and all the words, sang raucously:

> *"La sierra*
> *es una tierra*
> *donde tengo frio"*

—two fellow-guests limped in from the hills.

"We went for a ride and discovered a mine," they reported. "Got off the horses and panned gold with our hands—but while we were doing it the horses ran away and we had to walk back."

TAXCO—THE CATHEDRAL, FROM DOÑA BERTA'S CANTINA

XXVI · WHERE THE EAGLE ALIGHTS

"CUERNAVACA," said a resident of the Capital, "is known in Mexico as a *pocho* town."

The word *pocho*, I suspect, may be related etymologically to our term "pooch," and may be defined as "mongrel."

It is easy to guess that it was applied to Cuernavaca because of the foreign influences, North American and others, that have deprived it, in Mexican eyes, of authentic Mexican quality.

The ludicrously corrupted name itself unintentionally conveys something of the slur pronounced upon that city by my Mexican friend. For the place was known of old as Cuauhnáhuac, interpreted as "Near the Forest" or, more nobly, as

205

Pattern of Mexico

"Where the Eagle Alights." This dignified name was twisted by the Spanish tongue to the present ignominious "Cow's Horn."

Pocho or not, Cuernavaca is one of the most comfortable places in the Republic. Many Mexicans, as well as North Americans and other foreigners, live there or maintain homes there to which they can retire at intervals to escape the nerve-fretting altitude of the Capital and to relax in an easy climate amid the song of water and of birds and the fragrance of many flowers.

Cortés chose it as his residence, out of the thirty cities of his royal fief, and Maximilian wrote of its delights to his friends abroad.

Ancient stones are here: despite the Hollywood-Spanish architecture of the villas on its outskirts, Cuernavaca is full of them. The state capitol is the fortress-like, palisaded structure of dull-red stone where Cortés lived. Up its broad stair plod pajama-clad peasants, slender and high-cheek-boned, black-mustached, looking like the pictures of their hero Zapata, to tell their troubles to the governor. The capitol's wide balcony overlooks the valley, across a tropically leafy gorge to green rising hills and the farther snow of Popocatépetl and Ixtaccíhuatl.

It seems a quaint turn of "poetic justice" that this fortress-palace, which housed the conqueror, has been chosen to bear Diego Rivera's frescoes exposing the cruelties of conquest. They are ranged around the balcony walls: the sacrifice of captured Spaniards on a temple pyramid while battle rages below; the taking of Cuernavaca, as Spaniards and their Indian allies crept on a fallen tree-trunk across the ravine that had been deemed a natural defense; the enslaving and branding of Indians; Spaniards weighing gold and friars receiving natives' gifts; Indian slaves building this palace and the cathedral. Here a conqueror lolls in his hammock, while an overseer in a near-by cane field swings his lash over Indian workers.

Here hang, gibbeted, Indian patriots of the first insurrection
—and there are many other scenes of the Conquest and the
events that followed, up to the portraits of the independence
leader Morelos and the twentieth-century patriot Zapata.

Volunteer guides who infest the palace persist in pointing
out everything about the pictures except what is important—
their art. ("Now stand here, please, ladies; walk past and
watch Zapata's mustache. Now—see how he turns his head as
you pass!") But the guides' services are not compulsory; this
is a public building.

Perhaps one of these guides may be responsible for the story
of Ambassador Dwight Morrow's conversation with Rivera,
whom he engaged to paint these murals as a counterfoil to
his own gift for redecoration of a church: he wished to be
impartial to Church and State. Morrow, watching the work,
made the comment that Rivera's portrayal of priests was, to
say the least, unflattering. "Can't you paint some nice-looking
ones?" Rivera, according to the tale, said he had never seen
or heard of a priest of that description. But later he complied,
the story adds, by painting here Fray Bartolomé de las Casas,
friend and champion of the Indians, and Bishop Vasco de
Quiroga, who organized industries for the Indians' rehabili-
tation.

"Picture to yourself," wrote the Emperor Maximilian to
the Baroness Binzer in 1866, "a broad level valley, blessed by
Heaven, stretching out before one like a golden bowl, surrounded by a variety of mountain ranges rising one beyond
the other in the boldest outlines and bathed in the most glorious shades, ranging from the purest rose red, purple, and violet
to the deepest azure, some jagged and confused, piling crag
upon crag like the legendary coast of Sicily, others soaring
upward and thickly wooded like the green mountains of
Switzerland; beyond them the enormous volcanoes with their
snow-clad crests towering up like giants toward the deep-blue
heavens. Imagine the golden bowl filled at all seasons—or

rather, all the year round, for there are no seasons here—
with a wealth of tropical vegetation, with its intoxicating fragrance and sweet fruits, and, added to all this, a climate as
lovely as the Italian May."

He wrote, apparently, from the now decayed bungalow at
Apacingo, near Cortés' sugar-mill, two miles away, but he
might have said the same from his more commodious quarters
in the Borda Gardens, in Cuernavaca itself. Borda laid them
out formally in European style, but, as Charles Flandrau has
commented, with the usual rebelliousness of Mexico they refused to stay formal. Bougainvillea sprawls, glowing, over
the trees; bananas thrust out broad, wind-tattered fronds; the
mangoes that were Borda's pride decay on the ground under
bulging domes of foliage. And yet, with all its tropical disorder and its lack of care, the half-ruined garden retains a
trace of a spirit sylvanly discreet: the arches of Carlota's
bathing-pavilion are mirrored in the still pool.

The ghost of Borda still haunts the place, said Rosa King,
who lived for a time in the hotel into which the silver magnate's mansion has been converted.

"He was a rude ghost," she related, as we stood among the
antique pottery and glassware and stone images in her shop
near the plaza. "He would go into my bathroom and pull
the chain, and it would go on and on, and then he would wash
his hands in the bowl.

"Some friends of mine had the place for a while, and the
children got so used to the ghost that they didn't mind him
any more. All but Willie. Willie said, 'He never lets me alone.
He keeps telling me there is treasure. Money all over the
place, and he wants me to find it.'

"One maid quit because the ghost kept pushing her around.
Another, looking into a room, saw somebody asleep on the
bed, and reported the room occupied. No one was registered
for that room. The maid insisted some one was asleep there.
But when the manager went to investigate, he found no one.

Where the Eagle Alights

"For other people, he broke dishes in the kitchen. It must have been very convenient for the servants, to have the ghost to blame."

A washing was drying on the grass in the broad garden of the cathedral, between that severe, fortress-like building and the ornate Chapel of the Third Order at a corner of the grounds.

Franciscans built the cathedral in 1529 at the suggestion of Cortés, and the conqueror himself worshiped there. It is of the period—solid, heavy, with great flying buttresses and with pointed ornaments on its tall parapets. The tale is told in Cuernavaca that it was built by an old Indian method: a great mound of earth was heaped up to sustain the vault, and then carried away when the construction was completed.

Within, Indian-faced caryatids and short-legged Indian angels adorn an alcove; animal faces look out of long cylindrical bodies forming the ribs between the groins; ancient hand-hewn beams and hand-wrought Spanish nails hold the inner structure together.

Also like a fortification, and possibly having served that purpose, is the pyramid of Teopanzolco, near the railroad station—an adobe-colored pile of stairways and salients and slanting walls; even in ruin it is still noble, with remains of temple structures on the summit. It was war that disclosed its presence: federal cannon, mounted on a grassy mound to bombard Zapata's insurgents in 1910, shook away the surface soil and exposed the prehistoric stones.

Local tradition is that the Tlahuica tribe built Teopanzolco. Toltecs conquered them and carved a stone lizard to commemorate the victory, then dug a moat around the pyramid. The Tlahuicas retreated to Tepoztlan and built there the Tepoztécatl temple on a more easily defended height.

The house of the late Ambassador Morrow stands in a walled garden opposite a tortilla bakery. It is a Mexican house, iron grilled and almost blank walled like others; furnished with Mexican objects from various states, all in harmony and in excellent taste. Here are lacquer from Michoacán, pottery from Puebla and Jalisco, exquisite chairs, carved and painted chests, old paintings on wood, a votive "retablo."

The five gardens, set one beyond another like the three plazas of Uruápan, are cool, green, and secluded behind massive sheltering walls over which trails flamboyant bougainvillea: in one, there is a clear tiled swimming pool; in another a little shelter with table and chairs where, the caretaker informed us with a smile, Charles Augustus Lindbergh courted Anne Morrow. A place in which to dream, one thinks—and write poetry.

Life in Cuernavaca seemed placid and content: in the streets that turn at obtuse angles up and down hills; behind the tinted walls; under the many trees; in the plaza fragrant with sweet if funereal plumiera.

From the balcony of our room, the view extended over mottled rust-red roofs and the pink façade and tawny tower of a small old church; between tall slender poplars and an untidy tropical palm, it reached to cloud-wreathed blue-green mountains that notched the sky, cut by the straight swath of a power-line. To the right, thrust out the bare bones of the land, in the sharp, ragged ridges and castellated peaks of Tepoztlan. And beyond, when the haze cleared, shimmered the white tips of the two great volcanoes.

At twilight, more people were on the streets and in the parks. The crenelated towers of Cortés' palace loomed higher in gathering dusk. Trees in the plaza darkened and seemed to bend with weight of chattering birds. Mamas and daughters sat on benches, spooning up pale-green sherbets. Tired men in white pajama-trousers paused to rest on the carved stone bench beneath the statue of Morelos. Boys scurried through the streets, passing out handbills for motion-pictures at the Gran Teatro Morelos, with the ominous printed foot-note: "We will not be responsible for intermittency of the light."

Where the Eagle Alights

An Indian woman followed us around the plaza with an image carved of dense, dark stone, on which I fancied I detected the mark of modern steel tools; but it was well made after an ancient model. It was a squat figure, with hands on knees, and a large head with ornamented cap and ear ornaments, slanting slit eyes, and open mouth with out-thrust lips; the lower part of the face was full, like that of Indians in these parts to-day.

"Yes, señor, it is genuine, very ancient."

"But I don't want an *idolo;* I already have one. Besides, ten pesos is very dear.... So is five...."

She brought a smaller one, carved after the same pattern, from her woven bag.

"If the larger one is genuine, why are the two just alike?"

"This one, señor, is the son of the other."

"Where did you get it?"

"From the cave at the Ranchería de Terrero."

(I had heard that in the cave there was a "factory" for images, a thriving industry.)

"What did you pay for your *idolo,* señor?"

"Two pesos."

"Of what was it made?"

"Of tezontle stone."

"Ah, tezontle—that soft, porous, no-good stone! See, this one is of much better material. It should cost more, for it was more work to make. Yet I will let you have it for three pesos....

"No, the *idolo* has no history. Not all *idolos* have a history. ... What god? Who knows, señor? A sun god, a water god. ... No, I don't know his name. I am losing money, but you shall have it for two pesos, señor...."

I still think that *idolo* was a product of the factory at the Ranchería de Terrero. But later I saw his twin brother in a glass case at the National Museum, labeled, "Household god, State of Guerrero."

XXVII · DARKNESS UNDER THE EARTH

TO the caverns of Cacahuamilpa is a two-hour ride
through the "hot country" from Cuernavaca, in a
panorama of feathery coconut palms, exuberant
banana groves, mamey, mango, flooded fields of rice and
tangled thickets of sugar cane. Among them nestle high-
pitched thatched roofs above walls of adobe, of vertically laid
bamboo or reed, or of a criss-cross basketwork of sticks.

Ruined hacienda mansions stand in the fields; here and there
one has been reconstructed as a sugar-mill. Revolution and
counter-revolution trampled back and forth over all this country: what one party failed to destroy, the other did. Unlike the
practice in Hawaii, only one crop of cane is tended at a time,
and as it is a slow-growing crop, the mills are often idle for

long periods. The *hacendados,* said Señor Snyder who accompanied us, used to plant in relays for a more nearly continuous harvest, but now "it is not possible." He seemed not to know why.

Passing men at work on the road, we paused while they unloaded a truck of whitish lumps of rock. "It is perhaps the only place in the world," said Snyder, "where you can see them lining a ditch with silver ore."

Cacahuamilpa is near the head of an abrupt cañon, down which, in the wet season, rushes a brawling stream. A straggling hamlet of thatched huts clings to a steep slope, nearly every house offering bottled carbonated beverages and warm beer, but, in all that countryside, no coffee. A cable bridge spans the ravine, leading to steps carved to suggest natural limestone formations, between two tall artificial stalagmites, at the entrance of the cave.

These grottoes, the largest known in Mexico, were discovered in 1835, we were told. A fugitive—not, as is often said, a criminal, our informants insisted, but only a man hunted by the government—hid in the gloomy depths, and later, after the administration changed or his case was adjusted, revealed the existence of the caves. Doubtless the Indians had long known of them, but avoided them in superstitious dread of the "demon." This was a stalagmite shaped like a horned goatish monster, which dominated the first chamber until some vandal beheaded it.

Cacahuamilpa is like many another limestone cave—a series of vast vaulted chambers resembling cathedral naves, studded with pendent stalactites glistening in dim and unreliable electric light, and stalagmites rising giantlike from the muddy floor into which visitors have trodden a litter of bottle-caps. The more conspicuous formations bear fantastic names, which the government guide shouts in Spanish: the Dragon, the Thrones, the Hall of the Dead, the Organ, Dante's Head. One could invent one's own with equal appropriateness. For miles the passages wind under the mountain—farther than has yet been explored, the guides said—and the hollow sound of the floor at many points indicates still other caverns beneath. Two streams flow from these somber halls, to form a considerable river. Throughout, one hears sound of water dripping; pools lie on the floors.

Down and up we plodded, sometimes on what seemed to be a pavement, oftener stumbling and slipping over uneven footing coated with slimy mud, in a semi-darkness equivalent to faint moonlight. Two hours or more of this had gone by when, arriving at the "Throne Room," the guide announced—to the evident dismay of ladies who had rashly ventured in with white slippers and high heels—that we had visited seven *salas* and had thirteen yet to see.

There was no turning back; people must keep together lest they lose their way in the dim passages. On and on we went, the going becoming worse, to the last great "Gloria," another vaulted, shadowy chamber, rhythmical with the ceaseless drip of water. The guide climbed up at one side, saying, "Now I'll ring the bell of the Gloria," and struck a clear bell tone on the rock.

Little color was visible: the rock is mostly gray and white limestone, sometimes greenish black and sometimes glistening as if jeweled. Some formations are delicately lacelike; others massive; some, such as the Fountain, almost as regular as if sculptured by human hand. Animal and plant and human shapes loom fantastic and weird in the dripping stone, under the play of light and shadow in the flickering vastness of the halls.

We were unable to identify, in the Hall of the Palms, the inscriptions said to have been traced by two figures prominent in history. The guide had never heard of them, but Antonio García Cubás, in his *Libro de mis Recuerdos,* stated that he was present in 1874 when President Lerdo de Tejada, finding

Darkness Under the Earth

Empress Carlota's scrawled record: "María Carlota arrived this far," wrote beneath, "Sebastián Lerdo went farther."

We saw, however, the cairn of stones that marks the spot where an English explorer and his dog, exhausted with wandering in the dark mazes, died in this natural tomb.

As we started back, most of the lights failed, leaving only a sparse string of weak bulbs. We stumbled in near-darkness down a slippery, irregular stair of rock. Then, just as we entered upon a stretch of comparatively easy going, the lights winked out entirely.

The atmosphere was heavy, humid; we perspired and plodded on in damp desperation. Though the cave is large, I felt an oppression of breath, as if oxygen were lacking. The darkness rested upon us heavy and palpable, like a closed hand; the pitfalls seemed to move in around us.

Some in the party, however, insisted on advancing, holding lighted matches until they scorched the fingertips, tracing a few steps and trying to keep the scattered party together. The guides had vanished, presumably in an attempt to find the source of the failure of the light. The feeble bulbs flickered again, went off and on. As we stumbled out into daylight, a boy of the party came running up, breathless. He had made his way out ahead of us and had stammered to the guards at the entrance that they must "rescue" us. But the guards had only laughed.

Off the road to Cacahuamilpa, a city of mounds crowns a cluster of hills. On one rounded and moated summit, to which five terraces spiral up, stands an excavated and restored temple, rich with carving—Xochicalco, House of Flowers.

The Toltecs built it, Professor Palacios had told me, for the feathered serpent twines around its base, enfolding human figures and symbols of the New Fire; the plumes bear the halved snail-shell breastplate of Quetzalcóatl. The date engraved on the south side has been interpreted by the same authority as corresponding to 947 A.D.

Caverns and tunnels burrow beneath the hill; there are traces of a cylindrical shaft through which, it is conjectured, Toltec astronomers observed sun and stars, and captains sent smoke signals in time of war.

"I took an archæologist named Marsh to Xochicalco," related Garfíl, the talkative driver with whom we saw much of the countryside around Cuernavaca. "He was the foremost archæologist in the world, he said. I started telling him about the symbols on the pyramid. 'You're all wrong, my lad,' he said, and then he started telling *me*. Later I took a famous French archæologist to the same place, and started telling him about the symbols, repeating what Marsh had told me.

" 'You're all wrong, my friend,' he said. 'You've been reading Marsh.'

"So now I let them figure it out for themselves."

His real name, he said, was Orozco, but having served as "what you call a G-man," he had acquired the nickname of "Garfíl," which means, I think, literally a claw but is a slang term for a detective. He was capitalizing on it by advertising himself to English-speaking tourists as "William O. Garfield, chauffeur."

With him we set off, over a road in which we repeatedly bogged down, to Tepoztlan—a mud-colored town of tile-roofed adobe houses, set in a wild crag-rimmed valley among checkerboard fields, where urn-shaped granaries stand under their roofs of thatch. The paved streets, shading off into cobbles, are named and numbered: Nicolás Bravo, Guerrero, Matamoros.

The plaza, small and neat, has the inevitable bandstand, though I was told there was no band. On feast days, folk said, musicians came from Cuernavaca.

The market-place is primitive but orderly, offering wares in demand by Indians themselves: simple brown pottery, little

Darkness Under the Earth

pyramids of vegetables and fruit, baskets of corn, and a few toys, such as gaudy little guitars.

In Tepoztlan, only small boys were tourist-conscious. They clamored for a few centavos to "watch your car"; offered for sale tiny house-fronts carved of bark and terra-cotta figurines which might be genuine antiques. Their elders looked calmly past or through the visitors with monumental Indian indifference, recalling to our minds Anita Brenner's remark that the Indians survived the Conquest because they ignored it.

We found the church and former convent very old, massive, and empty. The convent cells were damp and musty; rain had seeped through the roof. But traces of black and white frescoes remained on the moldering walls, and the lift of the high flying buttresses was lovely, viewed through the rhythmic arches of the patio. The style was plain, severe, characteristic of the early period, the ornament concentrated in rich bas-relief of unusual design over the door.

We followed a steep trail, practically a long, rough staircase of rock, up the mountain, between tall pinnacles. Our feet crunched upon shards of pottery and fragments of obsidian blades. Above, the trail mounts even more abruptly between green walls of forest. A notched tree-trunk scales the cliff at one place, an iron ladder farther up. The heart pounds; breath comes in gasps; clothes are drenched with perspiration. The end must surely be around the next corner.... "We are half-way," encourages Garfíl.

On and up, to a clifftop where the dilapidated pyramid still keeps a trace of its ancient dignity. Even in ruin it is a noble pile, terraced with narrow steps; at the summit is the remnant of a shrine, inner walls carved with the sign of war and other symbols, the outer surface still holding patches of a white stucco covering.

The view is stupendous, across the sharp green-clad pinnacles called "The Three Marys," down to the reddish roofs of the town and over the valley to the long dark ranges.

Pattern of Mexico

This valley was the home of the Tepoztécatl, hero whose deeds are still celebrated in the village, his battles enacted in an outdoor theater, adorned with Indian symbols, near the market-place.

"He was born," related Garfíl, "of a virgin and of Ehécatl, god of Wind. It's hard to keep track of the wind. His two aunts, to hide their sister's shame, threw the child into a maguey plant. But he didn't die; the maguey fed him. Then they put him on an ant-hill. The ants brought flowers to wreathe him. The women threw him into a stream, and he turned into a sky-blue fish. An old man caught the fish, and then the Tepoztécatl turned into a baby again. The old man adopted him.

"The giant king of Xochicalco demanded victims for sacrifice, and the old man was chosen. The Tepoztécatl went in his place. On the way he picked up sharp pieces of obsidian, such as we find on the trail here.

"The king tossed him into a boiling pot. The first time the king lifted the lid, the Tepoztécatl changed himself into a tiger. The second time, he was a snake, and the third time the Tepoztécatl came out in his own form, laughing. So the king decided to eat him raw, and swallowed him at one gulp. But the Tepoztécatl cut his way out of the giant's stomach with a piece of obsidian.

"The king's soldiers chased the boy. Near Cuernavaca, he threw away a piece of obsidian, and it became a lake, which his pursuers had to swim. Farther on, he threw away his hair-brush, and it sprouted into a tangled forest behind him. The third time, he threw away his comb, and it became the cliffs of Tepoztlan.

"The king's guards couldn't catch him here. He became chief of Tepoztlan, built this temple, and fortified it; no army could capture it.

"The Spaniards sent for him to hang the bells in the cathedral tower at Mexico City. He called no helpers; he built no scaffolding. Everybody wondered how he was going to hang the bells.

"At the appointed time, he called on his father the Wind. When the dust of the windstorm cleared, the bells were hanging in place.

"As a reward, he demanded half the treasure of the city. He buried the box of treasure in Tepoztlan. Later a man dug the box up and opened it, and five pigeons flew out. They flew to Cuernavaca, Huaxtepec, Yautepec, Tlayacápan and Tlalmanalco, and all those places became prosperous, while Tepoztlan didn't. The Tepoztécatl said that if this hadn't happened, Tepoztlan would have become a greater city than any of them."

The latter part of the story is apparently somewhat out of time with the rest. For another tale relates that the first Spaniards arriving at Tepoztlan found the image of the Tepoztécatl on the pyramid, where he was venerated as a harvest god and inventor of pulque. Fray Domingo de la Anunciación had the image hurled over the cliff, but it did not break. Then he had it sawed in four pieces which were buried as cornerstones for the church. Rain ceased to fall. Grubs ate the crops, until the people prayed again to the Tepoztécatl to ask his father the Wind to bring rain.

Some say a treasure of jade and turquoise and gold is buried under the temple and that no one dares hunt for it, because it is guarded by spirits. Once a year, we were told, a fire is lighted on the mountain to guide the Tepoztécatl, for he will come back to lead his people.

XXVIII · ZAPATA RIDES STILL

THROUGH these valleys around Cuernavaca, in 1910 and the succeeding years, rode Emiliano Zapata, at the head of wide-sombreroed peasant warriors, shouting for "land and liberty."

They helped overthrow Porfirio Díaz and install Francisco I. Madero. Madero's government, from the agrarian point of view, was only a series of debates. Zapata remained in arms.

After Madero was overthrown and slain, through the treachery of Victoriano Huerta, Zapata fought Huerta. Pancho Villa and Alvaro Obregón swept down from the north. Huerta fled. Venustiano Carranza became president.

And still there were words—promises. Zapata and his armed peasants demanded action. Carranza, quarreling with

Zapata Rides Still

Villa, fled to Vera Cruz; Zapata's troops occupied the Capital and surprised the inhabitants by refraining from looting and violence, and by paying for what they needed. They fought, not for loot, but for "land and liberty."

Obregón defeated Villa, and Pablo González fought Zapata. The State of Morelos was laid waste.

Among the prisoners at González' headquarters was Colonel Eusebio Jaureguí, early captured by Carrancistas. The federals knew he was a Zapata spy as well as a prisoner. So they set a trap.

Giving him unusual liberty, they let him talk with visitors and permitted his messages to slip through to Zapata.

As Jaureguí was loitering near the general's office, Colonel Jesús M. Guajardo, a Carrancista officer, let the Zapatista overhear him complaining about lack of appreciation of his services. Later, confiding in Juareguí, Guajardo pretended to be planning to go over to Zapata.

Jaureguí passed the word on, in a watermelon carried by a vendor. A muleteer brought a letter from Zapata for Guajardo.

Guajardo gathered four hundred men, among them sixty former Zapatistas who knew the trails. Zapata demanded that as a proof of loyalty he attack Jonacatepec. Guajardo did so, and captured the town. As a second test, Zapata sent Guajardo into the front lines to attack the federals at Peña Pelona. This operation also was successful. Finally, Zapata demanded that Guajardo punish Victorino Bárcenas and the sixty other former Zapatistas as traitors, for their earlier desertion.

Guajardo shot them, all but Bárcenas, who escaped.

Zapata was convinced of Guajardo's loyalty. To celebrate, Guajardo invited Zapata to dine with him next day at Chinameca.

Guajardo's quarters were in the main house of an hacienda —a walled space, where but few at a time could enter the narrow gate. Six guards were posted at each door.

221

Pattern of Mexico

When Zapata appeared, with only a small escort, a cornet sounded a march of honor. It was a signal.

"Port arms!"

The cornet sounded again.

"Present arms!"

Zapata rode into the patio. Six bullets pierced him.

That is the tale that is told in Morelos.

At Cuautla stands his tomb, carved with an angel holding an unrolled scroll.

But there are other stories in Morelos. It is whispered that it was not Zapata, but a double, who was shot at Chinameca and buried in Cuautla. And the peasants around Cuernavaca insist that Zapata often is seen, from afar, riding over the mountain trails. He will return, when the time comes, they say, to call them to march again for "land and liberty."

XXIX · MICHOACÁN JOURNEY

THE train out of Mexico City, plumed serpent of this modern day, glided and coiled among rugged hills, from whose sculptured summits mounted stupendous pyramids of cloud. The way curved past exquisite lakes, unexploited and innocent of resorts, their groved shores studded with thatched villages, their turquoise or emerald waters furrowed only by the brown canoes of fisherfolk and the eddying wakes of wild fowl.

The scene grew wilder, fields fewer, forests more dense, as we climbed among the varied greens of the woods, through which glowed the red iron-oxide soil, and past far slopes mottled with changing light, as lucent battalions of clouds marched over the curved field of sky.

223

Pattern of Mexico

Downward we plunged into a broad valley circled with misty mountains, and along the reedy shores of Lake Cuitzeo, where the men of the thatched villages, two and two, were carrying great baskets silvery with fish. Past salt beds we went, with their conical hillocks of refuse earth, and through cactus-fingered slopes beyond; thence up again, until the twin cathedral-towers of Morelia pointed, stately and beautiful, from the inverted shallow bowl of the city's site.

Upward still, through sharp pink-tan terraces with deeply gullied banks; through cañons where waterfalls plunged, feathery, over fern-wreathed cliffs; past lakes nestling in folded hollows of the hills. Small volcanic craters coned skyward in the distance, beyond red-roofed villages and checkered fields.

Near-by, as we passed from place to place, each with its own local conditions, farmers were raising water with a crude, pole-handled irrigation apparatus, as in Egypt; reaping with machetes, furrowing the earth with wooden plows behind ponderous oxen, or uprooting weeds by hand. At one spot, horses, urged on by shouting boys, were treading grain.

Islanded Lake Pátzcuaro nestled, blue-green, in its horseshoe of forested mountains; the huddled roofs of Janitzio rose from the steep slopes of their island to the white colossal figure of Father Morelos, lifting a huge hand over the quiet water.

Climbing again, we followed the curve of the lake, lost it, regained it only to lose it once more, but to find exquisite, fairyland-like Zirahuén, gleaming emerald-bright in its girdle of green and tawny hills. It is a lake of mystery and legend: its waters are always calm, they say, since the Blessed Virgin washed her mantle there. Or do we prefer the older tale of the love-maddened Prince Cuitzeman, who dwelt among the wild beasts of the forest in a long search for his lost mate, at last to find her deathless spirit in the moon-silvered waters of this lake?

A SCENE AT COLIMA

Michoacán Journey

We skirted rims of cañons and passed small red-earthed fields and clusters of narrow-shingled, high-peaked houses that clung to the precipitous hilltops amid fanlike rows of banana plants. Do the dwellers in the almost Japanese houses at Aristeo, I wonder, appreciate the superb view they have every day from their humble dooryards among the broad, fringed fronds? Does daily use dull the keen sensation, or do they feel, as we do, that lift of spirit as wondering eyes contemplate the magnificent sweep of mountain and valley and scalloped meadow of sky?

"How is life in Uruápan?" I asked, in that city of running streams and singing birds and tropical fruit and flowers.

"Pobre—y alegre," was the reply: poor—and happy.

And I liked to fancy it might be so throughout the State of Michoacán, even in those precariously clinging hillside stations where tattered shreds of clothing, mended and remended until the original garment could scarcely be identified, hung from trees and fences, and men passed in shaggy raincoats of cane leaves, looking like animated stacks of fodder.

And so one winds down the hills into Uruápan, the Gourd of Flowers—itself a flower, nestled in its green bowl of valley. It is encircled by flat-topped, forested hills like temple pyramids, whose volcanic earth repeats the color-note of the tiled roofs piled around inner courts as in a Chinese city.

Clouds wreathe the far peaks and gather in pools of mist in the valleys. Cobbled streets climb steep slopes; flights of steps mount from age-mellowed doorways into moist, fragrant gardens and earth-floored patios. Pigs root among the cobbles; heavily laden burros plod down winding ways. Everywhere are fruit, flowers, the tinkle of streams. Across curving streets, Cupatitzio, the Singing Water, chants its lulling tone.

There is an atmosphere here of timeless, remote, easeful afternoons. Worries recede as the fevered, restless world recedes; as the spirit, submerged in the quiet of this scene, draws new strength from calm and contemplation. Scent of flowers, song of birds, flow of mist in valley-mouths, merge into a pool of restfulness in which the soul bathes and is refreshed.

"Poor—and happy." Here one can take unto one's self the words of that ancient royal poet of Mexico: "Praise then the singers, and the flowers that cover the earth, for they will intoxicate your soul."

XXX · ARCHES OF THE CENTURIES

HISTORY lies deep over Morelia, with its ponderous walls and arches, its carved stone façades and sun-lit patios with their aged monolithic columns.

"Here," says an inscription on the wall of a house, "was born José María Morelos, September 30, 1765." The city, anciently Valladolid, bears his name in memory of his struggle for his country's independence.

In another street, named for the same hero, we found members of the Morelos family still residing, as caretakers of the house in which he had lived, which had become a "national monument." It is large and dignified, with a beautiful patio. The rooms he occupied are preserved with some of their original furniture; his clothes hang on the wall; on hand-hewn tables lie the books he read. There are his rosary and flagella, and, in a glass case, the handkerchief that covered his eyes when he was shot, kneeling, from the back, at San Cristóbal Ecatepec on December 22, 1815.

The rear patio still shows the niche in a stone pillar down which roof-water ran to fill the cistern before a more modern water system was installed, and the slab of stone on which his mother washed his clothes looks to be still in use. The watering trough for his horse remains, and the projecting beam to which the animal used to be tied.

Melchor Ocampo had dwelt near-by and, farther on, another patriot, Santos Degollado. Another house had been the temporary residence of Maximilian, and still another was inscribed: "Agustín de Iturbide, liberator of Mexico, was born in this house September 27, 1783."

In front of a Colonial mansion, now the Hotel Virrey de Mendoza, that has been modernized within to a greater comfort than is usual in Mexico, is the inscription: "In this portal Matamoros was shot"—at the second pillar to the left, our host said.

Almost every important building in Morelia is centuries old: the city hall, with its twin-arched patio and majestic stairway, above which are murals of Michoacán fishermen and lacquer workers by Grace Greenwood; the museum with its ancient Tarascan picture-maps charting division of land, its prehistoric pottery and images, including the carved-stone goddess of creation, sitting to give birth; the technical school, formerly a Jesuit establishment, where talented pupils from all schools in the state continue their education on free scholarships with board and lodging—a place of tremendous patios and fountained gardens, simple and lovely, with the heavy plain arches that are characteristic of this city.

Another former church houses, among wooden sculptures of philosophers, the state library of thousands of ancient volumes. The School of Arts, with Marion Greenwood's murals of Pátzcuaro fishermen; the School of Law, with its chaste Greek-columned second patio, a reaction from the ornate style that followed the severe early period—all are variously beautiful. One convent has become a home for elderly people; another houses the highway commission; an expropriated estate lies, like a forest, behind a wall, being held for home sites for government officials on time payments.

From the balcony of the Virrey de Mendoza, the view leads down a broad avenue to the pink stone Plateresque façade and graceful towers of the Cathedral, reputed to be one of the most beautiful in the Republic. At one side of the broad atrium, which is enclosed in Colonial ironwork, stands in contrast a fountain of modern design: a stylized angel in white marble, the lines of the figure deftly harmonized with the contours of the stone.

Rich and quaint, if gaudy, is the little church of San Diego, with its bizarre decoration in painted and gilded clay, laid by the hands of Indian parishioners on almost every inch of walls and ceiling.

In the evening, the humble sidewalk cafés of the people, around the great plaza, were lively with business. The air was full of odors of cooking; a whole row of outdoor kitchens had been set up under the arcades. Around them sat or squatted groups of Indians or squads of soldiers, passing plates from hand to hand.

The life of Morelia's *portales* is rich and vivid, by day or night. In times of fiesta, booths are erected even in front of the leading hotel, facing the main plaza. Toys, pottery, red and black sarapes, all manner of wares are displayed, but most of all *ate,* the sweet fruit-paste of quince or peach or guava for which Morelia is famous. At night, we could see the outdoor merchants spreading their mats to sleep where they were, under the arches.

Near the door in the arched patio of the old-fashioned Hotel de la Soledad—whose owner, we were told, was so conservative that he refused to install electric lights until the government compelled him, and who still thought rooms with bath were an unnecessary foreign innovation—a sign, above the heads of students playing chess and of casual customers drinking the *café con leche* which is considered exceptionally good there, read: "Actors and bull-fighters not admitted."

The two hundred and fifty-odd arches of the aqueduct, on the eastern fringe of the city, are a monument to a Spanish Colonial work-relief program. For Bishop Fray Antonio de San Miguel Iglesias spent 400,000 pesos or more, it is recorded, in building it, for employment of the hungry of his diocese. He was the Fray Antonio of whom Don José Corona Núñez has written: "In time of famine he gave money for seed, and gave wise laws for the keeping of it...in time of pestilence recommended vaccination for smallpox, when he might have said it was a thing of Satan...the night is not entirely black."

Under those arches, of old, sword rang upon sword in duels for the favor of Colonial belles. And in the near-by grove, those ladies passed little scented notes to the gentlemen of their choice, at the Sunday promenade.

In this wood, even more anciently, wandered Characu-Miscuare, the Sad Boy King, fleeing from enemies and pierced by arrows when the rebel Cartzitiri stormed Pátzcuaro. Here he plucked a magnolia flower for a beautiful girl who was vainly trying to reach its high branch, only to be rebuffed by the girl, who without a word vanished into the forest. The petals fell away, and "the soul of Characu-Miscuare fell with it."

For the wind, sighing through the trees, seemed to chant: "You are a stranger in our land, and you have dared to raise your eyes to the Indigo Flower, whom the Pirindas serve as queen. You have offended the gods."

The Sad Boy King sickened and died, as the flower of the magnolia withered. Three days the Lord of Guayangareo and his captains remained silent before his ashes, and Súmac-

EIGHTEENTH-CENTURY AQUEDUCT AT MORELIA

Arches of the Centuries

Tzitziquín, the Indigo Flower, wept beneath the magnolia, kissing each flower that fell.

In recognition of her sorrow, the gods transformed her into an indigo plant, whose flowers kiss the faded magnolias that fall from the ancient trees. And they say in Morelia that a small bird repeats, over and over, in the wood, the ancient Tarascan song:

> Beware, beware
> of the Indigo Flower—
> the white flower and the yellow flower
> shall wither!

XXXI · LEGEND LIES DEEP

BETWEEN the village of Pátzcuaro and the lake a sculptured monument is inscribed:

"Death of Tangaxuhan II on the shore of the River Lerma, by order of the bloody and ambitious Nuño de Guzmán in the year 1530. 'See,' said Tangaxuhan to the warrior Ecuangari, 'the evil treatment they give me after I received them into my territory and believed in their gods. Take my ashes to my people, that they may keep the memory of their king.' "

And a later generation has kept that memory in stone.

The Aztecs never conquered the tribes of this region, the Purépecha—commonly called by their Aztec nickname, Tarascans. The Spaniards conquered them by diplomacy and treachery rather than by arms.

After Tangaxuhan submitted to Cristóbal de Olid, companion of Cortés, at "The Place of Humiliation," the young and beautiful Princess Eréndira, "The Smiling One," held out, besieged, in Pátzcuaro until all her people died "of hunger and rage." Only Eréndira escaped, and the people say she still walks on the mountain, with hair streaming in the wind, "calling her brothers to die for liberty."

Under the tutelage of the first mild missionaries, the Purépecha "accepted the new things, and flourished in industries and the arts.

"Then came Nuño de Guzmán, torturing and slaughtering, and the Indians fled. The work of the missionaries was undone."

Hence Michoacán blesses the name of Bishop Vasco de Quiroga, who strove in turn to undo the infamous work of Guzmán. He organized pictorial arts and crafts, and worked to make the Indians of Michoacán economically secure.

Up to his eightieth year, they relate, Don Vasco visited his entire diocese on muleback. Once, on his return, some one told him that in the farthest corner of his province, in the most rugged sierra, there was a tiny village he had not visited. " 'Then let us go there at once,' replied Don Vasco, 'for I do not wish to neglect a single place of those of my province where there are souls whom God has put under my care.' "

Thus legend enwraps the cobbled streets of Pátzcuaro that climb low hills between projecting eaves and carved roof-beams. Age and tradition breathe from those narrow, undulating ways, from the stout venerable arches of the *portales,* the worn stones of public fountains. It is a city of antiquity, a city of "New Spain."

Low, as if sunk into the earth by its weight, stands the house of Don Antonio Huitziméngari y Mendoza y Caltzontzín, first governor of Michoacán, on the site of the summer palace of his martyred father, the last king. It appeared, I thought, little changed by the impact of more than four centuries.

Here, when Don Vasco transferred the seat of the bishopric from Tzintzúntzan, dwelt Huitziméngari with his wife Mintzita, "who with her primitive beauty adorned and perfumed the lordly mansion with the freshness of a vase of flowers."

The princess did not feel at home in the Spanish-influenced court at Pátzcuaro; she longed for her royal house in the Place of the Hummingbirds. Only her love for her husband held her in the new capital.

She was sadder still when the Spanish women, in their sumptuous gowns, flocked flatteringly around the prince. Her obsidian eyes clouded as she saw him riding in his carriage with golden-haired Doña Blanca de Fuenrara, daughter of a Spanish landholder.

"Grandmother Cueróperi," she cried to the nature goddess, "why did you make the foreign woman so beautiful?"

Unable to speak Spanish or to associate on equal terms with the sophisticated court ladies, Mintzita fled.

On an island in the lake, she invoked her ancestral gods, begging them to change her beauty that it might be like that of this Daughter of the Sun who threatened to steal the love of her lord. In a hollow tree she set her loom to weave a garment such as no woman of her people had worn.

Huitziméngari reached the island at night. Mintzita stood on the summit of a pyramidal temple, under the full moon. A many-pleated gown flowed about her like a great fan; her breast swelled beneath an embroidered bodice, and from her head and shoulders waved a rebozo tinted with the blue of the sky and rays of moonlight.

" 'Don Antonio, my lord, I saw that your soul would abandon mine, and I have lived alone as does the Mother Moon. I asked her to whiten my skin like the skin of that woman who robs me of your love; I asked our father the Sun to give my hair the color of his rays, and the lake to give me the blue of her waves for my eyes.

" 'Look at my robe! I have made it myself to equal those she wears; I have tinted my rebozo where the moon shines on the water. See whether I am like her and you can love me now!' "

And Don José Corona Núñez, who retells the story, adds that this proof of her devotion won back the erring prince.

Since then, according to the tradition, Indian women of Michoacán have worn that costume: the many-pleated heavy skirt, gathered accordion-like at the waist beneath a wide sash; the brightly embroidered blouse, the oversize and brilliantly blue rebozo—on a young and pretty woman, indeed a lordly costume enough to have won the heart of a prince.

Around the corner from the ancient palace, a colossal demoniac figure guards the grand stairway of the "House of the Giant." Two centuries ago, the Count de Velasco set up the carved and painted guardsman "to frighten away intruders" from the arcaded patio and the carved doors. A later owner, it is said, opening the ample belly of the image, "found much gold."

Indians file in from the country in the early morning: men with heavy red and black sarapes dropping from a slit at the neck or tossed jauntily over the shoulder; wide, low-crowned sombreros over black straight hair; women in the legendary costume of the Princess Mintzita; children with large, appealing eyes.

They spread their mats around the edges of the plaza; lay out their lacquer-ware, carved and painted wood, pottery, and textiles. Rain falls in torrents, running down depressions at the sides of the narrow streets. As the first large drops strike, the Indians scramble to gather up their wares and bring them under the *portales*. One of them would not accept the paper currency I offered him for a heavy blue and white sarape. We had to enter a near-by store and exchange it for "hard pesos."

Pattern of Mexico

There was no water in Pátzcuaro, villagers said, until Bishop Don Vasco struck the ground with his staff, whereupon a spring gushed forth. One of the fountains, called "of the Bull," an old woman related, once stood in the middle of the Calle de Iturbe. But a soldier, riding past, was killed when his horse threw him against the curbing of the well. The authorities, with the formality of the times, "condemned" the fountain "to be removed from its place." As no one proceeded to carry out the sentence, the submissive fountain of itself retired to a corner, to avert further accident.

Down a rough street, a passage penetrated the crumbling walls of a ruined convent: vacant, except for one family who had made a few rooms livable, and the homeless poor who camped in the outer patios. Gardens bloomed in diagonal shafts of sunlight, untended save where my enterprising acquaintance had made his home. He had polished the hand-hewn planks of the floors, the heavy beams, and carved doors; hung the moldering walls with tapestries, furnished the rooms with heirlooms that were old "when my mother was a little girl."

"One family moved into the convent one day and out the next," he said. "They couldn't endure the visits of the ghost of a nun that haunts the place. My wife and I," he added, "have not seen her. If we did, I'd hail her and say, 'What are you doing here?'"

He paid the government a rental of about a dollar a month. The poor families who lived "like animals," as he commented scornfully, in the outer tiers, paid nothing. The old woman who was caretaker admitted them out of pity.

"One could buy the whole place for 10,000 pesos," he added, "but it would cost 40,000 to put it in repair."

Indeed, Pátzcuaro would seem one of the most economical as well as most picturesque cities in Mexico in which to live. His wife, he said, paid her maid less than a dollar a month for a half day's work daily. A fine house in the city could be bought for three thousand pesos or rented for twenty-five. Exchange in terms of United States dollars fluctuates, but at any time in recent years these have been comparatively insignificant sums.

A winding, rocky road climbs to the hill called El Estribo, whence stone steps—four hundred of them, according to rumor—mount to the look-out at the summit. It is a noble scene: the rippled lake, with its five principal islands and many smaller ones; around it, mountains mottled under clouds that pile dark and high, with lighter borders; fields and forests and towns, a panorama of rolling country in red and blue and green.

Nets hung, drying, like great gauzy butterflies, from the projecting roof-beams of Janitzio, island village of fisherfolk, as the launch from the Pátzcuaro landing approached the steep and stony shores. In dooryards sat men, women, children, plying wooden hand-shuttles, weaving and mending nets, or spinning cord on primitive wheels. At the water's edge, women in pleated skirts and bright sashes knelt to wash clothes on weather-smoothed rocks. Between huddled, hill-climbing houses, other women were spreading small silvery fish on mats to dry. One rose from her work to offer for sale a gorgeously embroidered blouse.

Guidebooks had represented the Indians of Janitzio as suspicious and unfriendly. But we were received everywhere on the island with smiles and soft greetings; the horde of begging children of whom we had been warned did not appear; men and women courteously gave us directions, answered questions.

A path of rough stone stairs winds up the rugged hill to the summit, where the colossal hollow figure of Father Morelos, heavy and squat like a piece of Indian sculpture, stands on its ramped platform, above a bronze plate bearing Morelos' declaration of the independence of Mexico. A sword rests, point to ground, in one hand; the other is uplifted.

Pattern of Mexico

"At night he is tired with holding it up all day, and lets the hand drop," people said.

A door opens into the interior of the statue, around which a narrow stair spirals up past five tiers of murals portraying scenes in the life of Morelos and in the Revolution, to the mosaic cupola and the look-out over the lake, the scattered islands, and the tiled roofs of the town.

Around the horseshoe of the lake lie a score and more villages, between which Indians travel by canoe rather than by road. The canoes are hollowed out of logs, square at the stern, sloping at the bow; thin walled, with stout supports across the bottom. Singing, the brown Tarascans wield short, round-bladed paddles, guiding the craft from the bow by a longer steering-paddle hung between loops of wood at the gunwales. In the afternoon, when fierce wind often ruffles the surface of the lake, they sometimes attach rude outriggers of planks, serving the same purpose of stabilization as the more finished and permanent outriggers of fishing peoples in Pacific islands.

Gnarled olive trees—planted, the caretaker said, in 1540, by Don Vasco de Quiroga himself—shade in melancholy grandeur the ancient church at Tzintzúntzan, a few miles from Pátzcuaro. Around the church clusters a remnant of the town. Six miles square the Place of the Hummingbirds stood in Indian times; on the ridge are mounds that mark its palaces, its temples, and its tombs.

Within the church, whitewash all but hid the frescoes, but the caretaker drew away the curtains to show the famous painting that alone draws visitors to this decayed town: a Descent From the Cross—of the type which Leonard Bacon has described as "looking like a railroad accident"—painted, according to legend, by Titian and given by King Philip II to Don Vasco.

It is unquestionably good painting: the miniature landscape in the corner, the face of the Magdalen at the lower left, and that of the Mother Mary bending over her dead, are all very fine. But the rich Titian texture is lacking in the robes.

The official directory of Colonial Monuments of Mexico says curtly: "In the church is venerated a picture falsely attributed to Titian."

They weave no more at Tzintzúntzan the glowing pictorial mosaics of hummingbirds' feathers. And on the hill at Zacapú the carved stones, the sculptured pots, lie hidden in the darkness of the mounds, in the tombs of the Purépecha kings.

We sat on the veranda of the lordly Posada de Don Vasco, at Pátzcuaro, as the sun sank behind the mountains over the lake, and quoted the words of the King of the Black Isles: "Some god has flung his mantle on the sky."

Between bands of robin's-egg and darker blue, a broad field of orange and saffron, striped with blue and black, in infinite shadings, frayed off, soft and woolly, into the blue, with fringes of pale yellow and white. Below loomed darker masses in lavender and purple and mauve, dipping to a blue-black thrust of duskened mountain and, near-by, the lake, reflecting myriad colors of the sky. A hush lay over lake and fields, accentuated, rather than broken, by voices of children at play, of birds, and the chirpings of innumerable frogs.

Changing, deepening, the sky watched as the sun went down to the caverns under the earth to renew his strength for the ensuing day.

It deepened to orange red, the upper blue graying, the lower remaining bright and reflecting in delicate shades on clouds that clustered about the hills.

Orange became pink, with deeper jets of flame. It faded gently, with notes of green in the upper layer of gray-blue; beneath was darkness, almost black. Pale lavender streaked the deep blue of the lake. The islands loomed dark, slowly merging with the farther shore. And thunder rumbled down from the rounded, wooded hills.

XXXII · THE GOURD OF FLOWERS

THE gardens of Uruápan, to which small boys begged
that they might guide us for a few centavos, rambled
in tropical disorder, rich with the pungent fragrance
of mangoes and the mingled odors of flowers. Only the National Park, green and wild beyond its small formal garden
at the gate, showed evidence of the care with which one re-
strains and tidies up Nature in more temperate climates. Paths
wound down to the river; the forest-scented air was merry
with the sound of running and falling water. There was profusion of tropical fruits: men were dropping heavy avocados
from the limbs of tall trees.

A rich odor of fermenting molasses hung over the luxuriant
banana fronds around the aguardiente distillery, source of

what was apparently the most appreciated local product. Few of the humbler folk, it seemed, indulged in any other luxury. Even during the three-day fiesta which had drawn us to that city, we saw few street vendors, and those were doing little business. Shops were poor and tawdry; churches were undistinguished—one of them converted into a lacquer factory and salesroom. People either were thrifty or had no money to buy.

"Many of the Indians are comparatively wealthy," said our host Don Alfredo Álvarez, who looks at the aborigine with the eyes of a Creole, "since the government has given them valuable timber lands. But it makes no difference in their living. It just means that they drink more aguardiente."

The city, however, with unusual lavishness, has not one but three central plazas, all in a row, shaded with tall trees. In the largest one a sculptured revolutionary hero, apparently Zapata, glares above formidable mustachios across the park. When we were there, the stone or cement was crumbling away, lending the statue a ludicrous appearance: the tight *charro* pants were falling off.

An enterprising local youth who had studied radio by mail had rigged up a loud-speaker, which blared all day the same half-dozen recorded popular tunes, over and over, interspersed with announcements of "bargains" at local stores. One merchant confided to me that people were already getting tired of the noise. Youths were playing basket-ball in the court between church and plaza. A file of burros passed, turning their heads to nibble at the alfalfa piled on their backs, which almost buried them from sight; behind them walked men under loads almost as large, whacking at the burros with long staves. A *charro* rode past, very handsome and conscious of it, in tight brown trousers, embroidered jacket and wide, silver-ornamented sombrero; on another horse rode his little son, similarly clad. Both turned to see whether we noticed and admired, saluting us with a broad grin and wave of hand.

Pattern of Mexico

"Very pretty," commented a Mexican near us. From the rest of his remarks, I gathered that he meant the horses.

Women were squeezing soap and grime out of clothes where thin streams trickled over the cobbles. Others were bearing bowls of corn to the neighborhood mill for grinding. In a wide patio was a small foundry of iron, brass, and aluminum; in doorways sat leather workers, embroidering belts with colored yarn, sewing, making shoes. In some streets, almost every patio was a home "factory." Yet even in the humblest, flowers blossomed, birds sang.

The street of the lacquer workers is Emiliano Carranza. Narrow-walked, it slants irregularly uphill, until the cobbles lose themselves in muddy clay. Doña Margarita Castillo de Navarete led us to the patio where younger people were working.

"I have been in this craft seventy years," she told us. "I have taught it to my children and grandchildren. I mix the colors; they apply them."

With pride she exhibited her best pieces, pointing out the fine qualities of the work and the details wherein lay the superiority of one bowl or tray to another. "José," she would say, "did very nicely with this one. But this, now, I would be ashamed to sell."

The designs, she said, had been handed down in her family, and were "very old."

The best work was done on gourds, though there were also some fine wooden articles, particularly small fragrant boxes. The irregularity of the gourd, or of the slab of wood when from a naturally asymmetrical piece, was pleasing.

Doña Margarita explained the process. The gourd is dried and polished, then sized with a compound of mineral earth, vegetable oil and *aje*—a secretion produced by a tree-dwelling insect—and the ground-color is applied in a fine powder. It is allowed to dry thoroughly, whereupon the process is repeated;

A MOUNTAIN TOWN

The Gourd of Flowers

then the gourd is anointed with oil containing a few drops of *aje;* dried again, and polished.

The colors she used, she added, were prepared from native earths; she scorned the manufactured oil paints used by less conscientious craftsmen.

As she spoke, girls were polishing gourds, thus prepared, and a young man was beginning the next step, tracing the design freehand, with a sharp instrument. Other girls were rubbing the powdered colors into the designs with the fingers and the ball of the thumb.

"It takes much rubbing. We never use a brush. Each color is applied separately, and the piece is then left to dry in the shade several days before the next color is applied. A large piece may take months to finish. Some people nowadays make a bowl in three or four days—but I will let no lacquer-ware out of my house in less than three weeks. If the work is hurried, the lacquer will crack."

Another lacquer worker in the same street led us to his kitchen: there were pottery and copper on the walls, but tin and aluminum showed more use; a grinding-stone stood in a corner, and a stove in the center, built up high of stone or brick, in a row of individual fireplaces arranged in **U** shape, for separate charcoal fires, one for each pot. "A horseshoe," he explained, "for good luck—or not to burn the frijoles."

A woman, asked at random in the street, led us to the house of Doña Isabel Cano de Álvarez, where lacquer-ware is not for sale, but only on display. Doña Isabel did the work herself, and she must have kept at it from young girlhood, to have filled the house with so much lacquered furniture, each room in a different color scheme, but all dazzlingly bright.

Later, in the state museum at Pátzcuaro, we saw how the art has deteriorated; it is not only the age-softened color, but also the finer patterns, the better design, that make the ware of a century or even half a century ago superior to that of to-day. But we never realized how good the lacquer of Uruápan is, even in its recent somewhat garish state, until we saw that of Quiroga, just beyond Tzintzúntzan.

Yes, it was a good-looking country, to the eye, around Uruápan, agreed the handsome, mustached Indian in the plaza, "but much worked—it won't produce without fertilizer." Whereas, "in my country" (in the hills beyond Zamora) "you only plow, plant, and weed, and the crop grows."

There were about three hundred Italians in Uruápan, he said, and some Germans, many of them "very fine fellows." The merchants, he added, were "Arabs," by which he probably meant Syrians.

He told me of the "eleven villages, pure Indian," on the truck road to his own *pueblo*: Juancito, famous for its pottery —the green with the black design, or the red with the blue and white design; Jacona, of the fruit orchards; Paracho, twice ruined by revolution, where musical instruments are made, and carved inlaid chocolate-beaters turned on primitive bow-lathes; and other places. Among them, Paranguítaro, whence orchids are shipped "to all the world"; Huetamo, in the "hot country" to the southeast, where plant lice are gathered to make the *aje* that gives luster to lacquer-ware; Nehuatzin, which builds canoes for Lake Pátzcuaro; Pichátaro, whence come the round-bladed paddles, and applewood for the throwing-sticks that add range and accuracy to duck-hunters' spears.

Through banana plantations and coffee groves bright with green and red berries the road runs from Uruápan to Tzaráracua, where the Water That Sings Like Birds leaps from a caverned cliff into a fern- and flower-fringed pool, spurting through crevices so fine that the delicate jets have given the cataract its name, The Sieve.

All the waters of Michoacán seem to have been born in legend. Near a spring that feeds the river, natives pointed out the print of the devil's knee. For, they related, the good Fray

The Gourd of Flowers

Martín de Jesús went up the mountain to speak with birds and beasts. The demon who haunted the place sent a wind that wilted all the flowers. A whirlwind enveloped the friar, wrenching the crucifix from his hand. But when the dust cleared, there stood Fray Martín, head high, arms extended, and at his feet knelt Satan, in consternation at seeing a spring pour forth where the earth had opened to receive the crucifix.

XXXIII · RAIN COMES TO URUÁPAN

IT was the time of the corn planting in Uruápan. Near the
small chapel, with its festival crosses of corn and green
reeds, a procession was forming. Wreaths of colored
paper and of flowers almost buried the oxen hitched to the
wooden plows. Ears of corn hung from their foreheads; rings
of bread encircled their horns.

Around them danced masked men, the red and gold flaps
on their black leggings waving as they leaped, striking out
with small whips at bystanders; colored ribbons on the high
head-dresses streamed in the wind. The lacquered masks were
black, but the carved features were not those of Negroes.
They were the faces, I learned, of the gods of the darkness.

Slowly the procession formed, marshaled by a ragged man

Rain Comes to Uruápan

who held his balance with a difficulty induced by fortifying potions of aguardiente. The hare-lipped man beside him had some mysterious influence in the rite. This was appropriate, for as any one in the State of Michoacán knows, only those born under a lunar eclipse bear the sign of the rabbit that lives in the moon, and such persons are close to the gods.

Three bands took their places: a very industrious ensemble of brass, a group of string-plucking *mariachis,* and a *"chirimía"* of drums and primitive flutes which played a barbaric music of Oriental fractional intervals. All three played at once, each stoutly holding to its own melody and rhythm.

Behind the oxen, young women in richly pleated woollen skirts, aproned in red or white, with embroidered blouses, brilliant blue rebozos draped straight down on both sides, and broad sashes, marched in a slowly wheeling advance, carrying on their heads lacquered bowls filled with fruit and bread. I should add that from the napkin that covered each bowl protruded the neck of a bottle of pink soda-water, rapidly approaching the boiling point in the noonday sun. They represented wives of farmers, carrying food to their men in the fields.

Deliberately, oxen and all, they marched the length of the street and back, pausing at the little chapel for the animals to be blessed in the name of Saint Anthony.

Young men mounted on burros rode ahead, to lurk behind corners and dash forth, striking furiously with light switches, enacting a "kidnapping" of another youth dressed as a girl. This bit of drama incited so much mirth that it was repeated again and again.

As the procession passed, handfuls of shelled corn were thrown over participants and spectators, an act obviously symbolic of the sowing.

Margaret and I became separated in the swirl of the crowd as I followed the procession, manœuvering for position from

247

which to snap photographs—into the foreground of which, at the crucial moment, thronged a medley of legs and sombreros and posteriors.

Later in the day I learned of Margaret's adventure. The crowd, densely packed on the high, narrow sidewalk, swept her along the hot, dusty street. She found herself in a throng of strangers, and she recalled that somewhere in that crowd I was carrying a considerable sum in pesos.

Disturbed by this thought, as well as by her own situation, she was carried on in that stream of people paralleling the procession. Uruápan, at that time of day, is a good place to sit in the shade. At nearly six thousand feet, it is high enough to make one tire easily, and still low enough to become very warm.

And suddenly, here came the oxen. The decorated animals, lumbering along, swerved to avoid a grating in the street. In a moment the lowered horns and plunging hoofs were crowding up on that narrow walk, heading straight for her. Jammed in the press of people, she could not avoid them by moving to right or left.

She felt herself falling backward. Brown hands drew her safely through an open window from which a group of women were watching the parade.

Recovering from this shock, she set out in search of me, over foot-battering cobbles in the swirling dust and the hot sun, and still engulfed in the confusing human swarm. She had walked thus almost the entire length of that long street, when a voice hailed her:

"Madam, may I be of assistance?"

By good fortune, Rafael—the only English-speaking chauffeur, as he proudly informed us, in Uruápan—had observed her plight. And it was Rafael who sought me out in the crowd still milling around the chapel and led me to where she sat in his car.

Rafael soothed her apprehensions of possible robbery:

Rain Comes to Uruápan

"That might happen in the Capital, but not here. In Uruápan, where one is as poor as another, there are no thieves."

"Where did you learn English?" I asked.

"In Oakland, California," grinned Rafael.

Returning, the celebrants filed into the patio of an abandoned hacienda. The girls shared with young men the food they had carried those weary miles in dust and sun. The bands played; men and women danced; slightly tipsy youths scuffled good-naturedly on the green.

"Stay; there will be more dances."

But dust swirled thickly; the sun beat down. We returned to the comfort of Señor Álvarez' El Mirador hotel.

Next day we went again in search of the fiesta. It wasn't easy to find. The chapel, the old hacienda house, the streets of the *barrio* that had been so lively the day before, were empty.

In a narrow way where men were threading green yarn into punched leather and women bent over sewing-machines in dark corners, a woman stepped from a rear doorway to listen. Ah yes, the *chirimía*—and she guided us up an unpaved, rutted alley to an adobe house whose owner graciously invited us to enter.

He was the *carguero*—the neighborhood official upon whom fell the honor and burden of defraying the expenses of the fiesta, roughly equivalent to some twenty dollars, which is a good deal of money in Uruápan.

Through a dark, narrow, scantily furnished room we passed into a sunlit, earth-floored patio between adobe walls. The small open space was gay with activity and sound. The *chirimía* musicians, ranged along one wall, were playing their odd melody, and, a little way off, the brasses performed prodigiously, cramming the patio with tone.

People were dancing around an open fire above which, propped on stones, rested a large iron pot into which women were dropping onions and chunks of meat. Masked clowns

249

postured among the dancers. One, dressed as a woman, became entangled in his skirts and stumbled over a stone, tilting the pot so that the stew began to spill. This caused only a momentary flurry as women ran to rescue the meal. Around them, the dance went on, stirring clouds of dust.

In a corner, other women were washing a few dishes; one was rubbing a shirt with soap, hurling it vigorously on a flat stone, squeezing and slapping it. Still another was drawing water from an open well with a crude windlass formed of an irregular log. From a near-by room came the rhythmic slap, slap of hands patting tortillas.

Our fellow-guests were as gracious as our host. As the dance gathered momentum, voices urged me to join in. And I recalled long-ago evenings on the coral-strewn beach of an atoll in the South Sea—moon-drenched hours spent in learning movements much like these, learning in pain and weariness at first, barefoot on the cruel pebbles of that harsh land.

In that patio at Uruápan, surrounded by a throng of furiously dancing Indians, I executed as best I could from memory a *kori* of the Tuamotu Islands.

Whatever the merits of the performance, it was apparently a success with this audience. At least it convinced them that this *gringo* was *simpático*. The clowns crowded around, slapping me on the back, shouting, *"Muy bonito."* The leader, followed by each of his men in turn, pressed my hand, thanking me. They were honored, he said, by my participation. One offered me a handful of tart little wild cherries—"very dirty with dust," as he cheerfully apologized. Then dancers and musicians formed for another procession.

All this was a recognized Christian festival, in honor of Saint Anthony. But it followed, in part at least, a ritual that must have been old in Uruápan long before the saint was known anywhere in Mexico. It was very evidently a planting

Rain Comes to Uruápan

ceremony; a prayer, after a half year and more of drouth, for rain.

As we walked back through the plaza when the rites were over, the first large drops spattered on the stones. A cold wind blew down from suddenly misted mountains; Cupatitzio murmured louder over its boulder-strewn bed. Those dancing brown feet—and mine with them—had not stamped the dust in vain. From the shelter of the arcades we watched the first rain of the season come to Uruápan.

Rain slants down into the gardens, where the mangoes hang heavy
          on the stem;
pools in the plaza reflect the tall fresnos in mirrors shattered
          by whirling drops.
The Singing River chatters over its stones; the mountain wears
          a rebozo of blue-white mist.
Don Simplicio wraps his sarape closer about him as the chill
          strikes down from the dove-gray leaning sky,
knees up, feet flat-planted on flagstones, liquid eyes gazing
          beyond the distractions of this life:
Don Simplicio has time for contemplation.

All day the masked dancers have trampled the dust of the patio,
          beating upon the doors of the earth for answer;
the oxen have marched, garlanded with flowers and bread,
          heavy with ripe grain;
the girls in bright gowns have twirled slowly, balancing on
          graceful heads the lacquered gourds piled high with fruit,
and the showered grains of corn rattled over the heads of dancers
          and watchers
in the ancient rite of the gods of earth and rain.

Now the oval pointed drops burrow down into the red volcanic
          earth, embracing the rootlets, trickling
into the open mouths of the small stone images buried in the fields.
The saints of the white and the brown man have answered:
          the rains come.

XXXIV · CITY OF THE ANGELS

THE road to Puebla climbs out of the Valley of Mexico, curving hazardously along the sides of darkly wooded mountains and winding valleys, beyond which the Smoking Mountain and the White Woman lift snow-encrusted heads. Up, up, it coils, to the scenic curve eleven thousand feet above the sea, between somber pines, and down again.

These forests were a haunt of bandits in Colonial and early Independence days. Robbery of the "diligence" to or from Vera Cruz was then almost a regular occurrence. Passengers were even stripped of clothes and continued on their way, behind drawn curtains, until, at the outskirts of their destination, they were met by accomplices of the bandits, who would accept promissory notes in exchange for clothing with which to enter the city.

I was told that on one occasion, a century or more ago, a foreign visitor, on taking leave of the president and the latter's aide, replied when cautioned to beware of robbers: "They won't get my money. I have it safely hidden in the lining of an old trunk, where they'll never think of looking."

When the robbers surrounded the coach, they went directly to the trunk where the money was hidden. The victim reported afterward that the robber chief "looked very much like the president's aide."

An opera troupe fared better. On learning that they were *"artistas,"* the bandits demanded only an al fresco performance, after which they sent the singers on their way undespoiled. Under the trees, *Aida* was sung, and members of the company declared they had never had a more appreciative audience.

We left the bus amid the busy tawdriness of the marketplace at Huejotzingo and walked toward the shell of the monastery, built by the mild Brothers of Saint Francis in 1529. Pointed-roofed chapels, like blockhouses of a fort, guard the corners of the vast atrium, where wild grasses struggle up between the stones. There is an Indian touch in the carving on the great doorway that leads into the high-vaulted church, facing a rich four-storied retable. In the hall adjoining, crude but interesting frescoes in black and white remain, some of them reputed to be portraits of the twelve Franciscans who first came to New Spain.

The carved doors open now upon emptiness beneath the noble domes, friars no longer trail their robes across the flagstones of the patio under the orange trees. San Miguel de Huejotzingo is a "Colonial monument," a museum-piece maintained by the government as an example of the ecclesiastical architecture and art of the sixteenth century.

Pattern of Mexico

The face of the great pyramid at Cholula is worn away with time; grasses and shrubs replace the plastered stone. The temple of Quetzalcóatl of the Air was long ago thrown down; the black image with its crown of fiery plumes and its jeweled scepter, gold collar, and shield of the winds, has vanished, as the Feathered Serpent himself vanished when the Toltec power crumbled. The god halted here at Cholula, on his sad retreat to the sunrise land Tlapallan; he lingered to teach the Cholulans the useful arts. . . .

"Looking toward Tula, he wept, and the tears hollowed and furrowed the rock upon which was resting Quetzalcóatl."

But beneath the crumbled earth, the roots, and the flowers; beneath the church of Our Lady of the Remedies with which the Spaniards crowned the colossal pedestal, lie ranks of pressed adobe, inclined walls, dizzying stairs, altar platforms —seven or more foundations, one upon another.

The tunnel driven by government archæologists was dim and dusty and smelling of old earth. These Mexican pyramids are solid, but an archaeologist always wants to know what is inside. And they have bored the pyramid of Cholula full of holes as if it were a giant cheese.

Through narrow corridors we tramped, tracing the worn outlines of what were once outer façades, setting feet upon steep stairs that mounted into darkness. The lights failed; men lit candles that faintly illumined the red and black frescoes on an overhanging wall—the symbol of Quetzalcóatl and the round-eyed mask of Tlaloc of the Tears of Heaven.

Age after age, as the fifty-two-year cycles moved around the sun, the temple foundations were augmented. In its ruined state, it is said still to be the largest artificial mound in the world—twice the size of the great pyramid of Cheops. There could scarcely be a more impressive monument to him who was revered as the Morning and the Evening Star.

The town itself has decayed since Cortés estimated it to contain forty thousand houses, and slew three thousand nobles

AT CHOLULA, A CHURCH SURMOUNTS A TOLTEC PYRAMID

in its plaza. The reputed three hundred and sixty-five churches which replaced the "four hundred and more towers, and every one a mosque" that Cortés counted, may exist; it is doubtful whether any one has had the hardihood to visit and enumerate them all. Visitors climb to the pyramid summit as much for the view over the maguey-studded plain as for the sanctuary that enshrines the venerated figure of Our Lady of the Remedies.

She is a rival of the Guadalupe, and her story is similar. An Indian chief found the crude wooden image under a maguey where one of Cortés' men had hidden it on the flight from the Capital after the Sad Night. As often as he took it to his house for proper veneration, the legend declares, it returned obstinately to the maguey plant. Obviously this was another miracle. Historically, the Lady of the Remedies has been associated with the Spanish cause rather than the Indian; she led the armies of the royalists against the rebels who rallied about the Guadalupe in the fight for independence.

From the pyramid the road runs to the plateau, surrounded by four volcanoes, on which stands the city of Puebla.

When the conquerors asked the Franciscans to found a city for a supply base between the Capital and the coast, a friar dreamed of two angels surveying a plain between high volcanic mountains, and by this sign from heaven—according to tradition—the site was chosen.

Nor did the angels leave the friars flat thereafter. Legend-loving Poblanos relate that when the cathedral was being built, as the work was not going forward rapidly enough, angels laid stone by night while the human builders slept. Although later a patriotic and anti-clerical officialdom named the city Puebla de Zaragoza, for the general who defeated the French here on May 5, 1862, Mexico still thinks of it as Puebla de los Ángeles.

The streets of Puebla are wide and straight and clean. I

was told they had always been so. "Every property owner is responsible for the tidiness of the street in front of his premises," a citizen explained. "He is fined if he allows it to become dirty or littered."

This civic spirit seemed to extend to nearly all matters. In few places did we see so many Colonial buildings so well groomed. And nowhere did we see such lavish use of the tiles for which Puebla is famous—descendants of the Talavera ware of Spain. In red, blue, green, yellow, cream, they adorned fronts of buildings or formed whole façades. The town was jeweled with color.

That was about all we saw of it the first day. For we arrived as members of a party of three hundred or more guests of the City and State of Puebla—an excursion of the twenty-seventh Congress of Americanists. The hospitality of municipal and state authorities was lavish, and official welcomes, in any country, take time.

Puebla was cheerful and bright in the morning. Busy cotton mills, modern schools and hospitals, spoke of progress and civic spirit; glittering motion-picture theaters contrasted with the fire-ravaged but noble structure which the mayor informed us was "the oldest theater in America—built in 1612."

The "sugar-paste house," a Colonial mansion to which all visitors are conducted, really did look a little like one of those cakes, for ornament only, sometimes exhibited in bakery windows: a façade of florid tiles with white decorations that suggested sugar frosting. Its interior had become a state museum, poorly lighted and ill arranged, with the exception of the tastefully reproduced Colonial interiors on an upper floor.

The old forts of Guadalupe and Loreto, also made into a historical museum, moldered on the slope above their dry moats, around their relics of battles long ago. From the height, we looked across the tiled domes of the city to snow-roofed conical mountains.

City of the Angels

Puebla, we thought, deserved the reputation of Cholula as a city of churches. Their bells chimed forth at all hours from the tiled towers. Indeed, the city has the reputation of being one of the most "Catholic," as well as most aristocratic cities in the Republic. The cathedral is rated one of the finest in Mexico—more coherent, though smaller, than the great cathedral in the Capital. Its paintings, though mostly by Mexican Colonial artists, included a head of Our Lady attributed to Correggio, and the tapestries in the Sala Capitular were said to have been designed by Rubens. Pedro Múñoz' wood-carving in the choir is reputed to be outstanding in the world.

Entering at mid-morning, we found the cathedral almost empty: a very few worshipers lost in its vastness, but a service in full cry, with bells and boy sopranos; brilliantly robed clergy moving in solemn and beautiful procession, conducting an impressive ceremony apparently just out of their own devotion.

The Temple of Santo Domingo was overpowering in its profusion of ornament; its famed Chapel of the Rosary amazing rather than attractive with its bewildering array of tiles, colored plaster sculpture, and the thick gold of its altars.

The monastery of the Company of Jesus seemed notable for its age and historical associations, rather than for its beauty. One could linger long among the twenty thousand books and manuscripts in its library, which may hold yet un-rediscovered treasures. Its church is of sentimental interest because of its association with one of Mexico's favorite legends. For there, according to the inscription, lies the original "China Poblana," whose costume, altered and debased with glittering decoration, has become identified in foreign minds with the "typical Mexican" fiesta dress.

The "Chinese woman of Puebla" appears, from the researches of José Juan Tablada, to have been from India rather than from China. Mirraha—"Bitterness"—was born in or near Delhi in 1610, the daughter of a "holy man" of the East. Before her birth, the Blessed Virgin, according to the story,

257

led her mother to a hillside and revealed a buried treasure of gold and jewels. In her childhood, Mirraha was lost on a river bank, to be found, after five days of frantic search, safe on a bit of driftwood in the bay. Seers prophesied that the streams of fate would carry her to strange lands where she would find a harbor of peace.

Invasion threatened, and the family fled to the seashore. As she played on the beach, Portuguese pirates captured her and carried her away to Cochin-China. Even then, at the age of nine, visions came to her: the Virgin appeared aboard the pirate ship to comfort her. In Cochin she was baptized, taking the name Catarina de San Juan.

At Manila the pirates sold her to an agent of Captain Miguel de Sosa, and in 1620 she was brought to Puebla to cheer the captain's childless home. Growing to womanhood, she devoted her time and fortune to helping the poor, and died in Puebla, greatly beloved, in 1688. In her memory, women adopted her costume.

She wore always, it is said, a skirt of red flannel, yoked and bordered with green, and a white embroidered waist—the reputed original of which is in the Puebla museum. The costume has suffered changes both in appearance and in use; it has been cheapened with spangles and adapted for carnival gaiety quite in contrast with the life of the pious Doña Catarina. In 1840, Mme. Calderón de la Barca was warned by conservative ladies of the Capital against appearing at a costume party in China Poblana dress, because of the frivolous connotations it had acquired.

Of all the churches of Puebla, we enjoyed most the graceful-towered San Francisco, with its rich but tastefully carved front, set with not too numerous tiles in flower shapes against the brick. Beautiful, too, was the fresh and clean tiled kitchen of the Santa Rosa convent, with its pottery in orderly rows— a seventeenth-century Mexican kitchen of the finest type.

A somewhat morbid interest attracts visitors to the former

secret convent of Santa Mónica. When these establishments were abolished by the Reform Laws of 1857, Santa Mónica went "underground" as did many another. Its distinction lies in its having existed undiscovered until a few years ago when, we were told, "a sacristan betrayed it for pesos."

The house, from the outside, looked to us like any other in an undistinguished street. But that house was only a mask, one room deep: behind it huddled forty or more cells, a chapel, two tile-walled patios with gardens. There was a windowless room where modest nuns used to change clothes in the dark; a dim cell adorned with skulls and scenes of torture to encourage pious meditation; the burial crypt, kitchen, refectory.

Even after penetrating the outer precincts of the place, the government detectives couldn't at first find its heart. By accident, it is related, one of them moved a vase of flowers in the dining-room of the house. Behind it was a bell push that swung back a row of shelves in an alcove, exposing the stair to the mother superior's study.

The government made the former convent a museum, housing relics from several similar institutions.

"What became of the nuns?" I asked.

"They continue their vocation in private," was the reply.

A couple of hours from Puebla, the ancient walled town of Atlixco zigzags up the hillside: Atlixco of the Waters, named long ago for its plenty in a thirsty land. Fields of corn and wheat lie green and golden about it; shady lanes wind to little orchards where fruits of the hot country meet those of the plateau.

Within its medieval streets, weavers ply the loom; *charros* ride out of the valley like characters from a romance of the ranchos; music of the dance throbs over the cobbled ways by night.

It is a Mexican hill town perhaps at its best, with its vari-colored market, its venerable *portales*, its severe Franciscan monastery against the conical wedge of the Little Hill of Saint Michael. Its widespread, thick-trunked ahuehuete tree must have stood here even before the Indians named the place for its abundant waters.

The church of San Francisco Acatepec is gone. Famed as one of the "jewels" of Mexico, it burned on New Year's Day, 1940. But Santa María Tonantzintla, also between Cholula and Puebla, is, in its way, even more interesting.

The name itself is eloquent: "Saint Mary," coupled with Tonantzin, "Our Lady" of the Aztec pantheon. The juxtaposition has been carried out in the décor. The exterior, with its red and white tile façade, might be a Spanish church of Puebla. But within, brilliance of color bewilders the eyes. Apparently every available inch of surface has been sculptured and decorated in violent hues.

One detects at once the Indian touch—reinterpreting the baroque, as Aldous Huxley has remarked, with neolithic mind. Sculptured angels with Indian faces draw bows across stringed instruments; cherubs wear feathers in their hair; monkeys, boughs of fruit, interlaced palms, recall Aztec symbols. The predominating colors are gold and red, but yellow and green tiles contrast with violent reds and vivid whites; cornices and salients are punctuated in black and gray.

Nevertheless, this fantastic scheme has been much admired. As Dr. Atl declared: "It is a little grotto of gold, in which the smoke of incense and the action of time have imparted a patina which harmonizes the brilliance of the gold with the greens, the reds and grays of the robes of the saints."

It is overelaborate for many modern tastes, but there is a joyousness in it; one feels that those Indian craftsmen had a good time doing it.

On those walls the Plunging God descends, in the moment of his fiery passage of the zenith, as he journeys north in May to bring the rains.

XXXV · JEWELS OF THE MAD HUNCHBACK

THE tiled domes of Tehuacan gleamed above a sandy valley between parched hills. The country through which we drove from Puebla looked like a desert, but the place, as we knew, is noted for mineral springs, and apparently they are the only reason for going there. Among Mexicans, it is a celebrated resort.

There we boarded a narrow-gauge railway train that crawled southward for twelve hours or more, among tawny hills clustered with giant cacti, and into wooded mountains and wild gorges lanterned with flowering trees. At last we emerged into a broad valley punctuated by thatched villages. Lone churches pointed stone fingers to the sky and fortress-like hacienda buildings frowned among the fields, around the city of Oaxaca.

The train was packed beyond officially recognized capacity with delegates to the Congress of Americanists, delegates' families, and people who knew a delegate and had gone along for the ride. Mexicans love traveling on trains: it's a prolonged picnic —chatting, singing, and eating. Leaning from car windows at stations, to buy food handed up by Indian women from the platform—melons, hands of bananas, baskets of small fruits—and munching them on the way, is half the fun.

In the forward car, which had been stocked by a generous committee with carbonated beverages and beer, Mexicans were singing the sentimental songs they love: everything from the few classics known fragmentarily north of the border to the latest tunes from Mexican sound films. They never tired, and seldom if ever repeated. Their repertory seemed inexhaustible.

We found Oaxaca a quiet but cheerful city, with ponderous buildings of greenish stone like old jade, a huge tree-shaded plaza facing arcades lively with street merchants and public scribes, and sidewalk cafes dispensing ices and beer. Beggars, if any, had been whisked out of sight. I saw just one, being led away by a policeman. The city and state governments were doing all they could to make us comfortable and spare us annoyance.

The city, among those of its size, has a flavor distinctive of the Mexican soil. We noticed that motors were rare in the broad streets around the square; Indian Mexico walked in from the threefold valley and the misty sierra to throng the market and to pray in the churches. Almost innumerable dialects sounded in the streets, most prominent among them the soft, round-voweled Zapotec and the clattering Mixtec.

Flat roofs and green towers spread between panther-crouching hills; in the thatched villages around these hills the Zapotecs still live their withdrawn, timeless life. And the

Jewels of the Mad Hunchback

sculptured stones of Monte Alban, the severe relief-mosaics of Mitla, crumble slowly beneath unchanging rain and sun.

The carved façade of the cathedral looks across at the Alameda with timeless dignity. As we entered, a shaft of sunlight gleamed upon red velvet and gold; choir boys lifted fresh voices. The life of the plaza stirred lazily outside.

The celebrated church of Santo Domingo was almost overpowering in its profusion of color and form. Heavy polychrome sculpture in high relief bulged from walls and arches as if about to swell and crush the beholder. Here the baroque had flowered into exuberant fantasy, culminating in a great tree design that spread its branches, fruiting with Virgin and saint, over the vault of the ceiling.

Santo Domingo has been extravagantly admired; authorities proclaim it the most superb example of baroque decoration in all Mexico. These ecclesiastical monuments should be considered not by the changing fashions of our day, but for what they are: the expression of their time, when no expense was too lavish, no piling of gold upon gold, color upon color, too extravagant to do honor to Our Lord and His saints. And the powerful arches of the adjoining cloister are, by almost any standard, a thing of enduring and functional beauty.

The brown façade of the church of La Soledad is like an altar-piece, with its deep niches, its images of saints in stone. On the altar within stands Our Lady of Solitude, patroness of muleteers and sailors and of the State of Oaxaca.

"It was in 1543," said the sacristan, "that an *arriero,* driving his mules to Guatemala, found, as he passed the hermitage of San Sebastián, that he had one more mule than those with which he had started.

"Lest he be accused of theft, he reported to the mayor, who opened the box on the back of the extra mule and found within it the image of Our Lady of Solitude. When the box was opened, the mule fell dead. On the spot where he fell, this church was built.

"Mule drivers used to come here in the early morning to pray, but so many mules were stolen while the drivers were inside the church, that a copy of the image was placed outside.

"The pearl in her forehead was the gift of a sailor, in fulfilment of a vow. In a storm at sea, he promised his most precious possession if he might be saved. And in his old age he brought this pearl.

"Look"—picking up a few grains of fine white sand—"the sea itself comes at night to do Our Lady honor. The sand of the ocean keeps falling from her robe."

Interesting as we found the inhabitants of Oaxaca, some of us were just as much so to them—and amusing, too. Crossing the plaza to rescue my wife from a sudden rain, I caused an apparently unaccustomed diversion and much hilarious comment, by unfurling her collapsible umbrella—especially when it collapsed at the wrong time.

This performance, however, was eclipsed by that of Margaret herself when she rustled through the market-place in a cellophane raincoat. Market women gathered from all sides, bubbling forth long and infectious peals of laughter. For all I know, it may have been the first garment of its kind exhibited in Oaxaca; at least it seemed to be one of the funniest sights they had ever beheld. One after another of our party succumbed to the contagion; soon we were all laughing as heartily as they. Margaret herself laughed until tears streamed.

Opposite that great central market, with its multicolored array of vegetables, fruits, and herbs, a tawny wall enclosed a block-square place lined with small sheds: the pottery mart. Some of the best pottery in Mexico, as well as some of the ugliest, is made in or around Oaxaca. The sellers seemed conscious of its superiority: apparently indifferent to business, they would scarcely trouble to lift a damaged piece to expose a better one beneath.

Jewels of the Mad Hunchback

Heaps and piles of bowls lay in variegated confusion: little and big, plain and decorated, mingled with clay toys and tinkling little clay bells, and flanked by big, bright-striped baskets. In these baskets buyers carry away the goods, packed in straw which must be thrown away and replaced by excelsior, paper, or some other non-contraband packing before they recross the border.

Attempting to point out to a most indifferent merchant a superior salad bowl, across a pile of mediocre objects, I kicked over and broke a pottery animal vaguely resembling a cow. The absurd, fragile, and misshapen creature immediately assumed a hitherto unheard-of value. One would have thought it was the most precious article in the shop. I had ruined, it appeared, a vital feature of the woman's stock-in trade. (We *gringos* are always blundering in and exploiting the natives. Mexico for Mexicans! *Viva México!*)

To still the clamor, I bought the monstrosity, then looked about for some means of disposing of it. Near-by stood a ragged small boy, his one good eye fixed in fascination upon the damaged toy. The look of joy that spread over his smeared face when I gave it to him was worth far more than the price. Even he made no attempt to identify its genus or species. Tenderly gathering up the pieces, he stroked them lovingly, murmuring in rapture: *"El animal, el bonito animal!"*—and turned to beg from Miguel Covarrubias a centavo for chewing-gum with which to glue the "beautiful animal" together.

Beneath a tremendous sky delicately flowered with cloud, the sacred city of Monte Alban, a few miles from Oaxaca, looks from a height over the valley. Across that valley, behind that distant blue range, dwelt the Mixtecs who overcame the city and superimposed their own structures upon the temples and tombs of the Zapotecs.

Like Teotihuacan, Monte Alban is arranged in a great complex of quadrangles, with a masterly sense of planning and, because of its scope and commanding situation, with even more impressiveness as a whole than that city. However, it is more difficult, because of its extent, to grasp its arrangement. Stone buildings, often with sculptured walls, surround broad plazas; wide stairways mount to ample platforms from which the eye falls upon still more templed squares, more grass-covered mounds whose excavation will yield further relics of the centuries that rolled along their way before history became tracks of black ink on a paper page.

A low entrance admitted us to the "Temple of the Dancers," so named by modern investigators from the postures of the figures on the walls of the inner chamber. As some members of the party commented, it might have been called the Temple of the Swimmers, for some of the figures appear in swimming motion.

This is but one of the more celebrated among many structures at this vast "site." Everywhere one looks, prehistoric stones jut from the dry soil, either singly, inscribed with glyphs of record or with a powerful portrayal of human and animal forms, or else ranked in walls and terraces and stairs. Some of the carved figures are upside down, or sidewise, or turned inward, indicating that later builders—the Mixtec conquerors, no doubt—regarded them merely as convenient building material.

A more recently explored structure appears to have been an observatory. It is polyhedral, shaped roughly like an arrow point, and oriented to the northeast. Within is a steeply vaulted chamber formed by inward-slanting slabs. The outer walls bear glyphs: the tiger god, a hill that may represent a place-name, and dates in the Zapotec calendar. I stood by while archæologists discussed the reading: the numerals alone are plain enough, even to a novice—the bar for five, the dot for one—and day and month signs can be identified by those who have given the matter somewhat more study, but the relation of this to other calendar systems is still open to varying interpretations, and so is a source of endless debate.

RUINS AT MONTE ALBAN, STATE OF OAXACA

Jewels of the Mad Hunchback

On a Cyclopean platform facing the axis of another plaza stand remnants of columns four feet or more thick, which once supported a portico roof. Across a sunken court, the platform faces a truncated pyramid, cut in cross-section by investigators to expose an earlier structure buried within. This is frescoed with representations, apparently, of the Feathered Serpent and of flowers.

Climbing a low hill farther on, we descended a ladder from a paved platform to a two-chambered tomb. The outer room was plain, except that above the doorway to the inner chamber stood an urn elaborately modeled in the features of a god of earth. Within, walls bore the snake symbol and a face.

The movable treasures of these tombs had been taken to the museum in Oaxaca for safekeeping. These included the jewels discovered in the famous Tomb Seven. In glass cases, under guard, they occupied the upper room of the museum: an amazing array of massive or delicate work in gold and silver, in jade and turquoise, in obsidian, rock crystal, jet. Here were gold breastplates, anklets, bracelets, ear ornaments, rings for fingers and toes. There was a cup of rock crystal, finely shaped of a material harder than steel—monument of a lifetime of patient grinding with crystal-dust and water; translucent goblets of alabaster; a jade pheasant, exquisitely carved, with golden eyes; fan handles of gold and jade from which the precious quetzal feathers had crumbled away. Gold and silver jewelry so delicate as to resemble filigree had been cast cunningly by the "lost wax" process; among them disks half silver, half gold, whose casting in such perfection must have involved a formidable problem, since the melting-points of the two metals are different. Great barbaric necklaces of turquoise, jet, and gold, of coral and jade and obsidian, were hung with pendants of huge pear-shaped pearls. Among the most exquisite were two small rings, one of gold, bearing the rising eagle of day, the other silver, with the descending eagle of night.

Pattern of Mexico

Dr. Alfonso Caso, who discovered these jewels in 1932, led us to the case that held the remains of their presumed owner. All these precious objects, he told us, were found in one tomb, and with them, these bones.

"A hunchback," he said, pointing to the deformed skeleton, "and mad, besides, for the skull shows disease."

The mad hunchback actually wore this weight of treasure —for the rings still clasped the finger and toe bones when they were found. He had been deified, it is conjectured, because of his madness and deformity—held as a reincarnation, perhaps, of Xólotl the Monster, an aspect of the great Quetzal-cóatl; Xólotl, who stole bones from Mictlan, Land of the Dead, which the gods bathed in blood to create man.

Looking upon those pitiful misshapen bones, the pitted, mal-formed skull, I could imagine that strange being: clad in rich garments of embroidery and precious feathers; loaded with these jewels; tended by retinues of priests; perhaps chanting mad prophecies; revered, and at last laid away with his treas-ures in the darkness at the heart of the hill.

Pottery and sculpture had been found in other tombs, but no other tomb thus far explored at Monte Alban, I was told, had yielded jewels.

Plumed dancers of Cuilápan were moving through their obscure rite in the sunlit plaza of Oaxaca when we emerged from the museum. Small, lithe men, their height was exag-gerated by tall head-dresses of many-colored feathers, in head-bands set with mirrors and disks of bright metal. They wore garments of barbaric hues, which were likewise mirrored and spangled in glass and tin—alien elements, these, but replacing, no doubt, native ornaments of more precious metals and of obsidian and pearl.

At a little distance, they were almost the "dancing figures" of Monte Alban, and the jewels of Tomb Seven come to life. To a monotonous tune played by a band of brass, they marched and swayed, lifting the feet, knees bent, in the animal-like gesture characteristic of the Indian dance.

They were from the hilltop village near Monte Alban, where rest, it is said, the bones of Princess Donaji, one of the last heroines of the Zapotecs. She was a hostage, the story goes, to the Mixtecs who held Monte Alban just before the Spanish Conquest. In the palace of the Mixtec king, propinquity did its work; the hostage and the enemy ruler fell in love. But the king went on a journey—some say to join the invading Spaniards—and it was Donaji's patriotic duty to smuggle word to the Zapotecs, her people, that it was time to attack.

A drama might be woven of the conflict between loyalty and love. The local legend is that she did send word, but that her people's warriors came too late; the Mixtec lord returned in time to save the city, and Donaji, by the law of war, was sacrificed in the temple. Her blood, flowing upon the lilies that hitherto had bloomed white, stained them purple—and so they remain, in memory of her.

The figures of the dance were few and simple, often repeated. For the Indian does not, like the white man, seek a literal interpretation, expressed in violent and exaggerated movements. He dances with a deeper inwardness, stylizing the interpretative gesture, choosing with fine artistic selection rather than attempting a mimicking appearance. D. H. Lawrence, who saw Mexico often through the glaze of his own illness and life-weariness, yet wrote a strikingly accurate characterization of the Indian dance:

"The curious, silent, absorbed dance of the softly beating feet and ankles, the body coming down softly, but with deep weight, upon powerful knees and ankles, to the tread of the earth, as when a male bird treads the hen."

The feather-dance has been interpreted as symbolic of the Conquest, its personages identified as Cortés, Moctézuma, Doña Marina—but the last also as the Flower-Maid, the goddess Xóchitl. There may be memories here of the lily-woman Donaji and her sacrifice. But one may suspect that underlying one or both of the symbolisms may be that of an older conquest, perhaps the triumph of Xóchitl of the Flowers over the drouth and barrenness of winter, at the beginning of the rains.

XXXVI · HALLS OF THE DEAD

THE way from Oaxaca to Mitla follows a broad valley of cornfields between delicately shaded mountains wreathed in mist. Cave dwellers inhabit the lower cliffs; from the road we could glimpse their barrier fences across the cavern mouths. In unoccupied grottoes, mountain people leave offerings to the gods. A cliff beside the road bears a carving of a horned snake.

"The great tree" of Santa María del Tule, on the road to Mitla, is remarkable for age rather than beauty, girth rather than height. A sabine, it is called, or "bald cypress." Its bulk, wide as a house, swells gigantically in the courtyard before the church. Estimates vary of the number of persons who, joining hands, can encircle the furrowed trunk. But it is the thought of its age that is really impressive. This tree stood here, it is believed, when Christ was born, and perhaps two thousand years before that. As the inscription upon it says, it has looked upon the history of a nation, the development of a race.

Cortés, according to local legend, rested under it on his march to Honduras, and some say it was from this very tree, "on the Tuesday of the Carnivals, at three hours before dawn," that he hanged the former Emperor Cuauhtémoc and eight other nobles. But this local legend does not agree with contemporary accounts, which place the event farther east, "on the bank of a great river, the same which flows to Coatzacoalcos."

The Great Tree needs no historical association to give it dignity; nor does the carved signature, in its bark, of Baron von Humboldt seem pertinent. Far better credit another local tradition, that the Indians secretly revere the tree as a god of growth.

Tlacolula, another stop on the way, is a sprawling adobe town around a large market and a city hall whose outer walls enclose a parked patio as big as the main plaza of many a town. Although Tlacolula is listed officially as a site of ancient ruins, it is so eclipsed in that respect by the near-by Mitla that its principal attraction is its lively Sunday market, where one may buy the famed Teotitlán sarapes without undertaking the difficult journey to the hand-loom village where they are made. This whole valley of Tlacolula is celebrated for its weaving— learned, they say, from the ubiquitous Quetzalcóatl on his way to Yucatán from the Toltec land.

San Pablo Mitla is a cactus-fenced village of thatched or tiled roofs above adobe or stone walls in which are embedded carved stones from more ancient structures near-by. The ruins are up a little slope, hard by the red-domed church. Residents say the church formerly stood in the village proper, but was so often shaken down by earthquakes that it was moved to the

RUINS AT MITLA, STATE OF OAXACA

ancient Zapotec temple area above, since which time the gods of earth have left it undisturbed.

Mitla is a city of the dead. The Zapotecs called it the Door of the Grave; the Aztecs, later, Mictlan—the name of their Hades. The entrance to eternity was believed to be in grottoes there.

The site is, fittingly enough, dustier than Monte Alban. And the architecture, the decoration, is more severe: abstract, geometrical friezes of zigzags and exact frets in two austere themes repeated in many varying combinations. A décor derived from textile design, Dr. Spinden thought; Huxley, translating the theory into imagery, called it "petrified weaving." Dr. Caso, as we stood in the unroofed, sunlit Hall of Columns, interpreted the basic design as symbolic: "Two elements: the stairway and the hook—a stylization of the Feathered Serpent motif. The stairway is the serpent's body; the hook is the head."

Unlike Monte Alban, these designs are not carved, but inset in relief: a mosaic of pre-shaped stones mortised so firmly into the walls that but few have fallen.

A stately stairway rises from a sunken court to a low door under a heavy lintel, in a wall decorated within and without in this precise geometry of stone. Room behind room follows, each with its low entrance: either the Zapotec builders were of short stature, or they bowed in entering the sacred precincts —as we to-day must bow if we would protect our foreheads.

Each of these rectangular chambers bears some variation of the same angular design. And in long rows stand monolithic columns, a yard or more thick, with bases buried far below the pavement. They have no capital: only the plain, smooth cylinder, from which an outer coating of plaster, probably frescoed, has fallen. Traces of frescoes, in red and black on white, linger on some Mitla walls. In 1922, more recent plaster fell from a structure behind the church—in which a priest was living—exposing the murals of an ancient temple.

Pattern of Mexico

In another plaza, under a ruined building, we entered the tombs, crouching as we moved through a tunnel-like passage to a dark interior, roofed with great slabs. In this protected crypt, color still adhered to the fretwork around the walls.

In one of these crypts stands the "Column of Death," popularly supposed to foretell the number of one's remaining years. By this criterion, longevity is inversely proportional to length of arm, for the expectancy is determined by the distance between fingertips of the two hands when embracing the pillar. Hence the jest that one long-armed visitor was surprised to discover that according to the Mitla oracle he had already been dead some years.

One feels, here, the infinite patience of the stone mosaic, laid away in the dark; the straining of innumerable backs to set the heavy roof-slabs in place. In the chambers and on the terrace platforms lingers the melancholy touch of deep antiquity, and echo the long-ago soft footfalls of the priests.

Outside, we found women with soft voices and pleasant faces vending clay figurines, bits of lace work, bright sashes worked in designs like those of the temple friezes, black jars like the pottery in the tombs. The woman selling heavy metal-inlaid sandals "of the Sierra" would not accept a torn five-peso note. She preferred the solidity of silver. But on the way back, I heard one of the party boasting of having bought an image with a counterfeit silver peso. "Fake money for fake antiques, it's a fair exchange," he said.

The kings and priests have gone their way to the darkness, but Mixtecs and Zapotecs remain, still viewing each other with suspicion. The Zapotec guide, who led Ralph Beals to the mountain villages where he studied the Mixe tribes, shunned Mixtec settlements in the region, as if still in peril of the sacrificial obsidian.

On New Year's Eve, I was told, people of San Pablo Mitla and the near-by country offer candles and flowers at the ruins, and little models of the goods they hope to acquire in the coming year. There, as well as at a stone cross in the fields a few miles from the village, God, Saint Paul, and the spirits of the ruins all receive offerings, with Indian impartiality. Until it was forbidden, sacrifices were placed on the big stone behind the Column of Death.

XXXVII · TEHUANTEPEC JOURNEY

SOUTH, where Mexico tapers toward the wasp-waist of the continent, the *macpalxóchitl* extends to the light its red finger-like petals, healing to the heart. Mexicans of to-day call it "the tree of the little hands."

Merchants of Tenochtitlán brought the flowers to the Aztec capital, and the flower-loving, power-loving Moctézuma sent ambassadors to demand the tree for the botanical gardens that were his pride. The king of the south refused; plumed warriors of Mexico mounted the passes in a storm of spears, and the crimson flower of death bloomed amid the inflorescence of the "little hands."

One tradition places the scene of this battle near the flower-pueblo of Juchitan, in the Isthmus of Tehuantepec.

Tehuantepec Journey

I went to Tehuantepec as Mexicans do—on the train that, once a day, plunges southward and westward all day and night through the jungles from Vera Cruz. It was an experience that most visitors neglect: a pageant of the life of the hot country, a glimpse into ways of living far from the thriving cities of the plateau.

Water lilies bloomed beside the track; yellow and orange butterflies hovered over the right-of-way; white herons stood motionless in marshes, as we crossed the vast green plain, studded with ragged palms, beyond Boca del Río. Flaming hibiscus and broad-fringed banana plants clustered around houses of vertical poles with roofs of thatch, where, leaning from car windows, passengers bought hard-boiled eggs, enchiladas, empanadas de carne, hot roast chicken-legs.... Beside the track at Joachín, water bubbled with slimy life and stank like a ripe cheese. Houses at Estanzuela had projecting peaks of thatch like the ridgepoles of a Fiji village.... Out of the flat plain, farther on, rose a bare, symmetrical mound, burgeoning in three palms that replaced, perhaps, the plumes of Quetzalcoátl whose temple may lie beneath.... At Tierra Blanca, a thatched shack was inscribed in whitewash, "Karl Marx School." On the station platform stood a metal drum, labeled "Water—for fire only," and containing sawdust.

The country buckled, as we moved inland, into low hills, with a blue ridge of mountains beyond. Jungles, interlaced with vines, alternated with fields of corn and bananas, or with grassy plains dotted by scattered trees. At Papaloápan, houses stood on stilts to lift them from the mud; streets were borne aloft on runways of planks high above a carpet of green slime. Under a house on a slight elevation, an Indian was working patiently, cutting a four-foot log with a handsaw.

On we moved in the gathering dusk, across slow gray-green rivers on whose banks clusters of thatched houses merged with the forest. Fireflies flashed brief lanterns; the night air was cool, smelling of moist leaves.... Lightning flickered against horizon clouds; across the plain moved the striped face of Tlaloc of the Rains. We closed windows and stifled, opened them and let the rain stream in.... A clouded moon filtered vague light over a vast wooded country. Through the open windows flowed the smell of the forest: now the aroma of sultry tropical flowers, now heavy rank odors of decay.

"Business is good," said the banana planter, who was wearing two sombreros, one atop the other, white suit, and boots, and carrying a plaited riding-whip. "Plenty of bananas, and large ones." He was full of *"negocios,"* repeatedly summoning two barefooted henchmen to conference, until they all left the train at a little station smothered in jungle.

The train stopped a long while by a dark crawling river, where we moved in the hot stillness to close windows against silent, dangerous mosquitoes that fluttered in.

Slowly we climbed through the darkness among precipitous hills to the divide at Chivela and down toward the Pacific upon which Cortés' men, like those of Núñez de Balboa, stared "in wild surmise," when at the captive Moctézuma's suggestion they sifted the streams of Tehuantepec for gold.

San Jerónimo Ixtepec is the junction where the decayed line across the Isthmus meets the rails that parallel the coast to the guarded back door of Guatemala. From a row of undistinguished buildings along the tracks, an unpaved sandy street —where long-snouted pigs prospect for garbage among naked children at play—curves between low adobe houses to the "center," a mile or so distant.

Into the market stride stately Tehuana women, in the regional costume that is worn, in these isthmian towns, not merely for festal occasions, but every day, and which sets off their sturdy figures superbly. It is a barbaric dress of contrasting colors: a loose blouse (*huipil*) cut low and square at the neck, commonly sleeveless, often gipsy red, with a hollow rectangle of embroidery at front and back, frequently done in bright yellow. Below it sweeps a long, brightly flowered skirt, perhaps of the vivid green of young rice, circumscribed a few inches from the lower hem by a broad band of white or of a contrasting color, and terminating in a ruffle or flounce. The feet are bare and shapely; the head bare, or wrapped in a light rebozo; the thick dark hair, braided down the back, is interwoven with strands of wool in green or blue, lavender or red.

These are their only garments—for when one lifts her arm to adjust the burden on her head, a smooth strip of gold-brown skin appears where blouse and skirt normally meet.

On festival days, as in Holy Week or in the great local fiesta that falls in September, they don a more elaborate costume of similar type, surmounted by the *huipil grande*—a tall white bonnet that looks like an inverted baby-dress. According to tradition, the prototype of this head-dress actually was a load of baby-garments washed ashore from a shipwreck.

They walk erect, heads lifted, in the sure pose of those who carry burdens balanced at the tip of the body's long axis; stepping soft and catlike, on confident brown feet. I saw one, in the market-place, stride nonchalantly under a full sack of grain and dump it into a cart with enormous wooden wheels, while her husband, burdenless, stood holding the oxen.

That scene is typical of the strength and self-reliance of Tehuana women. There, as rarely elsewhere in Mexico, the woman is the head of the family. She owns the property, conducts the business—and Tehuana women are shrewd traders. In their very appearance, radiating vigor, they contrast with the men, who have been described, perhaps not entirely without reason, as a listless lot.

However—"It is not true," said the young man who joined me at a lavish Sunday dinner in the hotel near the tracks—choice of five out of eight courses, with a marimba band, for the equivalent of twenty cents. "It is not true that the men never work. They plant and harvest corn. We have three crops of corn a year, although in all three together we don't get as much grain as they get from two crops in the State of Vera

Cruz, where five ears make a liter. But—three plantings, three harvests: that means the men work six times a year."

"What do they do between times?"

"A little cultivating, perhaps—but mostly they gamble and drink mezcal. The women don't drink, or rarely."

Every people has its division of labor, often derived from some obscure tabu. In the Isthmus, the situation is attributed to numerical preponderance of women, about five to one—traced traditionally to slaughter of the males in warfare, but accentuated by the exodus of men to the larger cities. Some scholars relate it to an ancient tribal matriarchate. However that may be, the social system of the Tehuanas seems to have worked reasonably well. "Among the Zapotecs," said J. de la Fuente, Mexican ethnologist, "there are no beggars."

One reads in many travel books that the Tehuana women are famed for their beauty. Some indeed are handsome in a savage tropical style—spectacular, I would say, rather than beautiful, and somewhat overpowering, like a heavy tropical flower. Perhaps it is their bearing, rather than their form and features, that gives the impression of beauty.

"My soul is a jaguar," sings an ancient poem, in that country where survivals of primitive totemism remain. And it is not inappropriate that these magnificently feline creatures inhabit Tehuantepec, the "Tiger Hill."

All these things are to be seen in somewhat more favorable surroundings in the city of Tehuantepec itself, or at Juchitan, but in San Jerónimo one is driven to walk about, observing them through sheer idleness. For, unless the condition of the roads is unusually favorable, one has no choice, if bound for Tehuantepec, but to remain in San Jerónimo overnight and until late in the afternoon of the next day.

I tried, throughout the Isthmus, to get a ten-peso note changed. Apparently no one had so much money. But the railroad official who consumed many a bottle of beer with me in

Tehuantepec Journey

San Jerónimo enlightened me: "They have it, all right, hidden away. But nobody dares to show money."

"Why?"

His answer was an expressive gesture: the gesture of grasping. The implication, I inferred, was that officials would find a pretext for fining so rash a person, or would extort a bribe for not fining him.

The train from Ixtepec lurched between sandy hills toward Salina Cruz, crossing the river at Tehuantepec, where nude bathing women lifted brown arms to wave a casual greeting. The Río de Tehuantepec at this point is less scenic than it is often represented: a shallow, scrawny, earth-colored stream, slipping between desolate sand-flats bordered by bare slopes of sandy clay.

There, from around three to five o'clock in the afternoon, women gather to wash themselves, their children, and their clothes—the tawny bodies harmonizing so justly with earth-brown water, tan-colored sand, and red-brown banks, that the scene is not at all surprising, but superbly natural. The men, I was told, bathe at early morning—if at all.

Salina Cruz straggles along a sandy slope between the sea and abrupt, panther-colored hills. From a large, wind-swept plaza, irregular, decayed streets wander up stony hillsides. The harbor, which I had come to see—having heard tales of a "Japanese pipe-line" to carry oil across the Isthmus and into imperial tankers—was small and neat, and without ships. Two stout moles shut off a calm expanse of blue water; a narrow and rather exposed entrance led into the basin. A drawbridge spanned the channel to the inner harbor, where two-score gaunt cranes stood idle, looking like skeletons against the sky.

"Yes, the dredging continues," I was told, though I saw no such operation proceeding while I was there. Some said sand sifted in continually, that the harbor never would be any good; others maintained exactly the opposite.

Pattern of Mexico

There was a pipe-line from the tanks on the hill, but no sign of its extension across the Isthmus.

Salina Cruz, all admitted, was a "ghost town," lingering on in memory of the days before the Panama Canal shortened the route between the oceans; when big-bellied sugar ships from Hawaii docked there, and their odorous loads were freighted by rail across the Isthmus to Puerto México on the Gulf.

"But Salina Cruz will come back," maintained the inspector of cars. "The whole Isthmus will come back. The United States will encourage double-tracking the railroad to provide an alternate route for the canal in time of war. The harbor work will be completed. Great ships will come again."

XXXVIII · WEDDING IN TEHUANTEPEC

THE city of Tehuantepec lies along a bend in the river, around the Hill of the Tiger whence, according to some authorities, the town derives its name. The legend is that long ago, man-eating jaguars (*tigres*) preyed on the people. A wizard, summoned from the Huave tribe, conjured a huge turtle from the sea, which met the animals as they came down the hill in double file and turned them to stone. Then the enchanter, afraid of the turtle, changed it also to stone. And there they remained: stone jaguars on the hill, a stone turtle at its foot.

It is a city of one-story buildings, heavy-walled to withstand earthquakes, and stuccoed in white or in soft pastel tints, around a great tree-shaded square. Near the station, the town has some of the tropical atmosphere one has been led to expect: groves of dome-shaped mango trees, row on row of banana plants, vigorous shrubs of red-flowering hibiscus— but as a whole the place is barren and sandy.

Save around the market, which is an all-day center of activity; and around the railroad station, at hours near the infrequent train-times, when women gather to sell tortillas, drinking-coconuts, and flowers, or to board the train with huge baskets of vegetables and other produce on their heads, for sale in neighboring towns—Tehuantepec rests in somnolent quiet. Few motor-cars stir the sand of its streets: there was, I heard, just one. The vehicles I saw were ox-carts that creaked slowly to the market on huge solid wooden wheels. Even the click of shoe-heels on the narrow sidewalks is infrequent; Tehuantepec is a barefoot town.

Only a fiesta or a wedding seems to awaken it—and yet, the inhabitants are, as Mexicans go, a joyous people. The women in the white-columned market-place chatter in a lively manner over their pyramids of fruit and vegetables, their stacks of large bubbly disks of toasted cornmeal.

Even the men roused themselves occasionally to jollity. Here I saw one—a bachelor or widower perhaps, with no wife to carry his burdens—trotting along, bent under the weight of a large bundle. A friend ran up behind him, playfully slashing at his legs with a slight switch. *"Arre, burro!"* the jokester shouted, with a toothful grin. *"Burro, por Dios, get a move on! Busca!"*

Tehuantepec is not notable for natural scenery, though the view from the railway trestle up the curving river to a blue distant sierra, where dwell tribes who speak no Spanish and live a primitive life of their own, is in its way enchanting.

In such a village Porfirio Díaz took refuge in his youth when he was a revolutionary against Maximilian. Later, when Díaz was president, he sent for the chief of that village, brought him to the Capital, and gave him two suits of clothes.

Wedding in Tehuantepec

The chief wore one of them as far as the railway station where he mounted a horse for his village, days' riding away in the mountain. There he changed to the baggy white cotton of his tribe, and the two suits, thereafter unworn, hung in his house the rest of his life; and no doubt they are venerated still. In another such village, when contributions were solicited to buy a testimonial sword for a revolutionary general, the elders replied: "If we want a machete, we buy it. Let the general do the same."

Near the railroad track in Tehuantepec is pointed out the house where dwelt a sweetheart of Don Porfirio. He would swing down, as the train passed, to visit her, incognito.

Nor is Tehuantepec notable for architecture, though the solid, squat structures fit in appropriately with the scene, and the ruinous but still used prison has stood since the Spanish conquerors built it in 1530. The interest is, rather, in the human scene.

I went to a wedding reception in Tehuantepec.

Band music called me to the street where a procession was emerging from the church and filing into a shelter of green branches before a house in a sandy lane. They were mostly women, as everywhere in Tehuantepec—gay in bright costume and, for the occasion, wearing small home-made paper flags that waved from their hair. There were fewer men, in the pink shirts and shapeless white cotton trousers of the hot country. Outside loafed a few vendors of food and drink, a group of children, and some young men who besought me to photograph one "Lola," who seemed to be the belle of the younger set. A man at the gate invited me in.

The guests had started a grand march through an arch of raised hands; women performed an animated square dance; a few paired off and danced the "fox." The men mostly lingered near the bottles.

The bride—resplendent in her best *huipil*—and the bridegroom, in more sober garb, sat stiffly on a platform, expressionless, immobile save when the bride lifted her blouse away to let the air cool her skin. The weather is nearly always hot in Tehuantepec.

Hour after hour the festivities went on, without change save as the dances became more boisterous, the men more tipsy.

When I returned late in the afternoon, the band was still wheezing in the shade of the green branches. Women were dancing a more robust figure. Two would lower heads and butt each other fiercely, until amid laughter one was driven to her bench.

"Why don't they dance the sandunga?" I inquired. For the sandunga is reputed to be the regional dance of Tehuantepec. Probably it was not being performed because few, if any, of the men were sober enough. But the one addressed didn't say so. "I'll go and ask the band to play it," he replied.

The sandunga has the characteristics of a step adopted from European sources. The music and words are Spanish, though I met some Zapotecs later who sang for me a sandunga song in their own tongue. Nevertheless, whatever its origin, it has become identified with the Tehuantepec country, and I wanted to see it in its own setting.

The man wandered off in the direction of the musicians, and did not return. No doubt he had found another bottle. An older man clung heavily to my shoulder, chattering a mixture of Spanish and Zapotec. Another tottered up to grasp at the other shoulder. The sandunga did not sound. Tiring of the affair, which appeared likely to continue, with increasing deterioration, all night, I left, declaring an intermission of my own.

When I looked in again, late in the evening, the party was still in progress. The bridal couple had disappeared into an inner room, but those of the guests to whom the liquor had left sufficient remnants of consciousness lingered with expectant air.

At last the bridegroom appeared, triumphant in bearing.

Wedding in Tehuantepec

"She was a *señorita*," he announced proudly.

A sputter of firecrackers and rockets replied, amid a clatter of congratulations. Everybody had to have another drink—several drinks. And the dancing was resumed, to continue, I was told, until dawn.

"The marriage customs are very strict," revealed a young professional man who joined me at dinner in Tehuantepec's only and primitive hotel—where the one bathroom bears a sign: "Guests who take both room and meals are entitled to bathe free of charge; others, fifty centavos."

Romance begins, he said, at the Sunday evening promenade in the plaza, where girls and men, walking in opposite directions, exchange eye-flashes, perhaps a few words, as they pass. In subtle ways, they convey to each other their sentiments. A couple of the young man's friends, older men, carry his proposal to the girl's family; or in some cases an elderly woman acts as matchmaker.

If both families approve the match, a party is given at which the engagement is announced. After an interval, civil and church marriage, and the feast, follow, culminating in the bridegroom's official test of his bride's chastity. If she proves to be a *"señorita,"* the bridegroom's friends wear hibiscus flowers in their hats for days afterward, in honor of the marriage.

"Nowadays," amended another man, "not everybody goes to so much trouble. The young man and the girl just go away together for a few days, and if the girl is a *señorita* and everything is satisfactory, they have, later, a civil ceremony."

A young man in San Jerónimo, however, cast a conflicting light on the situation. "Among my people," he confided, "a girl is not considered fit to be a wife until she is—what shall I say?—experienced. For that reason, a mother often sends her daughter to a friend of the family to acquire experience. Then she is considered marriageable."

I gathered that these apparent contradictions proceed from

287

divergent customs of different social strata and of various sub-tribes. The Zapotec country is large and diverse, and the Zapotecs are a numerous and varied people.

Our host, who dined with us, inveighed against what he considered the injustices of the régime.

"Everything is for the working people," he complained. "There is no chance for a businessman. I had to fire a girl who worked here, for stealing. Under the law, she collected three months' dismissal pay. From here she went to another job, from that to a third, and thence to still others. And from each, she was fired and collected three months' pay."

Business was bad, he continued. Prices, wages, were the highest ever seen, while his own rates, as he reminded me, were "less than a dollar a day, in your money, for board and room. An innkeeper makes no money; he only serves the public." A foreign guest, he related, once suggested that he equip his rooms with bath and toilet. "You can see, *señores,* what the times are, that one should make so preposterous a suggestion!"

In the old days, he continued, the working people knew their place.

"Yes," one of the guests reminded him. "They were slaves."

"It is true," he admitted. "I myself worked from dawn to sunset for a few tortillas and a handful of black beans. An employer could kill a peon, and no questions asked."

"That is the point," said Señor Oguita the dentist, referring to the fable of the golden eggs as a parable of developments in Mexico. "You are paying, now, for the goose."

Children gathered around me as I sat in the plaza opposite the market-place, watching the bright play of life between its fat white pillars. Laughter greeted the supposedly witty sallies they made in Zapotecan, doubtless at my expense.

Noticing my camera, a few made bold to ask in Spanish

PORTALES—ARCADES FRONTING ON THE PLAZA—ARE A
CENTER OF LIFE IN MANY A MEXICAN TOWN

Wedding in Tehuantepec

for a "portrait," and a small boy gave me an address to which to send the print.

An elder sister appeared, snatching up the children and exclaiming with outraged sense of propriety as another child told her of the occurrence.

"What barbarity! To give your face and name to a stranger!"

I ostentatiously erased the name and address, and she was soothed. Meanwhile her attention was diverted by a glimpse from the corner of her eye of a young man passing around the corner of the plaza.

"Quick, Pedrito"—to the small boy—"say, 'Chivela, Chivela, here comes your friend Rafael!'"

The boy repeated the phrase.

Rafael appeared somewhat indifferent. Men, being so few, evidently are at a premium in Tehuantepec. The children chorused repeatedly, "Chivela, Chivela, here comes..."

Chivela turned on them: "Tell him I'll kill him to-night!" she snapped.

Dusk deepened. The children scattered homeward; market women loaded baskets and gourds on their heads and moved majestically up the sandy streets. The thud of a drum approached from the farther end of the square, and a squad of short, chunky soldiers marched, with a file of prisoners in their midst, toward the crumbling, four-century-old prison.

"What's happening?" I inquired.

No one evinced interest.

"Criminals," was all any one would say.

Later, a group of young men of Juchitan sang for me songs of their country—songs, they assured me, that were "pure Zapotec," owing nothing to the white man. But in those melodies it was easy to detect European importations, as in the remodeled hymns that serve secular uses in Polynesia. The words were sometimes Spanish, but oftener Zapotec; the texts, like those of other Mexican songs, were of love and pain and death.

Oddly like Polynesians they looked, though there was no traceable language link with the peoples of the Pacific. But they sang without the boisterousness of the Hawaiian or the Tahitian. Eyes were closed in the lifted faces, and the sad, poetic words issued from their throats while the clever brown fingers rippled over the strings. "Woman's Pain" was the title of one song; they gave their own version of "The Little Mornings," and a "Juanita" very different from the sugary pseudo-Spanish lyric of North American school-days. And there was one song with a memorably fresh and beautiful refrain—did it keep in its reference a memory, perhaps, of the Feathered Serpent who was Morning and Evening Star?...

"Shine, Morning Star, on the path to my beloved!"

On a hill a few miles from the city of Tehuantepec rest mounds, buried in vegetation, cracked by roots of trees, but hiding perhaps another Mitla or Monte Alban. It is so in all that country: there is hardly a town that has not its buried ruins, its painted caves.

To the east, the jungles and tumbled mountains of Chiapas stretch away to the Guatemala frontier—a land of sugar and coffee and chocolate and precious woods, of orchids and indigo and rubber; of stone temples lost in forest; of villages, differing from one another in customs, costume, and speech, which are little known to the outside world.

The railway threads its way wearily along the coast from San Jerónimo to Tapachula under its two volcanoes, and on to the border. But most of Chiapas, Tabasco, and Campeche are reached by river steamers from east coast ports, or somewhat less arduously by plane—and then toilsomely on horse or burro or by canoe, through the insect dangers and pathological hazards of the hot country. Only an absorbing interest in archæology can sustain the trip—which amounts to an expedition

Wedding in Tehuantepec

—to the mounded temples of Palenque, with their cruciform symbols of the Tree of Life, their glyph-stones of forgotten history. Most visitors are satisfied with the more easily accessible Uxmal and Chichén Itza in Yucatán.

Outside Salina Cruz, through sparse herbage on sandy hills, is the path to the Bay of the Marqués—named for Cortés the conqueror who was Marquis of the Valley of Oaxaca. The bay is a deserted place, save for an occasional fisherman, and it has a haunting and melancholy beauty. Rugged rocks look out upon the Pacific; swells curl in from the great South Sea, whence perhaps the sewn ships of distant islands came, three centuries before Columbus, to this strand. I have heard it called the most beautiful spot in Mexico.

Those experiences are most memorable which crystallize into fragments of image and rhythm, which one can put together to convey the immediacy of the sensation more deeply than conventional prose can do. A page of almost illegible notes, scrawled on a ragged bit of paper, evokes this memory:

The mottled land
crouches between the sierras
where the stone gods grin in the darkness of their dream,
the forgotten darkness under the gray-green hills.

These towns that cling to the cable of steel track
lest they drown in the jungle that was not made for man,
bear names of rebels and martyrs and of saints:
Matías Romero, San Jerónimo, Jesús Carranza—
and the way creeps on over the slow dark rivers scrawling
a secret sign across the impassive face of the forest....

past the houses on stilts, like spiders stalking the river mud,
the flower-bright wings and the wing-bright flowers, and
        the stench of the jungle pools—
to the Hill of the Tiger, the painted gourds piled high
        with flowers, and the bathing women,
thigh-deep and nude, waving careless hands at the passing train;
the passion-red tunics, gold-embroidered over the gold-brown skin,
and the bright strands of wool lighting the midnight hair.

Pattern of Mexico

Do they remember the carven gods in the jungle mounds
who wait, smiling a timeless, a secret smile?

This is a secret land, and its men are weary
with the slow years, the unutterable burden of it,
bled deep with old battles, worn with breeding. Here
only the women keep the strength of the ancient soil
from which old sorrows mourn that are written
in the angular chiseled serpent-stones of the dead.
And the dark cry that sounds from the jungle night
is the cry that flames in their level sun-deep eyes,
tameless and proud as the tiger whose name they bear.

So the way winds over the worn bones of the land,
the dark vein-streams of its thought,
to the Bay of the Marqués, the beautiful loneliness
that looks to the vast, the unpredictable South...

and the bones of the Conquerors cry out, denying rest.

XXXIX · FLIGHT

THE vastness of Mexico unrolled maplike beneath the plane: from the Mexico City airport over the mud flats and shallow pools that are the ruins of Lake Texcoco, and up out of rain, the wings climbed into sunshine above white fleets of cloud. At the right, in cold sleeping dignity, the white woman-form of Ixtaccíhuatl reclined upon her fleecy couch.

Eastward, the mists thinned, and we looked upon the striped land: green, yellow, red, and buff; hills like warts; microscopic villages among their fields.

At this height, the plane seemed to move slowly, through the illusion produced by distance. At the rim of the valley, clouds were banked like snowdrifts. Below, checkered rec-

Pattern of Mexico

tangles of towns slid past, subdivided into smaller rectangles of patios, and scored across by roads like a network of ribbons. At the right again, Malinche thrust her pyramidal head through a fleecy sarape of cloud.

In low relief the contours of the land stood out: every town and village distinct, with its clear-marked shadow; the mottled pattern of a shallow lake, yellow and green and red.

We rose to cross the Sierra: el Cofre de Perote coffin-like at the left, Citlaltépetl at the right, masked in cloud. We climbed into high mist where only the wings were visible, and came down out of it above a country green and old rose, seamed with cañons, to the flat green coastal plain and Tejería, airport of Vera Cruz—a green field among pastures, with the lazily rolling Gulf beyond.

The roofs of Vera Cruz, the castled isle of San Juan de Ulua moved beneath; then Boco del Río, bitted with sand-bars across the shallow mouth, lavender-brown beach scalloped with creamy surf, and two streams winding Gulfward.

From the height, the surf flattened as we crossed a rounded point of land and leveled over the mottled Gulf water: green, blue, yellow, red—according to its depth, the formation of the bottom, and the shadows of the sky; dimpled, wrinkled like a skin, and flecked with small patches of white.

Innumerable winding streams crawled through a green and yellow plain splotched with irregular ponds. Long bars bounded wide lagoons. Inland again, as the coast curved, the earth was red beneath the green: streets of towns gleamed the color of old brick between the red roofs of tile.

Low hills of rounded contour rose, checkered with woods and fields and red-brown streams; the large still lake of Catemaco lay like a dark turtle on the land.

The forest thickened, a mosaic of mottled green, with here and there a cleared field, a tiny house, and great clumps of trees sunny with yellow blossoms, until the tall, belching refinery chimneys of Minatitlán notched the horizon.

Flight

It was hot and still in the thatched station, at twenty-seven meters above the sea. Rising again, we crossed the slow, broad, winding Río Coatzacoalcos and more forests flecked with yellow bloom.

From the air, the country appeared uninhabited for many miles where the Río Tonalá divides the State of Vera Cruz from Tabasco. No house was visible in the open forest, cut in curving patterns by winding streams, until, along another forest-shadowed river, clumps of thatched roofs followed the twisting of the water, among spear-battalions of corn and broad sheaves of bananas.

There was a brief halt at Villa Hermosa, a cluster of red roofs along a curve of the river. Thence we crossed a great wet region of ponds and marshes bright with green alga-scum; the Río Grijalva, named for a forerunner of Cortés; the Río Chilapa, a coffee-colored serpent writhing to the sea.

Beyond the Río San Pedro, waters lay rank-looking and stagnant in varying shades of green, brown, purple, and yellow, in an open, grassy country dotted with clumps of trees. The forest thickened again, broken by broad lakes, until we cut across a green lagoon to land at El Carmen, an island city fringed with palms and cooled by the Gulf breeze.

The Gulf was like a crinkled sheet of blue crêpe de chine, mottled with purple cloud-shadows, as we glided near the spot where the church tower of Campeche stood, noble, in the sun —and on, over yellow and red-brown reef to the low green shore and long forests.

The ancient city of Uxmal gleamed white, in orderly pattern, on its low hills: we saw the steep slant of the Castillo, the narrow arches of the Governor's House. In the clear light the carvings on the façades stood out; and roundabout, more ruined structures jutted out, mutilated, from their mounds.

And so down to the white or lightly tinted walls and myriad windmills of Mérida, capital of Yucatán.

XL · STREET OF THE ELEPHANT

THE house of the conqueror Montejo, facing the great plaza, still flaunts on its plateresque façade the sculptured Spaniard trampling upon Maya heads. But with belated justice the great boulevard of Mérida no longer bears the conqueror's name, but that of the Maya King Nachi-Cocóm.

Mérida is a clean city, neatly arranged in long, narrow streets of tinted houses, iron-grilled and built close to the curb. It covers an unusually large area for a Mexican town of its population. It is gardened with magnificent trees—ceiba, magnolia, African laurel—and gracious with parks and plazas. It is a city of fourteen wards, each with its own plaza, its church, shops, market, and theater.

Street of the Elephant

It is a Spanish city, with an Old World atmosphere: for centuries an island of European race and culture in the vast sea of the Maya. For here the conquerors did not intermarry with the people of the land to the extent that they did elsewhere in New Spain. Noble families allied themselves back and forth; their outward links were with Cuba and Spain and France.

The cleanliness, I was told, is a heritage from Maya times, when Mérida was the sacred city Ichkanzihoo. The Mayas in this region are still a neat people. I have observed, as others before me, that cleanliness tends to vary with climate. Dwellers in hot countries usually bathe more; in cold regions, less. Water supply is also a factor, but apparently a less determining one: for on the dry, streamless atolls of the South Pacific, the Tuamotuan laboriously carries water from the shallow, brackish village well for his daily and nightly bath. And here in Yucatán water is not naturally plentiful. The infrequent rain filters through the limestone of an ancient reef, to flow underground, visible only where a collapsed area of the surface discloses caverned *cenotes*—"sinkholes," they probably would be called in the States—that anciently were the only wells. But the Mayas, from earliest descriptions, seem to have been a cleanly race.

The city was encouraged to spread in area, I learned, by the fact that building material is obtained from the land on which a house is built: limestone dug out for cisterns is laid to form the walls. Thus, the larger the site, the more material is available. Since Mérida, at the height of the henequén boom, is said to have been rated the wealthiest city, per capita, in the world, its avenues are lined with large mansions, many decaying now with changing times: palaces of huge, high rooms, wide patios, deep hidden gardens.

But toward the outskirts, or along the remnant of the ancient city wall with its arched gates, are elliptical wattle-and-plaster Maya huts, with roofs of thatch, like those sculptured over doorways at Uxmal and frescoed at Chichén Itza.

Mérida is up early to enjoy the coolness of morning and the delicately tinted sunrise over the plain. Little flocks of goats are driven about, to be milked from door to door.

A few sculptured street signs remain, that marked the ways in early centuries for a people who could not read: The Street of the Elephant, of the Jaguar, of the Old Woman. Many Mayas still speak no Spanish. But the streets now bear modern and colorless numerals: "Calle 59."

The high two-wheeled horse-carriage ambled through broad boulevards and narrow streets, and past mansions with grilled windows, in soft tropical darkness. The silent driver delivered us back at the Casa Cámara in exactly one hour, and grinned when I complimented him on his punctuality. Without a time-piece, he knew so well the ways.

A merry, likable Maya drove us on another day in full sun-light through those streets, on which stood shallow pools from the rains; past exclusive clubs, and a great modern sports field, little used, behind its ornamental grillwork that must have made a fortune for some contractor with friends in the ad-ministration.

Turning a corner where, facing each other, two opulent palaces built by former governors stood, our guide commented wryly: "The people call this 'The Corner of the Two Thieves.'" Later, as he pointed out the rambling headquarters of the state police, I inquired: "Do they keep good order?" "Yes—but they are easily bought."

Characteristically, a brewer had one of the finest houses. Near it stood a mansion as big as a hotel, in a huge garden. "The owner couldn't pay his taxes, so the government took it and made it a school."

It may seem childish, but I enjoyed most in Mérida its liberal and appropriate use of the fruits of the land. No meal at our lodging was without its luscious bananas, sweet-fried

A TILED MANSION OF COLONIAL DAYS

or golden-baked; its salad of avocado, its pungent mangoes or pulpy orange-red mamey. Felipe, the Maya guide who later accompanied us to the ruins, led us to a café on the steaming plaza, which served, for the equivalent of three or four cents a plate, thin but delicious ice-creams of exotic flavors: fresh coconut, guayábana or soursop, nancén (which Felipe identified as "something like a crab-apple"), zaramullo or custard-apple, mango, mamey, melon—as well as the more familiar orange, pineapple, and chocolate. There were also mantecado, compounded with a richer cream, almond, crema morisca made with eggs, and, oddest of all, elote, studded with whole golden grains of corn.

In Mérida we dwelt literally "in marble halls." The Casa Cámara is the town house of a once wealthy planter, reduced by expropriation of his country estate to taking paying guests in order to keep up the mansion he built in more affluent times. It is a palace, lavish with marble floors and stairways; rooms the size of ball-floors, hung with French tapestries and furnished in the style of one or more of the Louis; family portraits on walls of vast twin double-bed chambers; cabinets filled with European bric-à-brac and miscellaneous souvenirs; marble-topped tables holding rich useless bibelots—the whole atmosphere of transplanted European culture that characterized the aristocracy of Yucatán.

Our hosts hovered nervously about, with painful unsureness of themselves in this altered condition; pathetically eager to please. They could not leave one to eat in peace, but must be darting from chair to chair with "Won't you have a little more of the guacamole?" They seemed to be crushed by the calamity of expropriation, and striving desperately to adjust themselves, yet living, by preference or without being able to help it, in the past. They showed us their picture album, worn out with handling: the lost estate in its avenue of palms; its bathing pool, its school, scenes in the fields and mill.

"Forty years it was ours," lamented the Señor. "Forty

years' work, gone overnight, by a stroke of a pen in the Capital. The labor of more than half a lifetime, given over to ignorant Indios; and we, in our old age, taking guests!"

Looking out from a dead century on this harsh, vital new world, they were bewildered, unable to understand their fate. But in their arrogant and exacting demeanor toward the Indian servants, who did everything in apparent terror and always on the run, one could read something of the underlying causes of what had occurred.

The young people of the family seemed less stricken, although when I remarked that Mérida seemed a pleasant city, a daughter demurred. It was *muy triste*—very sad, dull, she said. "There is nothing to do." Indeed, for these daughters of aristocracy, that is true: they scorn the *mestizo* ball; places of amusement are closed to women; Spanish tradition immures them. "I like New Orleans better," she added, a sad, brave light in her large eyes.

We visited an hacienda like theirs, typical of those operated by a total of forty-five thousand *ejidatarios,* former employees lifted by government order out of virtual serfdom. About it, on the flat plain, bristled swordlike leaves and tall flower-stalks of henequén, known to us of old in other lands as sisal or "Manila hemp." An agave, it thrives mightily in the limestone soil of Yucatán, where it is of ancient growth. The pre-Conquest Mayas twisted its fibers into ropes to haul the great stones of their temples. The Spaniards early found it useful. The industry grew. Before the first World War, Yucatán had a virtual monopoly on this fiber, as well as on chicle (the raw material of chewing-gum) and, to a large extent, on certain dyewoods. The Philippines competed, but at the time of the island insurrection, the price soared. At one time the world used half a million bales of sisal a year, of which Yucatán produced four hundred thousand. The price rocketed again in the years when the world fought—so much so that West Indian and East Indian islands, Panama, South

Africa, and other countries planted the crop. Then substitutes were found, and the market declined.

It was unfortunate, from the viewpoint of the social program, that expropriation of the henequén estates coincided with a period of depression resulting from these other causes. The laborers found themselves owners of a ruined industry; they complained that their share of the proceeds was often less than their former wages. This led to a suspicion that they were being cheated by officials or by the inspectors who apportioned the shares; once they petitioned the government to give the estates back to the former proprietors. In some places they were burning off henequén to clear the land for corn. Corn at least is a crop that one can eat.

Sprouts or cuttings of henequén are planted far apart. From about the fifth year, for several years, the plant puts forth rings of radiating leaves. The lower ones, which are older and of stronger fiber, are cut after being marked by the field manager, and are loaded into cars on small tracks and hauled to the mill.

The mill was an open shed, where bladed wheels were stripping away the green pulp, leaving a mass of yellowish fibers that slid out on a polished rail, whence an attendant dropped them into the cart that took them to drying-frames under the hot Yucatán sun. In another shed, a boy turned a large wheel which rotated a smaller disk. Another boy backed away from the whirling disk with an armful of fibers, twisting them in his hand, the twisting and rotary motions producing a tight cord, to be wound later into thicker strands.

The great house of the former proprietor stood vacant in its neglected garden. The hundred or so workmen who had become owners still lived in cottages along the farther side of the great compound; a few in the servants' quarters of the big, lonely house, with its high arched gateway and paved enclosure like an abandoned monastery.

The men seemed happy as they worked.

XLI · THE WELL OF THE ITZAS

IT was a four-hour drive from Mérida to Chichén Itza. The
road ran between low walls of gray-green jungle, silent
save for the small voices of insects and the occasional cry
of a bird. Blue wings flashed from a thicket; a wood-dove
mourned somewhere, unseen; a small eagle slanted past. The
jungle here is not as high or as dense as one would expect;
tracts are burned off at intervals for fields. A field is cultivated
for a few years, then abandoned, and new ones are cleared,
while the forest creeps in over the old.

In those open spaces, corn rustled, or gaunt stalks of henequén stabbed skyward. Among them stood skeleton-like watch-
towers, where in the dry season guards watch for sparks from
burning forest. A smiling Maya woman in a long, clean, em-

The Well of the Itzas

broidered white garment welcomed us into her thatched house of poles plastered with whitewashed mud, in a village along the way. It was elliptical like a Samoan house, and neat and clean within as a Polynesian home in islands uncorrupted by the white man. Like that, it had no furniture to encumber the smooth, slightly raised earth floor; only, at one end, a shrine, and, swinging from rafters, a few hammocks.

For the hammock has become, since the Spanish occupation, the bed of much of Mayaland—introduced, it is said, from the West Indies to replace the native mats of an older time. The Spaniards preferred the hammock for coolness, and for protection from ground-creeping insects and reptiles, and many Mayas adopted the fashion.

Hence the anecdote of the man from Yucatán who, on his first journey in a Pullman car, complained that the hammock was too small. Why, even a child couldn't get into it!

Gourds hung from the ends of rafter-poles outside. At a little distance stood the cook-house, just as bare and neat as the house, with a corn-grinding stone and pestle, a small fire on the earth floor, a bundle of wood by the door. Beyond, among trees of tropical fruits, the beehouse sheltered hives of hollow logs, plugged with removable stops of wood or clay.

The bees of Yucatán do not make a comb, I was told; the honey is stored in cysts like those made by bumblebees. And, it was added, they do not sting. "Once," said the gentle old man who showed us through the property, "a colony of North American bees was brought in, and before the owner could get rid of them they practically drove away the Maya bees."

A well, curbed with stone, took the place of the old natural *cenote,* since dynamite and drills had made it possible to pierce the limestone eighty feet to water. Fat turkeys strutted outside the fowl-house of vertical reeds.

Farther on, between jungle walls, a long dark-green snake lay across the road, straining to swallow an iguana lizard. At

303

our approach the snake slithered away; the iguana, as if stupefied, remained motionless.

"When a Maya is bitten by a snake," revealed Felipe, "he puts on the bite the first herb at hand."

"Does just any herb cure it?"

"They seem to think so. There's also a remedy made from the bark of a tree. But actually there are few snakebites. I've known in all my lifetime of only two or three. Perhaps that's because, as the natives say, the King of Snakes goes about, keeping order in his kingdom and killing the poisonous ones."

The natives fear tarantulas more than snakes, I was told, although a biologist assured me they are not venomous. I heard of a woman who killed a tarantula and threw it away, "and a hair of the tarantula poisoned her finger." Felipe said that in ten years he had been bitten "only once, and that was by a scorpion. The sting pierced my heel, and my tongue went numb."

They are most of all afraid of witchcraft. Witches, they say, float through the air, chanting spells. There are frequent complaints of sorcery, and the authorities imprison the accused for a while, "to avoid trouble." Much of the witchcraft is relatively harmless, having to do with love potions, or divining the missteps of erring husbands.

These revelations are not always reliable. "The squirrel," related Felipe, "came to the mourning-dove when she was sitting on her nest, and told her, 'Your husband is untrue.' The dove flew away to spy on her husband. While she was gone, the squirrel stole her eggs. Ever since then, the mourning-dove says, 'Ku-tu-tu'—in the Maya language, 'Squirrel, you lied.'"

Farmers passed, burdens on their backs, long guns at hand. "It's their custom. They come from the fields. They always carry a gun."

"For bandits?"

"No. They might see a deer."

The Well of the Itzas

Dusk nestled down upon the road; fireflies glowed in the bush, which loomed taller as we drew farther away from Mérida. The motor stuttered and stopped. Felipe nursed it down a slight grade into a village, where a dim light shone in a roadside store. He entered, speaking in low-voiced Maya with the proprietor, and emerged with a bit of twine, which served for emergency repairs. An hour or so farther on, the pyramidal bulk of the Temple of Kukulkán slanted into the night, gleaming white in the rays of a low moon.

Beyond, there was clustered what looked like another Maya village: the same oval white houses, thatched with palm leaves bound with vines. But, on closer view, windows, shaped after the Maya arch, pierced the walls, and within gleamed tile floors, beds and chairs carved in native designs, modern plumbing, electric lights. For when Señor Germón and the Barbichanos of Mérida designed Mayaland Lodge, they carried out indigenous motifs only so far as these would not interfere with foreign guests' ideas of comfort.

The atmosphere was rural, tropical, restful. Great poincianas, avocados, and other tropical trees—limes and cycads and clumps of bananas—shaded the grounds. The sounds of the countryside drifted in: the industrious orchestration of insects among moist leaves, unfamiliar bird-calls, distant braying of donkeys, vociferous voices of frogs whose croaking sounded like the gabbling of great flocks of ducks.

Perhaps it is the frogs that make the mosquito nets over the beds a concession to strangers' fears, rather than a necessity. Although the wet season was beginning, I saw no mosquitoes and indeed no insects of any kind within, save one large and clumsy tropical cockroach.

Morning was cool, with dew or remnants of night rain dripping from the trees. It was but a short walk to the nearest group of ruins, which enclosed a large plaza: at one side were the Temple of the Warriors and the House of Columns; opposite, the walled rectangle of the ball court, with temples at the ends and sides; near the road stood the great temple of the Feathered Serpent, and opposite, the smaller remains along the ruined road to the Sacred Well. The whole area, Felipe said, was probably once paved with stone, stuccoed, and stained dull red.

The pyramidal temple near the gate, known variously as El Castillo and the House of Kukulkán (the Maya version of Quetzalcóatl, the Feathered Snake) betrays the Toltec influence associated with the name—in its emphasis on mass and volume and inclined plane surfaces, and in its thinning out of the exuberance of Maya decoration.

Like the so-called pyramids of Teotihuacan, it is no true pyramid, but a series of terraces of diminishing size—nine of them, rising to a level summit which supports a stone temple. The corners of the base structure are rounded. A simple design of rectangles—fifty-two panels on a side—suggesting fretwork, adorns the terraces. Up the middle of each, when the structure was intact, slanted a raised stairway of ninety-one steps, whose sum for the four sides, together with the summit structure, equaled the days of the year. Two of these stairways have been restored. The one facing the Sacred Well bears on each side a carving of the Feathered Serpent, head downward, body writhing up toward the columned doorway. The broken heads are still in position at the base.

With quaint exactness, the builders designed these stairways wider at top than at bottom, to correct the optical illusion of perspective and make them appear of even width.

The temple on this mighty foundation is small, its doorways linteled in carved wood that has endured, unrotted, it is calculated, since the eleventh or twelfth century. Eyeholes in the stone provided, in the time of its use, a hanging-place for a curtain. The stone pillars facing the Sacred Well are carved. One bears the likeness of a bearded man: the Feathered Snake in the form in which he led and taught the people. Above grimaces a huge mask of the rain god: the round goggle-eyes of Tlaloc here squared, with pyramidal earrings at the sides; the nose elongated, curled up like an elephant's trunk.

An early investigator, I was told, mistook it for an elephant, and conjured up a pseudo-scientific fable of the Mayas riding on elephant-back across a vanished continent from Asia. Their ancestors, it is believed, did come from there, but over no vanished continent, and on no elephants. The Mayas, though differentiated somewhat, have been classified as American Indians.

A narrow door at the base of the pyramid opens into excavations which have exposed an earlier structure buried beneath. The steep, narrow stairway, at right-angles to the cramped passage, is dark and close, with the suffocating atmosphere of an ill-ventilated mine shaft or a tomb. We mounted painfully, feeling our way as the weak beams of the flashlights seemed to lose themselves in the dense, encroaching darkness, the heavy sense of tons of masonry and ancient earth around and above, the slight but oppressive smell of buried earth and stone, the breath of the remote past.

On and up we toiled in but slightly relieved blackness, until the pale rays lit up a frieze of serpents, jaguars, shields, and rosettes, and the iron grille—intensifying the dungeon-like feeling of the place—which shuts off the inner summit chamber since some vandal stole one of the jade spots off the red jaguar within.

The electric torches cut the blackness to reveal two barbaric sculptures: a Chac Mool, "the red-pawed one," a reclining human figure with staring eyes, and a sphinxlike head turned to one side, bearing on his abdomen a shallow bowl; and the monstrous jewel of that hidden place, the jaguar. The apparition smote us like a blow: in the flicker of light and shadow that jungle beast seemed alive, an incarnation of feral power.

It is life-size or more, its body a dull red, spotted with seventy-four disks of green jade, and glaring back at the torchlight with jade half-disks of eyes. Its teeth—real jaguar teeth,

Felipe believed, though other authorities described them as made of stone—gleam white; the tail is encrusted with jade. On the back is a round plaque of turquoise, exquisitely carved.

These formidable sculptures were seats of kings, said Felipe, and I later obtained apparent confirmation of this in an archæologist's copy of a fresco that has largely crumbled from another temple at Chichén: a plumed warrior seated on a jaguar throne. As for the Chac Mool, it is repeated many times at Chichén and in far sections of Mexico. From the bowl, or sometimes the flat plate, that it bears, some authorities have conjectured it to be an incense-burner. Professor Enrique Juan Palacios suggested to me that the bowl may have held the sacred liquor, *balche,* which priests drank before prophesying from visions of the gods.

On the rear wall of the inner temple, entwined serpents trace a cross, with heads branching to form arms—Maya symbol, perhaps, of the Tree of Life. Investigators found, in a chest in front of the inner stair, jewels almost as exquisite as those of Monte Alban.

As we stood in the doorway of the outer temple, some one remarked: "It is good that the Mayas are coming back into their own."

"Not yet," demurred Felipe. "Not very fast. We are still poor and weak.

"The politicians," he added, "make much talk of helping us, but they don't do much."

"Are you Maya?"

"Yes."

"You must be proud of your heritage."

Felipe's eyes filled with tears.

Below, a raised road leads past the ruined "House of Tables" and a row of pointed stone symbols—phallic, some say, or, according to others, representing flames—to the Sacred Well: an irregular oval pit, about eighty feet deep, with

The Well of the Itzas

forty feet or so of cloudy-green water flowing sluggishly, the pool of an underground stream.

A stone platform, hollow underneath, with a small opening in the top, stands on the side toward the great temples. Incense, it is believed, rose through the opening. From here, at the rain ceremony, the girl victim was thrown into the pool, perhaps after drinking a ceremonial narcotic in a small temple whose ruins appear at the right.

The rain god lived in a fantastic palace at the bottom of the pool. From far places, offerings were brought: cacao, colored shells, precious stones, jade and turquoise and gold. Bits of them are still found at the edge, where an archæologist dumped his dredgings. All were bent or broken before they were thrown in; pots were bored through to "kill" them. But the sacred virgins entered the pool alive.

Weighted with gold and jewels, richly robed, the girl stood on this platform, while the solemn chant sounded, the tinkling Indian music, the thud of drums. The priests prayed, no doubt, to Nohoch-Yumchak, begging him to accept the offering. Did she weep, or resist? They say not; it was an honor to be the bride of a god, to dwell in the palace under the green water, surrounded by fabulous delights. Perhaps she even smiled as the stern arms of the priests swung her out to plunge swiftly into the mysterious depths—that the god might be pleased and send rain.

We can not know, for no witnesses have left records so detailed. But the story is true enough. Sixty—some say ninety—skeletons of young women have been taken by archæologists from the pool.

If she struck the water flat, from that height, no doubt she was killed or rendered unconscious by the impact. But sometimes, Felipe said, she entered it "like an arrow," and rose again. In such cases, it was believed the god had refused her, but she was left in the pool (clinging, probably, to roots along the sides) until noon, lest he change his mind. If he had not claimed her by then, she was drawn out, feeling perhaps somewhat humiliated, but with a beautiful memory.

For she had seen, she said, the palace of the god, his attendants dancing about it, and heard their chanting. In fact, she really did "see" something of the kind, for centuries after the sacrifice had been abandoned and the temples fallen to ruin, an archæologist saw it when he entered the pool in a diving suit to search for relics. Refraction of light through the water built a fantastic structure out of the rocks and remains of temples on the brink; his own assistants, seen along distorted light-waves, assumed strange forms; their words came confused and altered, like a chant.

The ball court is a rectangle roughly the size of a football field, with raised grandstands on the two long sides and stone buildings midway of each and at the two ends, decorated in colored low-relief.

A carved stone ring was formerly set high in the wall on each of the long sides. One of them still remains in place. The end-sections and centers of the longer walls are painted with scenes depicting players, priests, and a sacrifice—for a victim was slain in connection with the game.

On the wall opposite the Jaguar Temple, the colors are still fairly fresh: one can trace the severed head and body spouting blood, designed in the shape of a flower—the flower of death, blood poured upon the soil that the flower of life might arise. Blossoms like morning-glories wreathe the scene: the symbol of life, or of the procession of the seasons. Among them a skull speaks to the earth. It is the ancient truth: all things must die, that all things may live; there is no life that is not fed by death.

The game, according to surviving descriptions, was played by seven on a side: four on the plaza, three on the terrace below the stone ring. The ball was of solid rubber. It was struck with shoulders, elbows, and thighs, which were padded, as can be seen in the murals. Those below fought for the ball and propelled it to their team-mates on the terrace, who tried to pass it through the ring.

If one of them succeeded, he could claim jewels and garments from the spectators; hence, when a "basket" was thrown, there was a sudden rush to escape.

The judges sat in a stone reviewing stand, opposite the temple. Steps mount the rear of the side platforms; spectators probably stood on top.

At one end, reached by a stairway from the wall, is an arched shrine, on a pyramidal base, with a columned front and the Tree of Life carved on its sides. The vaulted ceiling, partly restored, bears frescoes of priests bowing before what are apparently phallic symbols, intertwined serpents, and other ritual designs. Opposite, a more nearly ruined structure is believed to have been the place of sacrifice.

The Jaguar Temple, on the side toward the Kukulkán, is one of the most impressive structures at Chichén. A steep stair mounts from the outer plaza to a terrace, whence another stair ascends in the opposite direction to the temple. Feathered snake-heads guard the portal. Low-relief figures are carved on the columns and side walls; within are remains of frescoes, fallen away with time. One can distinguish houses like the Maya homes of to-day; warriors with round, blue-bordered shields; women grinding corn; a canoe whose paddles repeat the diagonal thrust of spears across circles of shields; a squirrel eating a nut, very lifelike, carved and painted in the stone.

Jean Charlot has pointed out why the figures farther away in this battle scene are painted larger, so as to fall into perspective when seen from below, as by one crouching in Maya posture on the floor; and how the illusion of movement is attempted by depicting the same man in different phases of a single gesture. The time it takes to shift the eye from one to another, he has calculated, is the time it takes to perform the actual movement.

Pattern of Mexico

The Jaguar Temple takes its name from the frieze of jaguars that walk, in lifelike positions, around the wall above the steep stairway from the ground. But the carved figures within are said to represent Ahau-kan, King of Snakes.

In the little chapel built into the Jaguar structure on the ground floor are some of the best-preserved of the colored bas-reliefs: plumed chiefs, priests with nose-ornaments and barbaric ear-rings, and, high where the broken vault begins to arch, a small leaping jaguar in red, wonderfully full of life and movement.

Wasps had hung their nests from the painted carving. Below lay jumbled heaps of still un-reassembled stones. Modern Mayas were playing baseball in the great court.

The Temple of the Warriors is so important archæologically that it has been made the subject of large volumes. It gets its name from the many representations of warriors in its decoration. Nearly all the names applied to these structures are derived from some such detail or from some fancied resemblance to buildings elsewhere. Of their names when in use, there is no record; even their purpose sometimes is doubtful.

A portico, roofless now, of square stone columns, bas-reliefed with these warriors and priests, stands before three great terraces. Two human figures, whose hands form rings to hold banner-poles, guard the broad stairway that cuts through the terraces to the platform and temple above. Near the foot of the stairway, I noticed a small convex-topped stone, evidently an altar for heart-sacrifice in the Central Mexican manner.

At the top stand two more banner-bearers and two feathered snake-heads; before the doorway, a Chac Mool. In the columned hall, foreshortened human figures support a stone platform identified tentatively as an altar or perhaps a seat for priests. Around the walls, the gods of rain and of war alternate in rhythmic repetition.

The Well of the Itzas

At one side, below, are the remains of another large portico. The columns change from square to round with square capitals, but all are carved, and most of them bear traces of color. Portraits, thought Escalante, one of the guides: a Maya Hall of Fame. Around two sides runs a ledge, on which it is believed pilgrims laid their mats and slept.

From the inner row of columns one could see, across a shallow ditch, the reliefs on the lower walls of the Warrior Temple: monkeys and jaguars, in lifelike procession, boldly carved.

A steep ladder led down from the Warriors platform to the inner so-called Temple of the Chac Mool, filled in by builders of the later structure and excavated by Carnegie archæologists. The frescoes have peeled from the walls, but not before they were copied by artists of the expedition. One was a battle scene at sea, in which dark warriors fought a lighter (reddish) enemy, men with long yellow hair strung with green beads. Victory was indicated by sacrifice of a yellow-haired victim. As reproduced, it is a moving and vivid scene, even to the swimmer being dragged by the hair into a canoe, and the fish and curious sea-creatures that ornament the spaces.

The so-called "market," half hidden in shrubbery near the Warrior Temple, may indeed have been that, or a lodging for noble pilgrims, or both. A stone ledge runs along a columned portico, where traces of a vaulted roof remain. Merchants who accompanied pilgrims from Northern Mexico and Costa Rica and Guatemala may have displayed their goods there as in the *portales* of a modern town.

Near-by is a bathing pool, in the days of its use probably filled with water from temple roofs or from containers borne by slaves. In another corner, grinding-stones and bits of pottery indicate a kitchen. There is also a steam bath: a paved and vaulted building with a low door; within, a fireplace and stone couches.

Guides tell a lurid tale of two almost completely ruined

313

structures, between the Jaguar Temple and the Sacred Well, called provisionally the "Crematory" and the "Cemetery." A wall around the latter is carved in representation of some two thousand skulls, no two, it is said, exactly alike, resembling a copy in stone of the "skull house" that was an adjunct of Aztec temples, adorned with crania of sacrificial victims. The "Crematory" bears carvings of eagles, warriors, and serpents; near it another ruin shows eight jaguars holding human hearts.

According to T. A. Willard, who seems to be the principal authority quoted by the guides, this place was the scene of sacrifice to the fire god. Victims placed their hands, it is said, on a stone disk covered with a wet red or blue pigment, and stamped handprints on the walls of their masters' or relatives' houses.

A great fire, according to the story, was built in the ceremonial enclosure. The victims were thrown into it, and, when slightly roasted, were dragged out again; their hearts torn out and offered at the feet of a stone image of the god.

Willard's account is supposed by the guides to be based on that of Bishop Landa, who, having destroyed the Maya books, remains the earliest authority. What Landa, however, as well as the "Relations of the Encomenderos of Yucatán," actually describes appears, rather, to be a fire-walking ceremony, a variant of rites performed in India, Japan, and certain islands of Oceania:

"They built in the patio a great arch of wood, and filled it with firewood, above and at the sides, leaving doorways by which to enter and depart." After dancing with bundles of sticks, in and out of the doorways, the next evening they returned and set fire to the wood. "When it was all live coals, they leveled it and spread it very wide, and among those who had danced, there were some who passed barefoot and naked through the coals, from one part to the other, and some passed without injury; others were scorched, and some half burned, and in this, they believed, was the remedy of their miseries and of evil omens, and they thought this their service was very agreeable to their gods."

The paved roads that once connected the buildings are gone. We walked through wet grass—stepping over marching columns of army ants, each carrying its round bitten piece of green leaf—to a group of temples some of which are attributed to the seventh century.

The purported tomb of Kukulkán is a small and badly ruined pyramid, sculptured with figures of two winged men. Bones were found in an inner chamber, beneath a perpendicular shaft. The Feathered Snake is supposed to have been buried there when he died after giving out the story that he was going away to the Sunrise Land and would return.

Apparently he was a historical personage, deified after death or identified in life with the god whose priest he may have been. A Toltec chief, some say, the Quetzalcoátl of Cholula and Teotihuacan, who spent his youth in the Maya land, returning to Central Mexico with religious and social ideas derived from the Mayas. His innovations appear to have caused a war of cults among the Toltecs, in the course of which he was driven out and returned to Yucatán.

The traditional blond complexion of this culture-hero is sometimes explained away as an afterthought suggested by his "return" in the person of the Spaniards. But the beard clearly is pre-Spanish, as shown by the portrait carved on his temple gate at Chichén, which was already deserted and falling to ruin when the Spaniards came.

One view regards him as a sun myth, his beard as the sun's rays. Another theory, resting on the epic which represents the Feathered Serpent as bringing fire and maize from the underworld, suggests that his beard is the tassel of the corn.

Romantic interpretations, though usually with the least scientific basis, are often the most intriguing. One legend brings him, with twenty followers, in a boat, to his first landing in

Mexico—the mouth of the Pánuco River, near the present site of Tampico. Taking blond beard and complexion at face value, romanticists have pictured him as a Norseman, and the feathered serpent his Viking ship with its dragon figurehead. Though improbable, it is not altogether impossible: Norsemen were in North America at about the time Kukulkán-Quetzalcóatl lived, and recent discoveries have indicated that they penetrated as far west in that time as Minnesota, whence it is not entirely unreasonable to postulate a voyage down the Mississippi and around the shore of the Gulf to the mouth of the Pánuco.

The most interesting building in the seventh-century group is the Snail Tower, so called from its shape. It is conjectured to have been an astronomical observatory. Broken steps lead to a terrace, a second flight to a round tower: there are really three towers within one another, so constructed as to support the roof vault, for the Maya arch was limited in width. Within, a ruined winding stair, narrow and low-roofed, mounts to the remains of a room pierced with windows that face positions of the sun or planets at various seasons. Here, it is believed, the astronomer-priests performed the intricate calculations by which they kept their feasts, in the complex series of interlocking lunar, solar, and Venusian calendars that provided a time-count more nearly exact than that which runs the world to-day.

Around the rim of the outer tower, the long-nosed rain god leers: degraded now to a foothold for tourists who climb to the shattered observatory cell.

In the House of the Dark Writing, red handprints preserve the signatures of a forgotten time. They may be, as Willard thought, the memorial of victims before sacrifice; another has suggested that they are the hands of Itzamna the Healer—or perhaps only the autographs of the builders. There are many mysteries at Chichén.

Richly sculptured without, the corridors and wall-niched rooms of the "Nunnery" sprawl over a wide area against the plaza of that ancient city. People lived in this great dormitory —for their stone beds are here, and the grinding-stones for the corn; near-by are their steam bath and the dry basin of their fresh-water pool. This was a palace of nobles, it is believed, and later the home of vestal virgins, one of whom, near the end of the dry season, went to wed the rain god in the Sacred Well. The rain god alternates, on the façade, with fretwork of stylized serpent forms; over the doorway is sculptured Itzamna, the Healer and Teacher. Great rosettes, resembling girasol flowers, are so arranged as to suggest a face, again as of the Lord of Rain.

There are so many structures at Chichén as to be almost confusing—the Red House, the House of the Three Brothers. . . . High on a mound are three small rooms, side by side, their walls tinted with scanty remains of frescoes.

"In respect to the kings of this epoch," wrote Bishop Carillo, "it is clear in history only that three princely brothers governed, with such admirable union that from this depended good government, their lives moreover being extraordinarily austere and exemplary. But, one of them being absent or dead, the two remaining princes corrupted their customs and their royal qualities, in such manner that by their iniquity and tyranny which they began to exercise over their vassals, the people rose against them, taking at one time both their scepters and their lives. It is probable that in this civil war was ruined the great city of Chichén Itza."

It was a two-mile walk through jungle to Old Chichén. Rain javelined down; the thin foliage under which we sought shelter dripped coldly upon us. Wet and chilled, we tramped on to the small but well preserved fourth-century buildings, to take refuge again in a temple carved with the ever-present rain god and snake, a tapir—once mistaken for an elephant—and crisscross latticework in stone reminiscent of Mitla. My clothes did not dry in all the days we remained at Chichén.

XLII · THE STONES OF UXMAL

THE House of the Dwarf, at Uxmal, whither we drove
on another day from Mérida, stands steep and high,
a carved rectangle on an oval base; below, in a long
arch at the rear, stares a splendidly enduring mask of the
Lord of Rain. Goats huddle for shade in the sculptured niches;
lizards slither over fallen carved stones.

As we sat in the Governor's House, while swallows twit-
tered above us in its empty rooms, looking out across a little
valley to still unexplored mounds, Felipe told the story:

"Over there" (indicating a tree-covered hillock) "lived the
Old Woman who kept the Sacred Fire. Lonely, she hatched
by magic an egg, from which a boy was born. He did not grow,
but he had an active mind.

318

The Stones of Uxmal

"He watched the Old Woman when she went to get water. Always, before she left, she built the fire high. When she wasn't looking, the dwarf boy broke a small hole in the water-jar, to delay her while she was away. After she had gone he raked away the fire and found a whistle under the ashes. He blew the whistle, fulfilling the first sign: for it had been prophesied that he who blew that whistle would become king.

"When the sound of the whistle was heard in the land, the reigning king sent for the dwarf and questioned him. 'I heard,' the dwarf replied, 'only the turkeys gobbling.'

"The king, thinking to get rid of the dwarf, decreed three tests.

"First, pointing to a ceiba tree, he asked, 'How many pods are on that tree?'

"Without hesitation the dwarf named the number. Officers of the court counted. He was right.

"The second test was an ordeal of flogging. But the Old Woman had anointed the dwarf with a magic oil, so that he didn't feel the blows.

" 'Bring twenty-four coconuts!' They were of a small and very hard kind. 'Break them on his head.' But the Old Woman had made him a silver cap, and the dwarf's head was un-harmed.

" 'Now,' proposed the dwarf, 'it's only fair that the king should take the same test.'

"Twenty-four more coconuts were brought. The first one broke the king's skull, and he died.

"So the dwarf reigned. Puffed up with importance, he tried to create life. First he made an image of wood, and tested it with fire. It burned. Then, an image of stone. In the fire, it cracked. The third image was of clay; in the fire it hardened, and thus he discovered pottery.

"Later, to show his power, he built in one night the temple that is called, in his memory, the House of the Dwarf."

Bishop Carillo, whose *Historia Antigua de Yucatán* tells

the story in more detail, adds that "in the city of Maní, seventeen leagues distant, is a deep well opening into a cave which leads underground to Mérida. In this cave, beside a stream, sits the Old Woman, a serpent at her side, under a tree, selling water not for money but in exchange for human beings with whom she feeds the snake."

This is an allegory, as the bishop interprets it, of the emergence of Uxmal from a weak Toltec remnant to leadership. The city of Mayapán was the "king" whom the dwarf overcame; the Old Woman was "the ancient fatherland, which agonizes and succumbs in internal wars ... this fatherland is buried beneath the Spanish dominion, because the Indians hold that their children no longer are born for the old fatherland, but for the new power which has subjugated them."

On the face of the Governor's House is carved the dwarf emerging from the egg.

Uxmal, too, has its so-called Nunnery, a large quadrangle around a sunken patio. Over the doors of one façade are carved thatched houses, like those of to-day; above them is the square-eyed mask of the Rain; around the court, stone lattices and fretwork recall Old Chichén and Mitla. Across another front writhe two colossal feathered serpents; over one door a human figure is sculptured in the round—perhaps a royal portrait. Fallen from a wall we found a turtle-shape with grotesque human face, seamed with wrinkles as of age.

At Uxmal, better than at Chichén, one may observe the Maya arch—the angular "false" arch without keystone, held together by interlocking the backs of stones as the sides slope inward, and closed by a flat slab over the top. At least this is the usual description, although Dr. Spinden differs: "The vault, like the walls, is a solid mass of concrete that grips the stone veneer and that must have been held in place by a false work-form while it was hardening. The so-called corbelled arch of overstepping stones was doubtless known to the Maya builders, but was little used."

The Stones of Uxmal

Under one of those arches, in the House of the Doves, we lunched on excellent food packed in Mérida, while a cooling breeze blew through the vaulted passage.

The House of the Doves is said to be named from the fretwork of its crumbling roof-comb, which looked to some one, from a distance, like a row of dovecotes. The structure beneath is choked with fallen masonry, for the building is very old—fourth century, perhaps. Projections in stone on both surfaces are believed to be phallic symbols.

"The purpose of this building is not exactly known," Felipe replied cautiously to a questioner. Later, when we were alone: "I didn't like to say it when the ladies were here, but now I can tell you. It is thought that here the high priest prepared young brides for marriage."

All about were other ruins: a building with a frieze of marching turtles; a skull wall; a cemetery; remains of ball courts; many grass-grown heaps still unexplored. It had been a great city, home of the Tutul Xiu dynasty, whose descendants still live a few days' journey away. A city built, it is said, three times, and thus "thrice sacred."

The little rancho opposite the House of the Dwarf still draws water from the well of the Tutul Xiu.

V · The Heritage of Conquest

UNFAVORABLE SITUATION

"*La situación*," said the professor, "*no puede ser más desfavorable.*"

And four dozen students wrote, in their respective languages, on the first pages of neat new notebooks: "The situation could not be more unfavorable."

A problem was unfolded: a problem of Mexico; a world problem, too, but one apparently intensified in that country where so many internal problems combine and clash and become intertwined with those of the rest of the world.

The second day, the professor, looking gravely over his aristocratic nose, announced the second subject, adding: "In this respect, the situation is dark indeed."

And so from day to day; from this aspect to that, of Mex-

325

ico's resources—natural, manufactured, animal, vegetable, mineral, human; from problem to problem—racial, economic, political. In all of them, we were told, "the situation could not be worse."

There came a day when the professor did not appear. The next day, too, he was absent. When the class filed out without him the third day, we were saying among ourselves, "The situation became so unfavorable that the professor just couldn't face it."

Eventually the story came out. The class of this professor, who was one of Mexico's foremost economists and sociologists, was followed in an adjoining room by that of another eminent scholar whose views on many matters were opposite to his own. Inquiring minds attending both classes had raised in one the question, "But Professor ——— says so and so. What about it?" And then Professor No. 2's words would be carried back next day to Professor No. 1.

Thus conflict of opinion was fanned into open feud. Professor A accused Professor B of being a "Red"; Professor B insisted that Professor A was a "Reactionary." And the situation between them became so unfavorable, indeed, that both resigned in protest.

That in itself, members of the class concluded, was a graphic illustration of one of the problems of Mexico.

XLIII · HUNGRY LAND

"IT is necessary," said the distinguished Mexican economist, "to dispel the myth of the 'enormous riches' of Mexico."

Under his guidance, we examined, one by one, the resources of the country, and compared them with those of other lands. We analyzed statistics, studied maps and graphs, swallowed one hard, angular fact after another. Each time the conclusion, from the premises presented, was inescapable. Each day, at the close of the session, the economist summed up:

"In this respect, we see that Mexico is not a rich country."

It is notoriously possible to prove almost anything by appropriately conjoined mathematical symbols. But one needs no statistics to see that Mexico is, as the economist so persistently impressed upon us, "not a rich country."

Pattern of Mexico

One has only to travel about, using eyes, ears, and nose. The outstanding fact, the fundamental problem, is poverty. The same is obviously true in varying degrees elsewhere, but Mexico is one of the countries where it appears accentuated.

Could Mexico become rich? The original legend has added to itself a corollary, that Mexico is poor only because it has not availed itself of its fabulous resources. I heard that opinion expressed, in varying language, throughout the Republic.

Looking from a train window between Tepíc and Guadalajara, the American businessman who shared my seat waved his hand at untilled fields.

"This part of the country," he declared, "could feed all Mexico. But the Indian won't raise a surplus. Just enough corn and beans to keep him and his family barely alive—he'll do no more."

The next day, on a bus trip through that same countryside, I learned in one of those cactus-hedged villages why the fields lay apparently idle. There had been no rain for more than half a year. It was not yet time to plant the corn. Meanwhile: "The men, señor, are all down in the tobacco fields near the coast, working for wages to keep themselves and their families until planting time."

It is true that the Mexican economy is largely one of bare subsistence, and that the Indian often plants only enough for his own needs. It is also true that in many cases that is all his land will produce.

It appears, further, from abundant testimony, that the large proprietors, when they controlled the greater part of the best land, allowed vast portions of their estates to lie unused. The hacienda was concerned less with production than with a safe return, and with ostentation. It has been charged that large areas were acquired not for use, but to prevent the Indians from using them, and thus to force those Indians to work in the fields of the proprietor.

But some Mexican economists are convinced that the im-

IN THE MOUNTAIN COUNTRY BETWEEN THE CENTRAL
PLATEAU AND THE GULF COAST

Hungry Land

providence of the peasant and the greed of the landlord have
been only contributing causes. The Mexican earth, they maintain, at least with the present facilities for developing it,
simply is not sufficient to feed the Mexican people.

Manuel Mesa, a director of the National Bank of Agricultural Credit, reported only 11.8 per cent of the soil of
Mexico arable, compared with 19 per cent in the United States
and 47 per cent in Germany and Italy. Daniel Cosío Villegas
placed Mexican arable land at only 6 per cent. In corn and
beans, the crops most planted and most used, the return is one
of the poorest in the world. The Mexican yield of grain to the
acre is estimated at only one-half that of the United States.

This comparative unproductivity can be charged in part to
unscientific methods: lack of crop rotation, fertilization, and
seed selection; use of primitive implements. There can be little
doubt that the land is capable of producing more than it does.
But this is not the whole story.

To begin with, nearly three-fourths of Mexico is desert.
Irrigation might save much of it for human use, and it is doing
so in some places, but the cost of irrigation requires resources
which the nation has not yet been able to apply on a sufficient scale.

Furthermore, Mexico is a victim of its geographical situation and physical conformation in still other ways.

As one economist said: "The topography of Mexico is the
result of a joke by Satan. He folded and creased it, wadded
it up, then tossed it down and said, 'Mexicans, here is your
country.'"

Behold Mexico: superbly mountainous, with a narrow fringe
of low land on each coast, and three great plateaus, each subdivided by mountain ranges into a multitude of lesser valleys.
This configuration impedes access to markets and cuts the land
into innumerable small economic units. Even where it is possible to grow a surplus, physical barriers often prevent transportation. Hence basic food crops are grown near the places

329

where they are to be consumed, even if the land is unsuitable.

Much of the soil is actually poor; most of it has insufficient or irregular rain. The greater part of the center of Mexico, where the bulk of the population lives, is dry, and 74 per cent of the precipitation occurs within a three-month period. That is, there is too much rain at one time, and too little the rest of the year. This has further impoverished the soil: dried out for three-quarters of the year, then suddenly deluged, the topsoil is washed down steep slopes to the sea or to the unhealthful lowlands.

Strangers seldom understand, a Mexican complained, why the "riches of the tropics" are not more exploited in Mexico. The tropical crops—sugar, coffee, bananas—thrive better than the temperate-zone crops. But most of them have suffered from foreign competition, decline of world markets, development of substitutes, and, in some cases, foreign domination. "The banana," said a Mexican, somewhat bitterly, "does not belong to Mexico."

Most tropical crops, indeed, are a stepchild of world economy: raw materials, produced profitably only on large areas and with extremely low-paid labor. In general, they are calculated to enrich a few large holders—in many cases foreign —rather than to reinforce the national economy.

The semitropical regions are more favored by Nature, but Mexico has not enough of them.

"Agriculture in Mexico," summed up the economist, "is a business in which the gains proceed not from agriculture itself, but from exploitation of the peon, who performs hard labor for an insignificant wage."

Profits, according to this view, have been possible, for the most part, only on large haciendas employing virtual serf labor at a low subsistence level. Other agriculture has yielded only a precarious and low-standard existence.

"The best for which we can hope is eventually, by means of irrigation, rural education, and improved technic, to produce

Hungry Land

enough for Mexico's own needs," declared Señor Cosío Villegas. "Mexico can not look to a future as an exporter of agricultural products."

But Mexico is a reputed treasure house of minerals—a leading producer of silver and petroleum, with some iron and other less important deposits.

Driving out of Cuernavaca, my companion, indicating the vast, tumbled landscape, remarked: "Scratch any of those mountains, and you'll find minerals."

"This, too," pronounced the economist, "is part of the legend. We have some important mineral resources, but it has not been demonstrated that Mexico is extraordinarily rich in that respect.

"In fact," he explained as I persisted, "nobody knows just what our mineral resources are. They never have been adequately surveyed. The few that we know have been exploited by foreigners. Mexico is not among the leading nations, in point of mineral resources, listed in surveys.

"There are rumors of gold in the mountains of Oaxaca, for instance. If gold were there, do you think the foreigners wouldn't have found it?

"It is possible that we have not exploited all we have. But a national economy can not be built on an unproved legend."

He forbore to add that silver, the metal of which Mexico mines most, has been profitable in recent years only because the United States bought it to bolster Mexican economy; that the iron mines, which are not extensive, are unaccompanied by coal deposits which would encourage industry. He did say that of gold and antimony, scarcely any is produced.

Mention of petroleum raises a controversial subject, no matter how it is approached. It can hardly be considered controversial, however, merely to report the historical fact that most of the oil fields passed, in President Díaz' time, into foreign hands—a circumstance which has been a source of contention since—and that world conditions just after their expropriation did not favor prosperity.

There remain industrial resources to be considered. Mexico has never been an industrial country. Industry depends on capital, which Mexico has always lacked.

Díaz tried to stimulate industry by inviting foreign capital. The result was, in the view frequently expressed in Mexico, that he sold the country to foreigners. From a historical standpoint it appears that by doing so Díaz erected a false front of national prosperity and "stability" which enriched those immediately around him, and the foreign exploiters, but which failed to help the Mexican people greatly or to found a genuine national economic structure.

There are two ways of obtaining capital. One is to borrow it. This has been done so many times that it has become difficult. Because Mexico is a poor country, and the borrowed funds have not always been wisely handled in the past, it has not been able to maintain credit. (The national external debt was estimated in 1938 as $275,000,000, plus the obligations of the nationalized railroads, estimated at $300,000,000, on which it was stated no payments of principal or interest had been paid in some years.)

The other way resembles the proverbial lifting of one's self by the bootstraps: it is the building up of capital by sacrifice on the part of working people. This has been done in certain European nations, with alarming results for the rest of the world and perhaps for the fate of civilization. It would be difficult in Mexico, where working folk have little to give.

President Cárdenas, I was told, once called upon the workers to coöperate in the formation of national capital by a sacrifice of wages. There was no response. To an observer it appears that such a recourse would be impracticable even if it were economically feasible.

Nathaniel and Silva Weyl (in *The Reconquest of Mexico*) suggested using proceeds of foreign trade to build up a modern domestic industry. One might suggest that first one would have to get the foreign trade. But, according to this plan, the government would control imports and the exportation of capital. Foreign exchange, if any, remaining after purchase of raw materials and essential consumer goods, would be applied to acquiring capital goods: machinery, industrial equipment, and such foreign engineering service as might be indispensable.

This would involve government control of private industry, compelling factory owners to invest a definite portion of their profits in maintaining and expanding their plant facilities. In return, the government would encourage long-term collective labor contracts, guarding against interruption of production.

My Mexican economist acquaintances, however, held that even if Mexico had or could obtain capital, powerful interests in the United States would discourage the development of Mexican industry as a possible competitor. In their view, Mexico is fated to remain a producer of primary materials and a consumer of manufactures, and thus to continue at a low level in the industrial scale.

This may not be the final word. Some Mexicans hold great hopes of modernizing both agriculture and industry so that their country may lift itself out of poverty. It will take a great deal of education, expenditure of much money, and large-scale planning.

Perhaps as important as anything else is the political factor. The complaint I heard most frequently from businessmen was that social reforms instituted as a political necessity had created a condition of insecurity. that was paralyzing business. Of course, such a view is not uninfluenced by individual selfish interests. At the same time, plans, however sound and honest at the source, for improving the condition of the mass of Mexicans—a primary requisite, one would think, for the national welfare—often have been frustrated by the selfishness of local politicians. Where a leader like Lázaro Cárdenas has shown the way, there have been too few to follow.

XLIV · MINGLED STREAMS

MAN, in the early morning of time, flowed in two directions—east and west, and developed two diverse cultures. In the New World, these met and clashed. Dr. Andrés Molina Enríquez has pointed out that, if we ignore for the moment certain eddies and backwaters of the human stream, we will find that two major tendencies developed: the Oriental mind, which was created by the structure of languages developed through visual memory—that is, picture languages; and the Occidental, by languages based on the memory of sound.

As the primitive family group expanded, the Oriental evolved tribal organization, the Occidental an armed camp

334

which became what we call a nation. The Oriental continued to think of land as occupied during term of use; the Occidental developed the concept of land as property, in the same sense as a spear or a garment, which could belong to the individual as distinct from the group.

To these fundamental differences has been attributed much of the conflict and confusion which trouble Mexico to this day.

For Mexico was the meeting-place of human streams from the east and the west; to-day it is the product of their mingling, and their national problem has always been to reconcile these opposite views of life.

Some Mexican scholars minimize the racial factor, choosing to regard the problem as mainly economic. Nevertheless we have here two racial economic theories, and it is probable that the clash between these two concepts of property is the root of many problems both in domestic affairs and in foreign relations.

In point of numbers, Mexico is an American Indian, and thus by origin an Asiatic, nation. The Spanish Conquest imposed upon it, in part, an Occidental language, a national organization, and a legal system which have not been firmly integrated into the masses. A million or more speak no Spanish; millions of others speak among themselves only Indian languages; the forms of Western government overlie but lightly, in many an interior village, the old tribal organization. The Indian in many sections still thinks in pictures, stirs the earth with a wooden plow, regards his neighbors in the next village as foreigners and the land as common property of the tribal group.

It is estimated that 300,000 Spaniards entered Mexico after the Conquest, to leaven a mass of six million Indians. Other foreigners have made a relatively slight racial contribution. Estimates vary, but the population is believed to be from 20 to 25 per cent "pure Indian," from 4 to 10 per cent "pure white," and the remainder of mixed blood. Thus Mexico is predominantly a *mestizo* nation, and, when the proportion of native blood in the *mestizos* is considered, an Indian nation.

What kind of person, then, is the Indian?

The frequent statement that he is "lazy, dirty, and stupid" is of course an unscientific generalization. He may be this or that, tribally or individually or according to his conditioning by climate, topography, and the productivity of his habitat.

One general statement can fairly be made: the Indian is poor.

Wallace Thompson, who is critical of the Indian and of Mexicans in general, makes a penetrating observation when he ascribes the Indian's apparent "stupidity" to a different view of life.

Employers complain that the Indian workman gets less done in a day than does a North American. Commentators who probe more deeply than the average employer—who is interested merely in how much he can get out of his working crew—attribute the apparent lack of industry to a fundamental apathy induced by climate, undernourishment, and in some cases alcoholism, and psychologically explained by a fatalism caused or intensified by centuries of oppression and lack of choice—"the psychology of slavery."

Industry, for the Indian, has not been notably profitable; what he has had above subsistence has usually been taken away from him; hence he has lost, if he ever had it, the idea that industry is worth while. His wants are few and simple; they have had to be; only thus has he survived. He is content with subsistence on a low scale, since for generations he has known nothing else—a circumstance which annoys brisk North Americans who want to sell goods in Mexico.

Practically all opinion is agreed that the outstanding Indian trait is conservatism, characteristic of "primitive" peoples, who are notoriously ruled by tabu. Everywhere in Mexico, "it is the custom," is sufficient reason for almost anything. We ourselves are not entirely free of this irrationality, though our life is less static than theirs.

The Indian, then, clings to tribal relationships, communal notions of property, patriarchal dependence upon local chief, employer, military or political boss, and prefers a steady job at a scanty subsistence level to one offering higher pay, money being less important to him—with reason—than daily tortillas. His history has taught him to be economically cautious. It has also taught him to be suspicious of strangers and not highly coöperative except within his own immediate group.

Another statement generally heard is that the Indian is morose and silent. His history has given him ample cause to be so, and I would not presume to contradict so many observers, although—especially in the warmer and more fruitful regions —I did not get quite that impression. Probably a geographical factor is involved here, too. "All the high country," wrote Jacques Soustelle, after a sojourn among the impoverished and downtrodden Otomíes, "is sad." But I suspect that in general, what is commonly interpreted as melancholy may be only the fundamental Asiatic calm.

The *mestizo*—what is not said of him? The most frequent generalization is that he is unstable, superficial, torn between conflicting heredities, incapable of thinking a problem through to its conclusion, and prone to mistake an eloquent program for a solution, a promise for a fulfilment. Such an analysis has been put forth by Mexicans, who tend, among themselves, to be more critical of one another than foreigners are of them.

Thompson, who synthesizes these views, along with those of Humboldt and other Europeans, considers the *mestizo* culture an unskilfully borrowed one, "based on the *mestizo's* peculiar picture of a European community" and his "peculiar conception of the white man's progress."

And so on. I am inclined to accept generalizations only with reservations. To me Indians, *mestizos,* Spaniards, remain fundamentally just people, as infinitely various and individually valid as Nezahualcóyotl's "flowers that cover the earth." A Mexican scholar has suggested that the *mestizo* gravitates toward the Indian or the European way of life and of looking at life, according to his environment and his economic and social opportunities.

It is no simple problem. It is apparent that a Mexican's mind does not work in just the same way as does the mind of a North American, or an Indian's mind like that of a Mexican of European descent. No question of superiority or inferiority is involved in this statement. Each likes his own way of life and thought because he is accustomed to it; that doesn't mean that it is better or worse.

In the case of Mexico, one may recall that up to the twentieth-century revolution, the *mestizo* was largely underprivileged, deprived of opportunity, with little or no experience in self-determination. It is possible that the asserted characteristics of the *mestizo* are attributable, in so far as they are valid, to this conditioning.

So much for the racial question. Professor Cesar Órtiz asserts that foreigners are inclined to overstress its importance. "Although certain factors of the racial elements must be considered," he said in an address in Mexico City, "the problem of the Mexican population is fundamentally economic.... The problem of the Indian is the problem of the land."

One might suggest that no national problem is so simple that it can be explained or solved by a single formula. However:

Before the Revolution, unification was retarded by the effort to keep Indians and *mestizos* down. Since the Revolution, there has been a determined, if not always wisely directed or efficient effort, to unify by education. At first the attempt was made to transmit culture solely in Spanish. As Professor Mauricio Swadesh recently pointed out, this effort often defeated itself because the education was not adapted to Indian needs.

Mingled Streams

More recently, teachers such as Professor Hernández y Hernández of Chihuahua have begun to take Manuel Gamio's advice. They are learning Indian languages and approaching education practically, studying the Indians' problems and co-operating in solving them, rather than trying to force upon them an alien and somewhat impractical culture. According to this view, it is more important to teach efficient farming and elementary hygiene than Spanish, which can come later.

There is also the view held by some Mexicans of the race-proud *criollo* type and by some North American businessmen. This view was eloquently expressed by Wallace Thompson, who wrote (under auspices of a North American oil magnate) one of the few treatises in English on Mexican psychology.

Thompson regarded the Indian as a totally strange, if not inferior, being, irreconcilable with the standards of the white and unapproachable by him; a being who, under a mask of apparent stupidity, "baffles us by his very simplicity."

The elements of the situation, according to Thompson, are: the Indian has always dominated; the Spaniards tried to assimilate him by racial amalgamation and failed, because the *mestizo* reverted to Indian type; since that failure became apparent, they have waited in vain for the Indian to "rise" to the white plane.

A North American oil man who shared a Pullman seat with me between the Capital and Vera Cruz expressed a similar view. "Educate an Indian," he maintained, "and he's still an Indian. The only hope for the Indian is to get as much white blood into him as possible."

And the only hope for Mexico, I gathered from his remarks and those of others of his type, was another "strong hand" like that of Porfirio Díaz, with reinstatement of the feudal system dominated by white Mexicans and by "new Creoles" from the United States. I shall not presume, as a pilgrim and a stranger, to propose solutions for Mexico's problems. All I have any right to do is to state the problems as Mexicans and others, of various schools of thought, have stated them, and as they appear to a neutral but sympathetic observer. Further experimentation and further study will be necessary before effective remedies can be worked out. As Manuel Gamio aptly remarked, "Nobody knows the social reality of Mexico," because the fundamental data for such knowledge is lacking.

I must own, however, to a greater confidence in scientific findings than in the more loudly voiced but less studied opinions of persons whose views may be influenced by personal economic grievances or by the difficulty of doing business in revolutionary Mexico.

At all events, the Indian and the *mestizo* are fundamental facts which must be faced in any intelligent program, and no national organization can endure which does not consider them.

Thompson sees the dark tide of the Indian, resurgent in the *mestizo,* rising to overwhelm the white. José Vasconcelos views the *mestizo* as "a new development in history . . . directed always toward the future," and reminds us that "all the great periods of history have been the work of a mixture of races . . . rather than of any privileged pure-blood nation."

To a mere observer, it seems clear that the *mestizo,* through temporarily superior advantages and perhaps readier adaptability, will continue for some time to lead, probably with a gradually increasing Indian participation. At the same time it is to be expected that mixture of blood will continue, tending eventually toward a more nearly uniform type, and that education, if wisely directed, will in time produce more nearly uniform standards and achieve, in some measure, national integration. It is to be hoped that this education will conserve the most socially useful Indian traits while imparting to them socially useful elements from the Occidental culture.

"We can't expect much from the present generation," said the governor of the State of Morelos. "It is too steeped in the tradition of four centuries of slavery—and in alcohol. Our hope is in the children in the public schools."

XLV · ONE MORE GOD

WITH reason," wrote Bishop Landa of Yucatán, "Spain can glory in God, since God chose Spain among other nations for the remedy of so many peoples, wherefore they owe that nation much more than to their founders or progenitors."

Spiritual conquest went hand in hand with physical: friars marched with mailed conquistadores. In conquered towns, temples were pulled down, and on their sites arose altars of the Christian God.

The Indians, after the first shock of sacrilege had passed, fell in rather readily with the new doctrine. Their pantheon was hospitable; it had admitted strange gods before, and there was always room for more. Indeed, the gods were known by various names in various districts, and in their different manifestations: it was easy to identify the local Christian saint with the local pagan god. Our Lady Tonantzin slipped readily into the robe of Mother Mary; Saint James rode the storm wind with Tlaloc of the Rain, and Ostocotéotl donned the raiment of Our Lord of the Caves.

"Among the idols and demons," wrote Fray Jerónimo de Mendieta, "were to be found also images of Christ Our Lord and of Our Lady, which the Spaniards had given them, thinking that with these alone they would be satisfied. But they, having a hundred gods, wanted a hundred and one more, if more were given them."

Did not the Spanish priests burn incense, give communion, hear confession, even as did the priests of the *teocalli?* Was not the Cross much like the ancient symbol of the Tree of Life? And were not the texts of many prayers in the two faiths much alike?

Indians were baptized in droves: no doubt the rite recalled the ceremonial cleansing-by-water of their own faith. And Mexico became, save for a few remote tribes, a province of the Church.

It has continued so. The old gods, under newer names, still bring the sunshine and the rains. But the prayers are said in the church under the cross, where, as many a tale relates, ancient images are tucked away in walls, or under altars, or within the molded likenesses of saints.

Apart from the destruction of an immeasurable amount of ancient art and architecture, and the loss of priceless archæological and ethnological treasures in the burning of the sacred books, the influence of the early clergy was, on the whole, benevolent.

The hand that held the crucifix often stayed the whip of the slave-master. The Church founded schools to impart new learning in recompense for loss of the old. Trades were taught; most of the popular arts of Mexico, so praised to-day, were

NO TOWN WITHOUT ITS CHURCH TOWERS, CENTURIES OLD

founded or preserved by friars or priests. What education there was in Mexico was conducted, until fairly recent times, by the Church.

Fray Bartolomé de las Casas refused absolution to slave-holders, and pleaded at court in Spain for the Indians. Fray Benavente Motolinia befriended them. Fray Pedro de Gante founded schools. Bishop Vasco de Quiroga organized the Tarascans into coöperative economic communities, rescuing them from the worst effects of the Conquest.

Efforts of these and other missionaries to ameliorate the lot of the Indians were often frustrated by the greed and power of Colonial grant-holders and by the corruption of officials. But in general the influence of the early clergy was exerted to help the oppressed.

Something of this tradition continued. Priests of the lower ranks, such as Father Hidalgo and Father Morelos, led the independence movement of 1810, apparently seeing in it a hope of helping the submerged folk of their parishes. Wealthy clergy opposed that movement, though later, out of hostility to the liberal Spanish constitution of 1812, they supported independence under Agustín de Iturbide.

In all times, there have been sincere and benign padres, serving their God by helping His children, brown as well as white. It is, however, a historical fact that any highly organized hierarchy tends to resent any interference with its prerogatives.

After Iturbide's "empire" collapsed, Church and State fell out over the distribution of "patronage." The hierarchy claimed to have inherited the privileges formerly held by the Crown, and to be independent of civil authority. That conflict has continued.

The Church by that time had become a vested interest. The historian Lucas Alamán estimated that in 1821 the Church already owned half the wealth of Mexico. Edward Alsworth Ross calculated that at the height of its power the Church controlled two-thirds of the production of wealth, dominated economic life, and monopolized not only religion, but also education and charity, which he classified as opinion-forming agencies. Mexican historians charge that the clergy shared with secular landholders the exploitation of resources and human labor. Historically, in the various revolutions and attempted revolutions, the Church has usually been on the conservative side.

Charges are hurled back and forth: that the clergy made salvation expensive for the peons, upheld the landholders' system of virtual slavery, and supported subversive movements; that revolutionary governments persecuted the Church, that "reform" leaders confiscated Church property for their own benefit, and so on.

Regardless of the merits of the controversy, the essential fact is that Church and State have been in conflict, off and on, from the time of Iturbide. Valentín Gómez Farías brought about laws to curb the clergy, whereupon the Church supported a revolution by Antonio López de Santa Anna—who, when in power, seized Church wealth to finance his war against the United States. It has been charged that the clergy then "betrayed" Mexico to the North Americans.

Benito Juárez separated Church and State; the upper clergy, as well as Napoleon III, supported his opponent, Maximilian. But Maximilian proved almost as much of a disappointment to them as did Santa Anna: he had alarmingly liberal notions, though he seldom knew quite what to do about them.

With the return of Juárez to power, liberal and anti-clerical legislation continued, but Juárez did not live to see that it was enforced. Porfirio Díaz, ruling Mexico for thirty-odd years, did not, on the whole, interfere with the Church as long as it did not interfere with him.

Between 1859 and 1861, Church property had been sold and Church loans called, but, as has been pointed out by historians, this action resulted only in a new concentration of wealth in other—and very few—hands.

The Church got along so well, on the whole, under Díaz that the conflict subsided. The revolution that overthrew Díaz was anti-clerical, to some extent atheistic. It is difficult for North Americans to understand the view of liberals in many Latin countries, who regard the Church as a national menace. Conditions among us are so dissimilar. But revolutionary leaders, as Dr. Ross has pointed out, considered the Church one of the main props of economic feudalism. It was allied with the landed proprietors, and thus was regarded as an enemy of the revolutionary State.

Quite naturally, the upper clergy supported Díaz against Madero, and later supported Victoriano Huerta, assassin of Madero. Later governments mainly adhered to the anti-clerical tradition. Previous reforms had not solved the problem; it was felt that something more thorough was necessary.

The reform government of 1857 had "lent" church buildings for religious purposes. The revolutionary government of 1917 seized them, making them government property—in which, however, in many cases, religious services have been permitted as a public function. The constitution of that year forbade religious organizations to own real estate or mortgages, have invested funds, maintain convents, solicit funds outside churches, or hold ceremonies outside churches, and forbade the clergy to criticize the government or take part in politics. The Church, in short, was to concern itself exclusively with religion.

In 1926, hostility flared into open revolt. Important clergy refused to recognize the constitution of 1917; the Calles government began to enforce the law more strictly, and the Church replied with a boycott and armed rebellion, in which the usual charges of atrocities were made by both sides. The "Cristero" uprising, failing, it is said, to receive expected aid from the

United States, was suppressed with ferocious severity, and the boycott failed.

As a Mexican pointed out to me, the boycott backfired. For the Indians found they could conduct services quite satisfactorily by themselves and save the priests' fees.

The government blamed the clergy for the assassination of Alvaro Obregón, former president and president-designate, in 1928, and the old dispute was revived from 1932 to 1934, when a bishop, whose arrest had been ordered, fled to the United States. When Lázaro Cárdenas became president in 1934, the Church again challenged the constitution, but a few years later State and Church reached an understanding, by which application of the laws was relaxed and the clergy refrained from active opposition.

Cárdenas, in a speech at Oaxaca, is said to have declared, "I am tired of closing churches and finding them full. I'll open the churches and educate the people, and in ten years I'll find them empty."

He was probably overoptimistic: the hold of religion upon Mexicans, particularly women, is not to be shaken so easily. But his immediate purpose was achieved: the controversy subsided; elements in the clergy supported his suppression of the threatened revolt of Saturnino Cedillo, and applauded expropriation of foreigners' oil holdings in 1938. His successor, Manuel Ávila Camacho, came into office on reputed good terms with the Church.

The Church, though deprived of much of its former political and economic power, remains a strong social force. I often found churches full of devout worshipers, whether their worship was directed to the ancient gods of sun and rain or to Christ and Our Lady, or to a mixture of both.

I found the churches sometimes artistically in bad taste, the sacred images often repulsive with Spanish-Indian emphasis upon suffering and death; but the intensity of devotion in the faces of those rebozo-shrouded women and sandaled men who moved on brown, road-soiled knees down stone aisles to the altars, was not to be denied.

And the churches, tawdry as they often seem to our more sedate notions of art, remain the only beauty in the lives of many millions in Mexico: the only refuge. "Opiate of the people," it has been called in another land—but without that opiate, how could they bear the burdens which Revolution has not, to a great extent, yet been able to lift?

Perhaps, in time, those burdens may be lifted to an appreciable degree; perhaps in a very long time revolutionary education will enable them to face life "neither leaning upon faith nor cringing under fear." But until then, the people need their faith, and until something adequate is given them to replace it, they will keep it.

XLVI · "OWL HOOTS, INDIAN DIES"

FROM poverty springs disease. The death-rate in Mexico has been estimated at twice that of the United States; infant mortality is even higher.

How can it be otherwise, when the per capita gross daily income of the peasant has been calculated at the equivalent of less than sixteen cents in United States money?

The majority of the people of Mexico, according to Mexican sources, are poorly fed, clothed, and housed; infested with insect parasites, and without medical care.

This situation proceeds partly from ignorance, which in turn proceeds from poverty.

The typical diet is tortillas (corn), beans, chile (pepper), and, in maguey-producing districts, pulque. Some Otomí families drink, according to Mexican estimates, seven quarts of pulque a day. It is, according to some authorities, one of the world's least sanitary beverages, although some Mexican medical opinion holds that without it the Indian would be even worse off; the stuff, which looks like thin mucilage and tastes a little like stale beer, is said to contain almost the only vitamines the Indian gets. One authority says the diet as a whole brings about vital degeneration at the age of fifty.

Whole villages are blind from attacks of a parasite that infects the eyes. Other whole villages are afflicted with goiter and deafness attributed to deficient diet. Jungle dwellers are spotted with *pinto,* caused, I was told, by a parasite which enters through the soles of the feet. There are districts, such as a part of the oil country, where 90 per cent of the population is reported malarial.

The sociologist Miguel Othon de Mendizábal estimated a few years ago that there was one physician to seven thousand rural inhabitants, and that more than 86 per cent of the villages of less than ten thousand population were without medical care. Physicians are concentrated in the Capital: one for six to seven hundred people, according to the records. In the State of Oaxaca the figures show one to sixteen thousand. Ancient knowledge of healing herbs has deteriorated, and new diseases have entered that herbs will not cure.

Water and milk in many rural districts are notoriously unsafe. Tourists and wealthy Mexicans drink beer or bottled water; the peon can afford neither.

The peon lies at night on his mat on the earthen floor, his hut tightly closed against the air, which he fears; his head muffled in his sarape. In the high regions, he sleeps cold; everywhere, save in the hammocks of the tropics, his bed is hard. Large families—and their animals—are crowded together. Bathing is believed, in many districts, to be unhealthful, except once a year, on the Night of Saint John, and actual lack of water prevents effective disposal of waste, as well as inducing the drinking of alcoholic beverages.

For example, the newspaper *Excelsior* of April 26, 1939, reported conditions found by sociologists in various communities, among them Paso de Ovejas, which was "without piped water, drainage, or septic tanks," in all of whose premises "exist manure heaps which perpetually breed flies.... This does not impede," added the report, "Paso de Ovejas from sending daily to Vera Cruz two thousand liters of milk which is obtained and prepared for shipment among the manure heaps."

Milpa Alta, only a few miles from the Capital, was another of many such examples reported.

The mere fact, however, that sociologists had been sent to investigate these conditions was encouraging.

The typical cases revealed another heavy load for the government to lift. As the Polynesian demigod Máui, after his first drink from the magic calabash, could insert only his finger-tips under the sky's edge to raise it, so here reform had barely got its finger-ends under the weight of disease fostered by ignorance and poverty. But it was, to the extent of the leverage it had, lifting.

Health missions were established in rural communities, teaching elements of hygiene. Vaccination had all but eliminated smallpox, save in the most remote areas. Every letter carried between post-offices within Mexico bore an extra stamp to help finance the campaign against malaria. Every few days I read in the press of sanitary water and drainage systems installed with federal aid.

Gambling had been abolished (hence the number of persons we saw in hotels playing checkers, about the only game still permitted). The president had wanted to abolish alcohol, but had not succeeded, perhaps because the government needed the revenue. As a compromise, abstinence was being taught in rural cultural missions and in schools.

In view of the conditions shown by surveys, and the examples I saw of those conditions, the Mexicans I met were, on the whole, healthier in appearance than one would expect. They are credited with being a hardy race; they have had to be.

The scope of the reform was limited; the government had no such resources as would be provided for any similar effort in the United States, and as would be necessary in order to make a deep impression. But apparently it was struggling along valiantly with what it had.

And one could hope that in time the Mexican Máui, with another draught from the magic calabash, would get his forearms under the edge of the drooping sky, and at last his shoulders, to lift it until it would no longer crush the trees.

XLVII · "LAND AND LIBERTY"

THERE is hunger in Mexico," I heard Manuel Gamio say, "not because of lack of land, but because the land is not in possession of those who cultivate it."

"Land and liberty" was the battle-cry of Zapata's peasant soldiers. It has remained the most insistent demand with which all governments of Mexico since 1910 have had to reckon.

"The fact that the land in Mexico belongs to a few," said Gabino Palma, however, "is due not to concentration of capital, but to geographical conditions and distribution of population."

The population is concentrated, and always has been, he pointed out, in the central region, the plateau, because of its more healthful climate and because of economic factors.

"Land and Liberty"

Therefore, he continued, "the agrarian problem of Mexico does not consist solely in redistribution of lands. First it is necessary to conquer the tropics and the desert, in order to make habitable enough land to be divided. . . . The tragedy of Mexico," he added, "is the illiteracy of its people, the geographical situation of the country, and the fact that its natural riches are in the hands of foreigners."

Another heavy load to lift. Irrigation, reclamation, drainage, mosquito control, are comparatively easy in a wealthy country such as the United States. In Mexico, which needs them so desperately, they are all but impossible. Yet large areas never will be habitable until these things are accomplished.

The government has shown evidence of realizing this. Its publications have been full of statistics—and photographs—of new irrigation systems, dams, roads, harbor developments, railway extensions, coöperative farms, works of sanitary engineering, agricultural experimentation, propagation of fish, reforestation, model housing, parks and playgrounds, hospitals and clinics.

They were on no such scale as would be possible if more means were available, and some of them looked better on paper than to the actual view. Some had been interrupted by lack of funds. Some may have been unfavorably situated or otherwise impractical. But an effort was being made. And I reflected that in that country, only a revolutionary government had troubled itself to any appreciable extent with such matters.

The task was so great, the means so small, that it seemed the height of courage even to attempt it. Indeed, I saw regions which the program could not hope to touch for many years to come.

Meanwhile, to meet popular demand, the government has been, with some interruptions, seizing land formerly held by large proprietors and distributing it to the Indians, from whose ancestors, in theory at least, it was taken by fraud or force after the Conquest.

The Cárdenas administration of 1934-40 accelerated this redistribution by millions of acres. One estimate, before the close of that administration, was 47,000 square miles, or more than twice the area redistributed by all previous administrations since the Revolution of 1910. It was further estimated that some 750,000 individuals and heads of families had received land.

Yet 1,900,000 were estimated to be still landless, and keen students of the situation were saying there was not enough arable land for all.

The constitution of 1917 also undertook guarantees to labor, some of which were put into effect in varying degrees by succeeding administrations.

Wages of the working majority in Mexico always have been low, whether measured in money or by the more just but less readily definable standard of what the money will buy. These wages, in terms of Mexican money, have increased over what they were in the Díaz administration. Meanwhile, cost of living has risen, and it is complained that many Mexicans are little or no better off.

In San Miguel de Allende, for instance, I learned that the prevailing wage for a caretaker, gardener, and man of all work at the summer homes of Mexicans or foreigners was the equivalent of eight and one-third cents a day in United States currency. A sociologist of my acquaintance quoted figures showing the average rural wage to be about three-fifths of that. The same authority calculated the minimum cost of living, for a rural family of five, as the equivalent of thirty-three and a third United States cents a day.

Thus, if every member of a family works, the total income may barely meet the most scanty estimate of subsistence.

The statistics may be unreliable, but the picture they present is apparently accurate. Much of Mexico performs, day by day, the seemingly impossible: it keeps life in the body on less than a minimum living wage. The human cost is, of course, enormous. Those who survive pay in suffering from malnutrition, dirt, disease, and lowered vitality. Industry inevitably pays in impaired efficiency.

Such gains as have been made are attributed to the organization of labor. Organized workers, with government encouragement, have fared better than the average, although I was told that part of the gain was lost through corrupt practices of grasping leaders.

In the old hacienda régime, before the Revolution, the proprietor maintained a general store, at which laborers were required to buy exclusively. Since the peon could not read or write, add or subtract, he had no way of checking his account, and was kept in a perpetual debt amounting to slavery. If he fled, the proprietor could send the rural police after him. When the peon died, his sons inherited the debt. In some districts, the proprietor, legally or otherwise, had power of life and death. The peon had no recourse.

Nevertheless, I have been told in all sincerity by some of my Mexican friends that the peon was better off in that condition than he is when he tries to make his way as a nominally free man. The proprietor, I was assured, felt responsibility for his peons; he would not let them starve. If his crop failed, he borrowed money on his land, to feed and clothe his workers. He considered himself a "father" to them (which, it is alleged, he frequently was in fact). When a peon grew old or sick, the proprietor took care of him. The hacienda, at its best, was like a large family group, a clan community.

If the proprietor had a good crop one year, the gains were likely to be wiped out the next. Most *hacendados* were chronically in debt. Andrés Molina Enríquez contended that the hacienda was "not a business," but a survival of feudalism, directed not primarily toward production, but toward maintenance of prestige, and thus operated with economic inefficiency.

All this is familiar reading to those who have studied the history of the North American "Old South." The same arguments were advanced for chattel slavery, and in many ways conditions were parallel. The Negro slave in the South, the Indian peon in Mexico, spared of responsibility, looked to the master—often in trust and affection; and no doubt many masters responded in kind. But in both cases there was opportunity for abuse, and among masters and overseers of the more brutal type, abuses occurred.

Both systems had the same characteristics: a decorative, gracious upper-class culture, with at its best a paternal regard for the humble who served it and who subsisted by its sufferance. Historically, both were anachronisms, survivals of an agricultural feudal economy which could not compete successfully in a modern industrial world.

The Revolution set about to change all this, and to some extent it did so. There are still haciendas, though they are fewer and mostly of smaller size. The same development has also occurred as in the United States: the sharecropper, doing the work of slave or peon without the slave's or the peon's security. There is also the small independent farmer, on his bit of land that clings precariously to the mountainside; often stony and sterile, often without adequate water; the poor soil scratched shallowly with wooden plow; the meager crop cut by hand with the machete; the miserable hut bare of all but the mat, the grinding-stone, and the griddle on which the wife bakes her laboriously-made tortillas.

And there are subsidized coöperative farm communities which the government has founded in an attempt to restore an ancient economic system of the Indians, reinforced to some extent with modern methods and machinery, irrigation works, and scientific services. Opponents of the program contend that these are inefficiently administered and economically unsound.

"Land and Liberty"

Government spokesmen quote impressive statistics to show that the projects, in the face of enormous difficulties and alleged sabotage by the opposition, have made tremendous progress in bettering the lot of thousands of peasants.

Theoretically, this system should be more advantageous than small independent farming, since it facilitates the engineering projects that are necessary to render much Mexican land arable—as well as scientific methods, expert planning, and use of machinery. It should be more economical to cultivate land in large units than in small ones. Critics contend, however, that in practice abuses have nullified the advantages; "the bureaucrat has taken the place of the large proprietor."

Near Torreon, I saw the project of La Laguna, where 30,000 *ejidatarios,* as farmers under this type of organization are called, were working the land on this basis. Methods through much of the 270,000 acres under cultivation were still relatively primitive. But the houses were neat and better furnished than rural homes in many regions of Mexico; the people, on the whole, seemed more confident, and there was an atmosphere of hope.

The engineer in charge showed me the figures: an increasing yield each year; so many tractors installed; so many pumps; so much gain in cash return year by year.

He explained the operation of the project. Government experts drafted a coördinated plan of sowing, calculated the capital necessary, and advanced it to the farmers according to acreage cultivated and amount of labor necessary. The government further advanced a peso and a half a day to each farmer, the remainder of his share to be determined by the proceeds after the harvest. (A critic of the system stated that most of them received only the peso and a half, and that for some months about one-third of them failed to receive even that, because the government didn't have the money.)

The government furnished machinery, fuel, and lubricants, to be paid for out of returns over a five-year period. The

357

National Bank of Farm Credit marketed the crop. Its value was then divided: after expenses were defrayed and the year's share of the loan repaid, the remaining profit was apportioned among the farmers.

Under the old private ownership, the engineer told me, the peon received one peso a day, and that only on days when work was available and when he worked. Under the new *ejidal* plan, he was guaranteed a peso and a half and as much more as his share of the crop might yield after expenses were paid. Some received, he said, a thousand pesos or more in the course of the year.

The whole matter, I found, was controversial. Yes, merchants in Torreon said, the people were more prosperous since the project had got under way. Stores were selling merchandise —much of it imported from the United States—that their customers had not hitherto been able to buy. The former proprietors, said the president of the Chamber of Commerce, spent their money abroad, and their peons had none to spend, but the new peasant proprietors spent their money in Torreon. The United States consul confirmed the statement that business had improved, that financial, educational, and health conditions were better.

I asked people about it at random in the streets. *"Parece que va,"* they replied: "It appears to be going (well)."

I quoted this to a former resident of Torreon, a businessman representing a Mexican industry in the United States.

"Va," he exploded scornfully, *"al diablo."* ("It is going to the devil.")

The Laguna country, he added, had been spared repeatedly from expropriation because it was felt that a project there would be unwise. Only under the Cárdenas administration was the land seized, and then because, my informant contended, it was already developed and one of the richest agricultural areas in the Republic. The former private owners, he insisted, had put vast sums into irrigation and machinery; then the government seized it in order to "make a record at the former owners' expense."

The peons, he asserted, received higher wages under the former private ownership than they received from the government guarantee and their share of profits under the coöperative system.

Said the daughter of a Chihuahua *hacendado,* speaking of expropriation: "You can't understand what it is until you've been hit by it."

"There are abuses, naturally," I replied, to draw out her views.

"Yes, nothing but abuses. . . . When the governor of the State of Chihuahua went to Parral to campaign, he met my grandfather, and my grandfather said: 'I know you; I've met you before.'

" 'Where?' the governor asked.

" 'Oh, you were the one who stole my favorite horse in the Revolution.'

"We have lost our land, but we still have to pay the teacher in the school that is on the land. Another family is still paying taxes on land that has been expropriated.

"My father still has a small rancho, but the peons take the crops, and the government does nothing about it, because the governor wants to be reëlected."

I mentioned La Laguna.

"The Laguna peons made as high as two pesos a day under private ownership," she asserted. "They had model housing and medical care, and the *hacendados* took care of the peons' families in the inactive season. Mules from Chihuahua were used on the plantations. Now there is no money to buy mules, and the mules of Chihuahua are dying."

"What is your greatest problem here?" I asked the head engineer at La Laguna.

"To get the farmers to sell their mules and buy tractors," he replied.

Pattern of Mexico

There you have the contradiction one finds throughout Mexico.

What do the peons themselves think? Some of them complain of favoritism on the part of the work bosses. Some live far from the area assigned them to cultivate. All plans that look well on paper are subject to the incalculable tangents of human factors.

But some of those peons, who are not as ragged as many elsewhere, answered: "Life is better, now. The land is ours. We are free."

RUINED CHURCH AT COLIMA, LOOKING TOWARD THE VOLCÁN
DE COLIMA

XLVIII · UNCLE SAM'S SHADOW

IN the atonal symphony of modern world life, a nation no longer can be a solo instrument. It becomes more and more difficult to adjust domestic problems without involving relations with other powers. The operation of economic law becomes more and more a negation of national law, as economic principles conflict increasingly with the old anarchy of nations.

Mexico, in economic history, has been the colonial preserve of foreign exploiters. Hence, most of the efforts the nation has made to redeem its economic status and promote the welfare of its people have offended powerful commercial or industrial interests in other countries.

A Mexican administration has to maintain the delicate bal-

Pattern of Mexico

ance of a tightrope-walker. On the one hand, revolutionary tradition, which no politician may openly flout, demands "land and liberty" for the centuries-oppressed millions; on the other, foreign powers resist any attempt to encroach upon the interests of their nationals in exploiting Mexican resources.

Often the popular demand has been met by large promises and as near a minimum of fulfilment as has been considered safe and as the apathy of the people has made possible. The external problem has been met by taking advantage of conflicting foreign interests to play one foreign power against another.

In this welter of cross-purposes, the most prominent factor in Mexican foreign relations has been, because of its geographical position, the United States.

The United States, for its own protection, long ago declared itself guardian of the Latin American republics against Old World aggression. In doing so, it accepted a degree of responsibility for these republics' conduct toward other powers.

Now Latin republics, although in emergency they accept the protection of their northern neighbor, do not relish the notion of a guardian. It offends their pride. Nor do they welcome interference with their ways of doing things.

This situation again is particularly acute in Mexico, because Mexico is nearest to the United States.

Thus the United States is regarded in Mexico with a mixture of suspicion—not entirely unjustified by history—and conciliation. North Americans individually are treated, commonly, with courtesy and kindness, but collectively with considerable reserve. Mexicans have not forgotten the North American conquest of 1847-48 which lopped off more than half their territory. They remember the bombardment of Vera Cruz in 1914, and the Pershing invasion of 1916 in pursuit of Pancho Villa. They recall the procedure by which the Republic of Panama was detached from Colombia to create the Canal Zone; the occupation of Haiti and Nicaragua by United States marines; the doings of the private armies of North American oil companies in the Huasteca region.

If they are thoughtful, they remember, too, that a North American threat pulled out of Mexico the French army that held Maximilian on his shaky throne; that North American guns and bullets made Pancho Villa's *Dorados* formidable in the Revolution; that the United States, for the last hundred years, has kept other nations reminded that it would regard an attack from Europe or Asia upon Mexico as one upon itself.

That is one reason why Mexico has an extremely modest navy and an army whose function is that of an internal police force. Whether Mexicans, or we ourselves, like it or not, Mexican defense is inseparable from defense of the United States.

The Mexicans resent this fact, even while they welcome it. And always there is that troublesome question: as the Latin proverb puts it, who will guard the guardians? The notion seems ridiculous to most North Americans, but many Mexicans can't quite put away the thought that their country may sometime be swallowed by the "Colossus of the North."

Thoughtful people in both countries realize, of course, that Mexico would be, for that "Colossus," a highly indigestible mouthful. We have enough problems of our own without taking on those of Mexico as well.

"I have always felt," said Professor Daniel Cosío Villegas, "that the history of Mexico would be very different if its wider territorial boundary were with Guatemala instead of with the United States—with the weaker instead of with the stronger nation.... Mexico would be more tranquil if the United States frontier were smaller."

But, in Guatemala the Mexican border, and in El Salvador and Honduras, the Guatemalan border, are watched with similar anxiety. The smaller nation distrusts the larger.

Moreover, North American influence is felt not only in foreign affairs, but in internal matters as well, introducing a complicating and sometimes determining factor into Mexican politics and social action. It has been stated, with corroborative evidence, that no successful Mexican revolution has been conducted without aid from private or other sources north of the Río Grande.

I was told again and again in Mexico that a national administration there stands or falls according to the extent of its support from Washington. This support can be given or withheld in various ways: by granting or refusing diplomatic recognition, by permitting or forbidding export of arms and munitions over the border, by buying or not buying Mexican silver, by a hostile or benign attitude in trade relations, by a minimum or maximum objection to the social programs that are considered necessary to maintain the prestige of a Mexican government among its own people.

Some Mexicans resent this, too, even while they take advantage of it. Naturally enough, they would like to determine their own destiny, unimpeded. But the world becomes increasingly a complex of checks and balances. It may still be possible for a very large and powerful nation to be self-contained and self-sufficient, but only at great domestic sacrifice and, as recent history has shown, at the risk of foreign war. For a relatively small nation, it is impossible.

So Mexicans watch United States elections. A liberal administration in Washington may be expected, they feel, to support within reason a liberal administration in Mexico, and vice versa. As recent examples, the opinion has been expressed in both countries that the Cárdenas administration was enabled to conduct its rather drastic social program as boldly as it did, largely by the friendly attitude of the Roosevelt administration in Washington, and that Cárdenas' successor, General Ávila Camacho, was confirmed in office and a possible revolt by his opponent General Juan Andreu Almazán averted, by Washington's prompt and emphatic recognition of Ávila Camacho's election, expressed by sending no less a personage than the Vice-President of the United States to attend the new Mexican president's inauguration. It was obvious at the time that considerations of hemisphere defense were involved, and it was also believed that modification of the Mexican nationalistic social program was contemplated.

It has been calculated that 53 per cent of the wealth of Mexico is in foreign hands—mainly British and North American—and of this percentage, more than half is owned, or claimed, in the United States. Figures vary, but the table immediately before me estimates United States investments in Mexico at more than a billion dollars.

Now the United States Government naturally feels an obligation to safeguard this stake, regardless of the means by which some of it may have been acquired. And it is equally obvious that social programs in Mexico since 1910 have tended to threaten some portions of this investment.

Foreign landholders, including North Americans, had to give up some rather large tracts as a part of the program of returning the land to the people. This caused relatively little disturbance, for Mexico has been paying for some of the expropriated land. (Domestic landholders were not so fortunate; they were allowed to file claims, which it was predicted never would be paid.)

Some industrial enterprises as well have passed from foreign control into the hands of workers, under government supervision. This also created comparatively little friction, since many of the enterprises taken over were, in existing conditions, no longer profitable, and some foreign owners of such properties were glad to escape.

An instance in point is a sugar estate in south central Mexico. I heard Mexican conservatives and North American businessmen lamenting the fate of the former owner who, they said, had thus lost the fruits of his life work. But one of the members of the United States consular staff smiled broadly when I inquired into this case.

Pattern of Mexico

"I'll take you out to meet J———," he said. "He's a friend of mine. He thinks expropriation is the best thing that ever happened to him. The government turned his property over to the workers; it now supports it, and has hired him to run it. He gets more in salary than he got in profits when he owned the business, and the government takes all the risk."

The most serious conflict, however, arose over the oil lands. I do not intend to become embroiled in so controversial a discussion, and it is not for me to say who is right or wrong in the complicated web of conflicting interests. But, as a mere matter of history, it can't be omitted entirely.

Petroleum had been known to the Indians before Cortés, but the oil industry in Mexico, in modern times, dates from the beginning of the twentieth century, when oil was "discovered" near Tampico. The next twenty years saw a mad scramble for concessions, and a period of virtual anarchy. In the history of that period, oil appears mixed freely with blood and gold. The documents are full of stories of Indians shot in the back and their lands acquired from the widows, or simply occupied; of bribes to officials of the Díaz government and tribute paid to bandit chiefs; and of political and international intrigue.

These things are not peculiar to Mexico or to the oil industry; nor is the right hand in New York or London necessarily conscious in detail of what the left hand doeth in Tampico or Cuba or Honduras. The advance guards of large-scale industry are expected to get results, and they get them, "or else." It is only fair to add that, as stated by Frank Kluckhohn (who cultivated so detached a viewpoint that he was expelled from Mexico for "blackening," as the phrase is, the nation), much of the property seems to have been acquired by procedure that was "legal, even though ethically questionable."

But when the gunpowder smoke settled, British and North American interests held the greater part of the oil fields of Mexico. Edward L. Doheny alone, whose involvement in certain matters connected with oil reserves in his own country is a matter of record, had concessions in Mexico totaling 600,000 acres. It has been alleged that he supported the Madero revolution against Díaz in 1910 because the Díaz government favored British interests, and that the same Doheny gave Venustiano Carranza $100,000 in cash and $685,000 in fuel credits to fight Victoriano Huerta.

It was the Díaz administration, however, more than any other, that turned over Mexican resources to foreigners. Probably this policy was partly selfish, for the enrichment of officials through bribes, and partly a necessary method of building up industry and creating "prosperity"—for it is doubtful whether the resources could have been developed without foreign capital. The existence of petroleum had been known in Mexico for some centuries, but it had not been developed.

To transfer the oil fields to foreigners, Díaz had to violate a fundamental principle of constitutional law, inherited from Spain. For the Colonial grants vested ultimate title to the land and all its products in the Crown. Surface and mining rights were separate and revocable. The Law of the Indies, in 1523, provided that the resources, to be held, must be used. (This accorded also with the theory generally attributed to pre-Conquest Indian practice.) The constitution of the Mexican Republic in 1857 stated that "in the nation is vested direct dominion over all minerals—solid, liquid, or gaseous."

But Díaz' mining law of 1884 yielded to the property notions of Anglo-Saxon nations by declaring subsoil products the exclusive property of the owner of the land. Another law in 1892 granted perpetual subsoil rights in petroleum.

Article 27 of the constitution of 1917 reversed Díaz' law by reaffirming the principle of national ownership, subject to concession for use. Thus the Spanish-Mexican concept of national domain again came into conflict with Anglo-Saxon ideas of private property.

The history of the controversy, in detail, is a series of

manœuvers and compromises and reversals that it would be tedious to repeat. Mexico placated the United States for a time by declaring the law non-retroactive and allowing the companies to keep what they had acquired under Díaz. It was, however, inevitable that the basic conflict of the two principles of land tenure should recur.

In brief, the foreign companies' statement of their position has been that they acquired the land in good faith, under existing Mexican law, and spent large sums in developing Mexican resources which otherwise could not have been developed. The Mexicans assert that the lands were acquired by fraud or force and large profits extracted from them, of which very little went toward promoting the welfare of the Mexican people.

The show-down occurred when the oil industry clashed with the Mexican program for improving the condition of working people, under the Cárdenas administration. (It has been charged that this program was a pretext and that "nationalization" of the oil properties had long been contemplated.)

"Equal pay for equal work" was the principle involved—a principle that is of necessity controversial. Mexican workers contended that they were producing more oil, at a lower investment, and at lower wages, than workers in the United States, and that the American companies were getting higher prices for their product in Mexico than in the United States.

In 1936 the foreign companies rejected a demand for wage increases and certain social services guaranteed by Article 123 of the constitution. Some of the demands would be considered, in this country, extreme; but any one who is familiar with collective bargaining knows that it is customary to ask for more than is likely to be received.

The companies refused the demands as unreasonable, though it has been stated that later they made an offer incorporating the less extravagant ones. A general strike started in May, 1937.

Uncle Sam's Shadow

The government, intervening under the law, declared the conflict technically an "economic" one and appointed a committee of experts to study it. The committee reported that food costs had increased 89 per cent between 1934 and 1937, and that real wages in Mexico had decreased 16 to 22 per cent in that time, while in the United States they had advanced 7.8 per cent; that the companies charged 193.4 per cent more for gasoline in Mexico than elsewhere, and that their profits in Mexico averaged 16.2 per cent, while their profits in the United States averaged 2 per cent.

The commission therefore found the companies economically capable of granting a wage increase totalling 26,000,000 pesos, or, according to exchange at that time, some $7,200,000, annually, which the workers accepted. After the award was sustained by a labor tribunal and by the Mexican supreme court, the companies, according to Mexican sources, still refused to accept it. (The companies contended that the wage increase, together with the increased workers' benefits awarded, would total $11,600,000.)

Frank Kluckhohn, then correspondent for the New York *Times,* reported that the companies eventually offered to abide by the award, except for that portion which gave the workers a voice in management of the industry. The labor board held that the companies must accept the award in full.

Under Mexican law, refusal to obey the award made the companies liable to cancellation of their labor contracts and to payment of three months' dismissal pay to the workers. The principle involved here is that of the worker's equity in his job, a principle which is gradually being established in this country. Continued resistance placed the companies technically in "rebellion" and, as in the case of other industries, to reassertion of constitutional government dominion.

On March 18, 1938, President Cárdenas signed a decree expropriating seventeen British and North American oil companies, whose investments they had themselves calculated at some $400,000,000.

In accordance with Mexican law, the oil workings were placed in the hands of organized workers, under government supervision. The workers, it has been stated, got from 15 to 25 per cent less in wages and other benefits than the tribunal awarded them, and even this, the government contended later, proved to be more than, under present world conditions, it could pay. But they gained, technically at least, in ownership and control of the industry. The expropriation, at the time, greatly enhanced Cárdenas' prestige and was hailed as a victory over foreign imperialism.

It has been suggested that both the Mexican Government and the oil companies were "bluffing." The government, it is said, was relying upon competition between British and North American interests, which had been turned to advantage before, to make them submit to the Mexican rulings. In this, the government was overoptimistic. British and North American companies made common cause against the threat of interference with their exploitation.

It has been suggested that the companies hoped for a last-minute compromise that would save their prestige and at the same time make the necessary concessions. A more radical theory has been formulated, stating that they forced Cárdenas to take drastic action, in the hope of bringing about a conservative revolution. Against this contention, some commentators trace a long-continued government policy leading to expropriation, and declare that the government was determined to expropriate, no matter what concessions the employers might offer.

There are in the Mexican archives sworn statements and photostats of correspondence that purport to show negotiations between oil company representatives and the Fascist "Gold Shirts" for financing of the abortive "rebellion" of General Saturnino Cedillo.

Uncle Sam's Shadow

Whatever the reliability of these documents, the Cedillo counter-revolutionary movement, which may have been purely an individual's selfish attempt at aggrandizement, came to nothing. The more serious results, for Mexico, were a breach of relations with Great Britain and an unofficial economic blockade of Mexico. Britain and France boycotted Mexican oil; North American interests embargoed tetraethyl lead, without which high-test gasoline can not be made, to Mexico; Mexican cargoes were attached in foreign ports, and large concerns refused to sell equipment to Mexico—despite the lingering depression in United States industry—lest they lose the business they were doing with the oil companies.

Mexico, as President Cárdenas explained, had to sell oil somewhere, and the concerted boycotts and embargoes forced it to barter with Germany, Italy, and Japan for goods, when it needed cash. After the second World War started, much of this market also was lost, while the barter customers were owing millions to Mexico.

Meanwhile, efforts were made to settle the controversy. Mexico had offered to pay to the companies, in oil, over a period of ten years, the value of their properties. But the Mexican evaluation and that of the companies didn't agree. The old conflict between the two concepts of property was involved: Mexico would pay only for installations, not for the land itself.

On the morning of August 11, 1939, we read in Mexico City newspapers that the oil question had been "composed," in the happy Spanish phrase. The industry was to be administered by a board of nine members, of whom three would be named by the Mexican Government, three by the United States Government, and the remaining three chosen by these six from a list of nine proposed by the two governments; if no agreement could be reached on these latter appointments, the three remaining members were to be chosen by lot.

The announcement proved premature. The companies rejected the cumbersome plan, in the hope—it has been suggested—that a change of administration in Mexico, which was due shortly, might give them better terms.

But on that August morning, it was believed in Mexico City that the *"problema del petroleo"* had been, if not happily, at least workably, compromised.

"Mexico," said Professor Gabino Palma to his class in the National University, "has yielded in part, and the companies have in part yielded. Exploitation of petroleum in Mexico by foreign companies will continue, but by common accord and with mutual benefit.

"This arrangement has been brought about, not because the justice of the Mexican position is recognized, but because it is convenient for the North American and British governments in the uncertain world situation. Rumors of war have become more insistent. This makes us see that somebody needs our petroleum."

The professor's remarks have since been supported by world events, even though at the time the petroleum conflict had not been settled, as he believed.

The "oil controversy" involves fundamental differences in concepts of property and of social equity. By one view, natural resources are the property of the nation; they are inalienable, and any rights to exploit those resources are temporary and revocable, contingent upon continued use which does not jeopardize national interests or violate national law. The opposite conception is that natural resources are the property of individuals who have acquired them and who can rightfully do with them what they please, subject to such laws for their regulation as may prove enforceable.

The social principle is equally subject to conflict. The one view exalts human welfare; the other, property rights. In the former view, industry exists for humanity; in the latter opinion, labor exists for industry.

The idea, which has been expressed in high quarters in the

Uncle Sam's Shadow

United States, that an industrial enterprise which can not pay its workers a living wage does not deserve to exist, is in Mexico the law of the land. There is, of course, room for argument as to what constitutes a living wage. The oil companies contended that they paid the highest wages in Mexico, and the workers replied that living costs in the oil region were the highest.

The two conflicts are related. The first merges with the second; both boil down to property rights versus human rights, and the conflict is fundamental and world-wide. In our own country, we compromise as best as we can between the diverse viewpoints. The weight of authority has been historically on the side of property, but it has been mitigated by popular demand in the interest of humanity. Achievement of balance between the two is probably the function of democracy.

For it has been argued plausibly that the conflict is more apparent than real; that untrammeled industry creates prosperity which to some degree filters down through most of the population, easing the human lot. On the whole, the history of our own country tends, though with some reservations, to support that contention.

It is asserted, in rebuttal, that prosperity in the United States has been the fruit of abundant natural resources, the exploitation of a hitherto sparsely occupied continent; and that benefits to humanity in general have been incidental—derived in spite of, rather than because of, the advancement of property and of its manipulation.

Theoretically, the greater the amount of goods produced, the more there is for each citizen; the larger the number of dollars available, the more can go in the pay envelope each week. Somehow, a prodigious number of these dollars and a large amount of these goods tend to get sidetracked, but the notion is obviously not entirely devoid of truth. The difficulty is that we have solved problems of production more rapidly than problems of distribution. It is considered in some quarters a prime function of democratic government to clear obstructions away from the channels of distribution, so that not too large a proportion of the population shall be hungry at any one time. I am aware that this notion is regarded in other quarters as impious and worse: confiscatory, and savoring of what conservatives are pleased to call "bolshevism." At any rate, Mexico has the same problem, in a more acute form.

And Mexico is similarly divided: conservative opinion would develop industry and exploit resources, for private profit, on the theory that prosperity would thus accrue, in some measure, to all. Liberal opinion, in theory, seeks to build prosperity from the bottom, by placing industry increasingly in the hands of those who turn its wheels.

Neither view, in practice, has proved its validity in Mexico. Under Díaz, prosperity didn't trickle down. Under the Revolution, it hasn't trickled up; in fact, there hasn't been much prosperity. Mexican conservatives say that has happened because the theory is impractical; Mexican liberals attribute it to the fact that Mexico has been in turmoil, weakened by years of civil war, and hampered by conservative sabotage of reform, and that there has not yet been time for the seed to develop into the fruiting tree.

Meanwhile, in the last years of the Cárdenas administration, storm broke upon the world. Strange and new aspects of old conflicts had arisen, accentuated by dynamic and alarming nationalisms. Stalin had perverted Marx; Hitler had perverted Nietzsche; Mussolini had recast both in the mold of Machiavelli. Japan, awakened from isolation a century ago by North American enterprise, had adapted the mechanisms of Western civilization to the uses of its feudal system and its fanatical imperialism.

War trod with steel soles over Europe, Asia, Africa; continents on the other side of the earth shook with the concussion. It soon appeared that no nation, or, at most, only those favored by peculiar circumstance, could be entirely neutral.

Uncle Sam's Shadow

The American republics had to decide on which side they were to be counted. (Even before the war began, a Mexican economist said to me: "Mexico must choose between two imperialisms—European and North American.")

The United States early showed its sympathy for the embattled democracies. Most of Latin America followed suit—roughly in decreasing ratio to their distance from the United States. Their problem was not simple. They had trade relations with the totalitarian powers, and some of them had large population groups more or less associated with those powers. Some of the larger South American nations produce products in competition with the United States. And there were other reasons for hesitation.

Most of them, however, fell early into line. In times of relative quiet in the world, Uncle Sam may be regarded, by some other American republics, as a bully whom it is wise to placate; a rude, tactless neighbor to be secretly despised and openly flouted to such an extent as seems safe. To some Mexicans, he seems a potential conquistador, to whom no foothold may be safely given.

Nevertheless, from the start, Mexico continued its traditional policy of favoring the more liberal nations. United States opinion had its influence, no doubt, but the official attitude probably represented the sentiment of a majority of articulate Mexicans. It is quite likely that in such times our Latin neighbors reflect that perhaps North American imperialism has alarmed them mainly because it has been close to them; that, after all, North American imperialism hasn't been consistently predatory, but has been mitigated by relative liberalism, and that, anyway, it is preferable to the European or Asiatic brand.

So they begin, even as we, to suppress within their countries foreign elements who are suspected of anti-American activity, and adopt a more coöperative attitude toward Uncle Sam. He's a heavy-footed, blundering busybody, but at heart not a bad sort. In emergency, it's a good thing to have a big fellow on one's side.

Meanwhile, the United States, for its part, has been putting forth increased activity in its somewhat belated "good neighbor" policy, and it is likely that more negotiation has been going on than has appeared on the surface.

In the Mexican presidential election of 1940, both important candidates declared for coöperation with the United States, and although both were committed, as any Mexican candidate must be, to guard the principles of the Revolution, and one of them to continue the liberal policies of the Cárdenas régime, both were understood to contemplate easing up on the pace of the social program, so as to avoid annoying the "Good Neighbor" north of the Río Grande.

As both candidates put it, in effect, they were for "consolidating the gains" of the Revolution, without subjecting the national economy to further strain. Accession of President Ávila Camacho was attended by unusually cordial manifestations on the part of the United States Government, and by negotiations with Mexico, as with other Latin American governments, tending toward closer coöperation in defense of the entire hemisphere, in which the United States, having the greatest resources, must bear the greatest share.

In world politics, Mexico is bound to be associated more or less closely with the United States. It is increasingly recognized that the larger interests of the Western Hemisphere demand United States leadership, or at least United States defense. Our own security is held to involve a degree of responsibility for the entire area. So our relations with the two score republics continue to be close. And that is particularly true of the nearest of them, Mexico.

May these relations continue friendly, and may friendliness increase. May each nation grow in sympathetic understanding of the other's problems, and, without arrogance or domination, aid in solving them.

VI · Art of The Centuries

XLIX · POETRY IN STONE

WITH the first-planted grains of corn, the brown men
sowed the seeds of art. For, since sunlight and rain
in just proportion were vital to this economy of the
soil, their imagination evolved gods who sent the sunlight and
rain, and who must be nourished and kept in good humor by
prayer and sacrifice.

So arose temples—made of earth at first, in the image of
the cone-shaped mountains; then, as men grew more ambitious
and more skilled, of stone, in the squared and terraced geometry of those shapes—stone hewed with tools of stone and
carried and set in place by the unaided red muscle-flesh of men.

They carved the stone in the images of men and gods;

379

painted it with pigments of plants and earth; covered walls with plaster and frescoed rich scenes into its wet surface.

Tribes came and went; old temples decayed, and new ones were built upon them. Conquerors came, and the stones of the old gods became foundations for the temples of the new.

Rain and wind, blown dust, débris of dead leaves covered many an ancient shrine. Jungle roots writhed up between the stones to overthrow walls. Man builds, and time erases. The stone gods slept, unseen and but little remembered, under the mounds.

But Nature preserved even as it destroyed. The blanket of leaves and earth protected carven traceries; fallen archways saved frescoes from the attrition of sun and rain. Broken and disordered, often, but sealed against decay, a mighty art lay locked away in the earth.

By accident here, by vague memory there, or by deliberate quest, the sacred places were discovered. Men tunneled into green-scarved hillocks, skimmed soil from slanting walls, and laid disassembled stones again in their places. The ruins were sacred no longer to earth and sun and rain, but to the study of man and of the arts that ennoble his spirit and enrich his life.

Almost every town in Mexico has its *ruinas*. Almost any tree-covered mound may hide still unexplored structures of ancient times. The Archæological Atlas of the Republic of Mexico enumerates, in more than three hundred pages of fine type, "archæological sites." And it is said that those numbered and named are but a fraction of those which exist.

"All the earth is a tomb," sang Nezahualcóyotl, and all Mexico is a tomb in which lie treasures of prehistoric art.

Primarily, this art served the gods. The people, save for a few nobles and priests, dwelt in huts not unlike those of to-day. Edifices that remain are public buildings: temples, ball courts, palaces of the ruling class.

I have already described several of the most prominent and readily accessible examples.

TOWERS AND DOMES AND BUTTRESSED WALLS OF CATHEDRALS
LIFT POWERFULLY INTO THE MEXICAN SKY

Poetry in Stone

A characteristic form is the rectangular terrace, the truncated step-pyramid: this is a foundation rather than a building, an artificial mountain on which to plant the temple nearer heaven.

The tribes of the central plateau evolved a massive, simple architecture of heavy, solid proportions and an impressive interplay of plane surfaces. Terraces arose like graduated building-blocks, cut perpendicularly and diagonally by great stairways set off one from another with varying widths and angles to form a harmonious composition.

In such centers of religious and national life as Teotihuacan, the structures were placed according to a comprehensive plan; each group was orientated around its individual axis, and the whole was orientated to a central axis believed to have been determined by the inclination of planets or of the sun.

The people whom their Aztec successors called Toltecs, or "Builders," carried this architecture to its highest development. At Tula, Cholula, Xochicalco, and elsewhere, but most notably at Teotihuacan, they left their monuments; these were apparently influenced at one period by the more florid art of the Mayas, whom they in turn influenced in the symbols of the Feathered Serpent whom both revered.

In the southeastern jungles the Mayas at first heaped up their buttressed quadrangles of rubble coated with decorated plaster, and later built in stone. They developed the corbel, or false arch, to construct long, narrow rooms borne on thick foundations. Later still, they took some of the weight off the roof-vault by erecting a narrow, pierced wall above the partitions, which permitted a widening of the rooms. Again, they supported arcades upon carved and painted columns.

Deep in the south, the Zapotecs and Mixtecs built their cities in what is now the State of Oaxaca. At Mitla, groups of stone buildings around sunken plazas are decorated with stylized fretwork in mosaics of separate stones so finely cut that they remain in place without adhesive. Compared with the temples of the central highland, they are relatively low and broad; their lintels, resting on heavy monolithic columns, allow wider rooms than do the narrow vaults of Yucatán.

At Monte Alban, early Zapotec architecture seems to have been overlaid with structures of the People of the Mists. There is less of the fret motif; walls are carved with human and animal figures, and the glyphs of written language.

These are the principal types. They had many variations, here and there merging or borrowing from one another.

Engineering, architectonic planning, artisanship of a high order speak from their mutilated surfaces—and so does the aspiring soul of man, who sought thus to rise nearer to the spirits who gave him life.

Few Aztec structures remain, but from fragments that exist, and from contemporary descriptions and drawings, they resembled broadly the Toltec style from which they are believed to have been derived.

In most places, temples functioning at the time of the Conquest were torn down, and the stones were used to erect churches which are the most prominent feature of any Mexican town.

Early churches and monasteries, and palaces of the Conquerors, look like fortresses, as indeed they were: high, bare, thick walled, topped with pointed stonework like oversized spike-ends, they have heavy flying buttresses, narrow, deeply recessed windows; carved decoration reserved mainly for doorways; within, heavy columns and arches around garden patios, long corridors, small dwelling-rooms, and vast vaulted chapels. The dominant impression is of strength and solidity: these things were built to endure.

In adapting this alien architecture from Europe, the hand of the Indian workman kept a memory of his ancient craft. Walls often slope, retaining a suggestion of the pyramid; carving repeats Indian motifs, or European motifs are subtly tinctured with Indian style. We saw saints and angels, on sixteenth-century churches, of which the squat shape, the very posture and flexing of their limbs, were almost identical with the form and posture of figurines found in prehistoric tombs. The sign of the sun, the rabbit of the moon—many a symbol of the old faith adorns the temples of the new.

Later, Renaissance architecture emphasized the dome, often ornamented with colored tiles; the style became more decorative, lighter.

As the Church grew wealthy, the early simplicity was vitiated. Decoration became more elaborate. The baroque style of Europe was intensified in Mexico into florid carving and heavy encrustation of gold. Churrigueresque baroque, in Mexico, became more Churrigueresque than José Churriguera himself.

In interiors, sometimes in façades as well, it appears to have been felt that every available inch must be decorated, every line broken. Form and color ran wild. The result is, to modern taste, often an architectural bad dream, a confusion to the eye.

It is almost impossible to grasp so much detail of carving; the gold crushes with its weight; the gilded and daubed saints leave no rest for the sight.

An authority on Colonial architecture explained to me very simply the distinguishing characteristics of the principal styles or substyles:

Plateresque—derived, as the name indicates, from the designs of silversmiths—runs to straight horizontal lines.

Baroque affects curved lines, or straight lines broken by curves; ornamented panels; round or twisted ("Solomonic," he called them) columns.

Churrigueresque squares the column, increases the decoration, breaks and re-breaks all the lines. Pilasters are fractured in a series of inverted pyramid forms.

One will find few examples of any style unmixed. Builders and decorators borrowed from all sources, The octagonal chapel with alabaster cupola in Tepotzotlán shows elements of at least five European and Asiatic styles, mingled with American Indian symbols.

Still later came a revival of Greco-Roman or neo-Classic style—columns and capitals of the Greek orders, polished surfaces of colored marble, and other features that often harmonize but poorly with the walls of an older time that enclose them.

There are Byzantine influences, and Moorish: the Mudéjar style with its polychrome tiles and modified Arabic decorative motifs; here and there a touch of Gothic. But nearly always there has been a hybridization of foreign styles subtly modified by native influence—the lingering craftsmanship of the pyramid-builder, the spirit of the Mexican earth.

More recently, urban architecture has begun to go "modernistic," following what is probably a temporary trend copied—often badly—from German and North American models. Wealthy suburbs are full of hollow cubes of concrete intended to be "functional." At their worst, they are ugly; at their best they might qualify as a modern and more hygienic version of Mexican adobe architecture.

Villas of Cuernavaca and certain other places repeat the "California Spanish" of Hollywood.

But there is dignity in the perpendicularly extended step-pyramids of modern "set-back" office buildings, such as those which rise incongruously between old-rose Colonial palaces and mellow-tiled Mudéjar façades in Mexico City. They are modeled after prototypes in New York and Chicago and San Francisco, but it is not difficult to imagine that the temple architecture of ancient Mexico might have developed, with time, in some such direction. Here again are the outlines of the volcanic peak, the skyward thrust of the cliff, the soaring walls of the barranca. Such an architecture, though it clashes with Colonial surroundings, has in it something of the character of the landscape.

Poetry in Stone

So from the stepped pyramid, through the flowering stone and writhing exuberance of a style afflicted with architectural "proud flesh," back, even if by an alien influence, to the stepped pyramid in a new exaltation: that is, briefly, the story of building in Mexico.

L · FACE OF THE LORD OF DAWN

IN the National Museum at Mexico City there is a prehistoric sculptured head in hard greenish stone, simple and massive, but delicately carved. The features are strong but gentle; the expression is one of repose; the eyes look out with a deep serenity, an Oriental calm. It is said to represent the Feathered Serpent in his aspect as Lord of the House of Dawn. And the statement that sculptors of other lands have not surpassed its quality might reasonably be defended.

It seems to say that the little irritations and distractions pass, but the deep, tenacious rhythms of Nature and of human life go on.

Few of the ancient gods imaged in the enduring stone are so attractive to look upon. For in ancient Mexico, as in most

386

parts of the world, a god was esteemed in proportion as he was feared. The faces of most of the sacred images are deliberately hideous, emphasizing the harsh, irresistible powers of Nature. It is noteworthy that the actual features, in many cases, do not appear: the gods are masked.

Xipe-Totec, in his garb of human skin; Tlaloc, with his face covered by the writhing snakes of the rain, or looking through round or square goggle-eyeholes; Huitzilopochtli of the gold-speared sun of war; the serpent-skirted mother of the gods— all are in varying degree frightful.

But art is not concerned solely with pretty things, nor with literal interpretation, but with ideas, with principles that are considered fundamental truths of Nature and of life. The mother of heaven is claw-handed because she devours corpses of men, but her breasts are flabby because they have fed with the milk of life her children, gods and men. She is the union of opposite principles of Nature: birth and death, creation and destruction, the earth giving life to all and receiving all life back into itself. Xipe-Totec wears the flayed skin of a sacrificial victim because he symbolizes renewal of the earth's garment of growing things in spring. Tlazoltéotl is depicted as a scavenger because she eats the sins of men, leaving the spirit pure.

Works that are presumably human portraits are often comparatively realistic. The Feathered Serpent himself, in his human form as Kukulkán, looks with grave, mild eyes, from his worn features, above un-Indian beard, from his doorway at Chichén toward the Sacred Well. The so-called "Sad Indian," in his dignified simplicity, might, if we did not know his history, have been carved by a modern artist of any land. In his functioning life, he upheld a banner before the temple; now, in reduplicated miniature, he serves as a book-end or a paper-weight.

Whether realistic or symbolic, or distorted for ideological or esthetic reasons, the ancient sculptures of Mexico were conceived and executed with profound feeling for proportion and form, for rhythm, for all the plastic values. Those anonymous masters could be literal enough when they wished: an Aztec dog, an ocelot, a frog in dark stone, worn into proper shape and texture by untold days of patient rubbing with sand, are as lifelike as if cast from living models. The highly imaginative concept of the Divine Mother, fantastic as is its general scheme, is executed with fine precision of detail: every scale of her serpent skirt, every severed hand and plucked-out heart of her necklace, every fold of her pendant ornament, is carved with meticulous accuracy.

This elaborate art has been admired by high authority. I must confess that I am more drawn to the simpler, quieter strength of certain early Maya heads, the serenity of the jade-skirted Lady of the Flowing Water and of Chicomecóatl, red-skinned goddess of the corn.

Before the rhythmic stone came the clay figurines that are found in the tombs and scattered in the fields—individual portraits, some of them must be—and along with them, little clay dogs so lifelike that the characteristics of the breed may be traced. They were modeled at first by hand; the Toltecs later cast them in molds, and tourists at Teotihuacan buy, along with perhaps a few ancient relics, recently made ones cast in the same or similar molds.

Stone was more difficult to work with primitive tools, but in time the art developed a skilful technic. After one becomes accustomed to the Maya notion of filling all available space with design, the procession of nobles and priests on the walls and pillars of Chichén Itza acquires nobility of form. And the little leaping jaguar on the ruined vault of the lower Jaguar temple, the animal frieze along the Temple of the Warriors, are marvels of truthfully portrayed action.

Perhaps its setting, in the darkness of the buried temple under the House of Kukulkán, enhances the dramatic impressiveness of the "Red Tiger." It is a bizarre creation: a simplified body in red stone, bearing spots of inlaid green jade; jade eyes

Face of the Lord of Dawn

blazing back at you above bared white teeth. But that stone jaguar in the tomblike darkness at the top of the buried stair is one of the things I shall remember longest from Chichén.

The Spaniards brought the art of another faith, which felt in turn the impress of the Mexican spirit. Churches are full of suffering saints and tortured Christs, whose wounds and expressions of anguish are depicted with a harsh realism.

For still the god must be frightful. These are but frightful in a different way. The suffering of humanity, in that land of hunger and cold and disease and long oppression, is chiseled and molded into these forms of wood and wax, of plaster and stone. The old consciousness of the harshness of life, the imminence of death, is in them as in the skull-wearing Mother of the Gods, the blood-drinking Child of the Hummingbird. They are the saddest gods I have seen in any land.

The Indians prefer them so. The story is told of a wealthy lady who gave a comparatively attractive saint to the church of the town in which she was sojourning, to replace one she thought unspeakably hideous. The following of that saint suddenly fell away; in time the new image disappeared, to be replaced by the old and ugly and beloved one that was nearer to the Indian heart.

Perhaps a psychological principle is involved. The tortured saints, having themselves suffered, understand human sorrows. Juan and Pedro, María and Conchita can talk to them in confidence; they will comfort, they will not fail.

Of them all, only the Holy Mother walks consistently in beauty. It is a various loveliness: Our Lady of Solitude at Oaxaca wears the beauty of a high-born lady of Toledo or Seville; she of the Remedies has the form of a crude doll; but the most beloved, the Dark Madonna of Guadalupe, blesses mankind with the Indian features and the gentle calm of the Jade-Skirted Mistress of the Flowing Water or the Seven Serpent Woman of the Corn—a serenity equal to but more human than that of the green Master of the Morning Star.

Pattern of Mexico

In life there must be beauty and terror and sorrow; so then the gods, being fashioned in the image of man's thought, must be beautiful, terrible, and sad. In few places is this more true than in Mexico, where beauty and terror and sadness walk so swiftly in their visible forms across the harsh face of the land.

Mexicans still carve in wood, in ivory, in stone. Some of their work follows European themes and technics: Mexico has rather more than the usual rash of stiff bronze generals and statesmen in its public parks. But some late sculpture is definitely of the land. They no longer carve the ancient gods, but the roots of their art are in the soil that produced those gods; the works are fashioned with the same instinct for rhythm and form.

I have before me a foot-high figure carved in some mellow, creamy, fine-textured Oaxaca wood. Around its base it bears still the brown, striated bark. Cut back in the peeled wood, bare toes peep from beneath the severe but flowing lines of a long skirt. The arms, the outlines of the body, are hidden under the shawl, whose few simple folds follow the curved grain of the wood. All is simplified, plain, clean. Only the face is sculptured in detail: the face of an Indian woman, head slightly to the side, eyes downcast, features serene but unsmiling, the surface worked in fine pits and lines, as of smallpox or of age. The hair, straight, parted in the middle, and drawn back over the ears, flows at either side of the low forehead in the delicate colored lines of the wood; the grain of the wood swirls into a tiny knot at the top of the head.

It is sad and serene, like the more gentle of the holy images, and with a beautiful plainness, a restful simplicity. It is carved with a true feeling for the material, adapting itself to that material, preserving the clean nobility of the wood.

It is signed "Ruíz." For the art of Mexico is no longer invariably anonymous as when the friezes of Uxmal and Chichén were carved, or the serpent façade of Teotihuacan.

Rain was spearing down into the patio of the Free School of

Face of the Lord of Dawn

Plastic Arts, and we had taken shelter in a shed that served as an atelier in which Guillermo Ruíz was instructing young workers. Their exercises were scattered about: tastefully simplified animals in stone, heads and figures in clay, wooden statuettes similar to mine, if less distinctively done. In another shed, they were casting a colossal bronze; across the way, Máximo Pacheco was directing eager young painters.

On the work-bench stood, perhaps as a model, perhaps the employment of his spare time, this bit of sheer beauty from the hand of Ruíz himself. It shares my affection with a small prehistoric goddess in porous gray volcanic stone, to which the gray soil of Ixtapalápa still clings, and a little, black, squat basalt household god of the Tlahuica tribe.

The modern piece is more sophisticated, perhaps; of finer workmanship, certainly; but all three have that monumental simplicity, that patient serenity; all three are truly functional, integral with their material.

LI · COLORS OF DEATH AND LIFE

THE ancient peoples of Mexico wrote in picture; their sacred books and histories are a panorama of color and form. They decorated vases with human and divine figures as well as with geometrical design. They painted, as well as carved, façades and colonnades, and they frescoed temple interiors.

I have already referred to the prehistoric paintings at Chichén Itza. On the wall of the lower chamber of the Jaguar Temple there, a procession approaches an altar of the Feathered Serpent. Time has worn away the stone, and perhaps dulled the colors, but the stately forms, the robes and feather headdresses, spears and spear-throwers, nose-jewels of jade or turquoise, still are clear. True fresco is more perishable, but a little remains of a historic scene on the wall of an upper room in the same temple: elliptical thatched houses, the sea and canoes, fighting warriors—with repeated motifs of circle and diagonal in round shields and slanting spears.

All this wasn't just art for art's sake. It told a story or imparted a doctrine. The artist wasn't free to follow his own fancy. The form and garments and color of each god or hero were prescribed by tradition, leaving the artist little latitude. But working within those limits, he often achieved considerable freedom in spite of them. Nearly always, he created a work that has artistic value to-day when the lesson it was intended to teach may be no longer legible.

A woodland scene, now crumbled away from the wall of the Temple of the Warriors but preserved by an archæologist's copy, is an example of what could be done with stylized trees and animals in a beautiful relation of form and rhythm. An altar frieze at Teotihuacan reduced sacred symbols to pure design of high decorative quality. A battle scene in a Mixtec picture-history, portraying an army attacking an island town, stylizes forms of aquatic life with clever plastic sense.

Christianity brought European art. Almost every church of consequence has its copies of Murillo and other Spanish masters and their Colonial imitators; and the San Carlos galleries in the Capital are said to have more "old masters" than any other collection in the Western Hemisphere.

Mexican painters of the Colonial and early Republic periods imitated, for the most part, foreign models. Their art is often finely executed, but it is mainly a softer and weaker version of Spanish style. One wearies of round-faced, pink-fleshed cherubs and insipid Madonnas, as well as of gruesome saints and livid Christs. The Mexican contribution in those periods was, with some exceptions, a sentimentalizing of the more pleasant scenes and a morbid heightening of the unpleasant ones.

Later, Mexican art still imitated foreign art. The predominant influence was French. Much of the product was pretty but sterile, having no roots in the soil.

This situation continued until the political Revolution of 1910 was followed by a revolution in Mexican art. One result of the ferment in the air was the rediscovery and revaluation of the indigenous Mexican, the Indian.

Artists began to adapt to native material what they had learned abroad, fusing the foreign with the native and remolding it in the Mexican image. Prehistoric art was rediscovered and viewed with new respect. The ancient Mexican process of teaching an unlettered people through art was revived to serve the Revolution. Art became a medium of political, economic, and cultural propaganda.

Most art that is vital has a purpose. At least, purpose doesn't invalidate art. A modern Mexican style began to take form. José Vasconcelos, as minister of education in the Obregón government, gave the artists walls on which to paint. And thus the art of fresco was reborn.

Artists of Mexico remembered, then, the painted walls of Chichén and of Teotihuacan, the squat, expressive human figures in Aztec codices, scenes on ancient vases from Guatemala and Yucatán. They remembered, too, the decorations on Uruápan lacquer, the satiric woodcuts of pamphleteers and illustrators of popular ballads. They recalled the crude but forceful murals on walls of pulque shops, the quaintly pious votive paintings in humble churches. Some remembered also the Italian primitives, the Byzantines. Art of Old World and New flowed together to form something vital and indigenous and new.

To many North Americans, Mexican mural art means Diego Rivera and José Clemente Orozco. They have been considered preëminent in their own country as well, but there were and are many others. For a time it seemed that every wall in Mexico would be emblazoned with revolutionary slogans in fresco. I saw, however, a number of murals, begun years ago, which remained unfinished. I understood an art authority to say that this was because governments often forgot to pay the artists. But at least they had walls to offer them.

Many people disliked this dynamic art, disagreeing with its social purpose. Students from conservative families mutilated Orozco's frescoes in the National Preparatory School; acid scarred Rivera's pictorial history in the National Palace; even some of the panels in the Ministry of Education have been marred.

The initial wave of mural painting in Mexico has passed, but I saw several formidable projects in process, including some as powerful as any in the earlier period. In another chapter I describe briefly the great works of Orozco in Guadalajara.

Though, as stated, Orozco and Rivera are giants in Mexico as abroad, there are dozens of other significant artists in that country. It would be tedious to enumerate them or to attempt to describe their work; it must be seen to be appreciated.

The feeling has begun to be expressed by some critics that Mexican art is repeating itself, the Revolutionary movement crystallizing into its own academicism, the creative impulse gone stale, and there are evidences that this is partly true.

But the interesting thing is that new talents continue to appear, often in unpromising surroundings. Fernando Castillo, for instance, no longer young, but distinctive—a Mexican primitive, who reads and writes, I was told, only with difficulty. He sells newspapers on the streets and in his spare time carries on in his own way the heritage of the folk art of *pulqueria* paintings, retablos and codices, in naïve detail that recalls the meticulous dream-forests of Rousseau le Douanier.

And there are sudden bursts, like Guillermo Meza.

Inéz Amor told me of him, as we sat in her studio whither much of the finest modern art of Mexico finds its way.

"A young Indian came to see me," she related. "He had shown some of his paintings to Rivera, and Rivera, who is kind to young artists, sent him to me.

Pattern of Mexico

"I believe that young Indian, Guillermo Meza, is one of the greatest talents ever born in Mexico.

"He is what you call in your country a 'natural.' He is entirely self-taught. He had no family background of art. The son of a tailor, he has never been out of Mexico City. Until he came to my studio, he had seen no art except reproductions of a few Italian classics, which his own work does not at all resemble. It resembles, in fact, nothing he could ever have seen.

"He has drawn, he tells me, since childhood, but began to paint only recently. He is a born surrealist, though he had never heard of surrealism or seen a surrealist work.

"Some one remarked that his work suggested that of Van Gogh, and asked him if he knew the work of that artist.

" 'Who is Van Gogh?' " he inquired.

"An American artist who was present invited him to her studio. He was delighted, for, he said, 'I have never seen an artist at work.' "

When one sees the quality of art produced by children in the schools, who are purposely left free of formal art instruction, one begins to understand how all this amazing activity is possible. The Indian instinct for form and proportion, for color and rhythm, is welded with the Spanish instinct that filled monasteries and cathedrals and palaces with plastic expression.

What makes so much modern Mexican art significant is its vitality, rooted in the ancient art of the land and in the contemporary life of the Mexican people. In that strength, much of it should endure.

LII · PICTURED WALLS

EVEN if one accepts Jean Charlot's doctrine that art is vital in proportion as it is purposive, many North Americans will appreciate the greater part of Mexican mural art only by separating it from its subject matter. Neither approval nor disapproval of the characteristic theme of "the rich reveling while the workers starve" is properly involved in one's admiration of the strength and directness of the drawing, the glow of color set deftly against color, the balanced harmony of composition, the answering chorded sweep of rhythm.

There is a panel in the Secretariat of Education that glows before me even now as I sit these thousands of miles from it. It is night: men in uniform pore over a book. In the foreground, men in sarapes and broad curving hats, women with rebozos around their shoulders, and barefoot children huddle, asleep. Here is tenderness and strength, the deep pulse of the heart of Mexico, the crimson flow of its blood. The inclination of the sleeping forms, the lassitude of the reposing bodies, the relaxed droop of the hands, are supremely just and quiet and right.

The bulk of Rivera's mural testimony, apart from its doctrinal trend, is one great pageant of Mexico: its history, its geography, and above all, the life of its people. Nor did he, while painting under the auspices of a revolutionary government, slavishly glorify his sponsors. The left-wall panel of the National Palace stairway is a keen criticism of the fruits of the Revolution, as borne in the administrations of Calles and Obregón.

I saw peasants, sombrero in hand, sandals planted firmly on stone floors, standing mute and reverent before this tremendous triad, or in the loggia of the Cortés palace—and, too, before Orozco's colossal Padre Hidalgo at Guadalajara: reading, like their ancestors, their country's story on its walls.

"There is a contrast, don't you think? Guadalajara so quiet and peaceful, and my frescoes, they are not so."

José Clemente Orozco was speaking, beneath the tall thrust of the chapel dome at the Hospicio in Guadalajara—scaffoldings rising like gallows about him, the murals sprawling in eloquent violence along the vast walls.

Indeed, these powerful swirling compositions do seem, at first sight, shattering, with their livid cadavers, tormented faces, visions of starvation and slaughter. One becomes accustomed to them, however; the anatomical fragments fall into their places in the orchestrated composition, so cleverly adjusted to the architectural space.

I had been warned locally that Orozco was "difficult" and "unapproachable," but I found him as kindly and open a man as I had met in Mexico. From behind the thick lenses and the deep-contoured, oddly converging planes of the rugged face looked out a personality sensitive, it is true—whence, no doubt, the legend—but simple, quiet, charming, and modest, though with a wholesome consciousness of his own great talent.

"People say he is bitter," commented his wife. "That is because they do not know him. He is bitter in his art, yes; but in his own life, no."

And yet one can see that the tormented, stormy fury of his compositions must proceed in part at least from a fierce resentment within: for the wrongs of the masses in Mexico since the Conquest; for the graft and oppression of some "Revolutionary" governments which have meant, often, merely a change of masters. More than likely, too, the accumulated wounds of his own harsh life speak: the poverty of his native village in Jalisco; the maiming blast of a firework that tore away an arm in youth; public misunderstanding of his work, and neglect of governments to pay him for months of contracted professional labor.

Orozco has done three great projects in Guadalajara: the auditorium of the University, the stairway of the Government Palace, and more recently the chapel of the Orphanage—a tremendous work, this last, covering walls, ceiling, and dome of a hall as big as a city church. It was, he admitted, his largest fresco project to that date, involving new problems of space relations and of the use of a spherical surface.

In the University rotunda, Man the Thinker, the Builder, the Scientist, the Rebel, confronts himself in the flaming swirl of the cupola, while below, the False Science cowers before the Awakener, facing the problem of human suffering, and the soldiers of the Revolution lay down their rifles and take up tools to build anew. At least, this is the rough conclusion one may draw for those who demand a story; the artist himself deprecates such literal and confining interpretation. These are forms, elements of design, not symbols, he insists.

Pattern of Mexico

Perhaps he "protests too much." For any one can recognize, to the right of the stair of the Palace, certain widely publicized dictators among what one commentator has identified as "the clowns misleading the people." "And the people misleading themselves," Orozco added when I quoted the commentary to him.

But on the vaulted ceiling, above scenes of battle and massacre and a scaly monster disgorging weapons, there is no mistaking the heroic figure of Hidalgo, father of Independence, a flaming torch in one hand, the other uplifted in a sweeping gesture over the noble head. Appropriate enough, too, for in this very building, it is recorded, Padre Hidalgo "signed freedom for the slaves."

The orchestration of color and form in the Orphanage, however, is more complex—at first sight, even confusing. "Hispanic forms," said the artist, "and Indian forms treated in an Hispanic manner, to make Mexicans conscious of their heritage, their national unity, their national personality." Only this, no detailed symbolism. Or, if you prefer, to each beholder his own symbolism.

"All the interpretations are right," he declared. "The important thing is that a work of art shall say something to each one who sees it, awaken some response in him."

The mailed horsemen of Cortés thunder across the wall, their lances aligned with the plunging hoofs; the blood-and-gold banner of Spain is reflected in a sunrise behind a great wheel rolling over fragments of archæological remains; an Aztec priest lifts high a dripping heart—and so on through sixty or more contributory units that lead up to the swirl of human bodies and fire that fills the inner surface of the dome with light.

For these huge, powerful panels are but the introduction, the supplement, to the vaster conception above: the four elements—Earth, dark and pensive; Water, fluent and fecund; the great green head of Air, and, dominating all, at the apex, the tremendous glowing figure, perhaps the divinity in Man, of Fire.

In the rotunda of the University, he seemed interested primarily in the problem of adapting art to architecture.

"Painting a fresco," he said, "is a process of logic, of reasoning. One has the space, the architectural dimensions, and adjusts one's work to them. It is similar to the architect's problem: he can't see the building until it's finished, but he knows how it is going to look. It exists in his mind. So with a mural."

The problem at the University was "to preserve the spherical space, not flatten it. Too many murals are just a series of landscapes or of figures, lacking structural unity and structural composition."

The theme, according to an analysis by Luís Cardoza y Aragón, which analysis, when I asked him, Orozco said was "as good as any," is "man, his plastic expression within the materialistic concept, abandoning trite and childish procedures and facile and worn-out allegories . . . the enormous theme of man confronting himself, without gods."

Four huge figures sum up the philosophy: the builder, with compass and rule; the cadaver on the dissecting table; the hanged figure of rebellion, and a man with five faces—the philosopher—looking with scientific curiosity in all directions.

Orozco recalled that when the late Leon Trotsky saw this work, he pointed to one of the "false prophets" in the lower panel, saying, "That is Jouhaux, isn't it?"

"In a way, perhaps," replied Orozco. "I don't know Jouhaux; I've never even seen a portrait of him. I just wanted to portray some false leader."

"It's he to the life," confirmed Trotsky. "Even to the way he wears his hat."

But, as Gómez Robledo has pointed out, all this "analysis" is secondary; the great quality of the work is its internal dynamism.

Pattern of Mexico

Birds were flying in and out through the broken cupola windows of the Orphanage, where Orozco, with deliberate movements, was painting a freshly plastered section of wall.

"They come to see the pictures," he said.

At the base of the opposite wall lay a *petate*—a Mexican mat—resting-place of the master when he took his siesta.

He showed us his "cartoon" for the section on which he was working: a very rough draft, a mere suggestion of forms, with not even the color filled in.

"It's in the mind first," he explained. "Most of the work is done on the scaffold. The application is more or less mechanical; that's why I can work eight hours a day."

So, day by day, he was welding that huge space, with its multiple vaults and arches, into a unified whole, preserving the architectural form.

These human figures with robot limbs, wheels and levers growing out of mutilated bodies: the juggernaut of industry, perhaps, crushing human life, feeding upon human blood?

"Just parts of bodies," he said, "—for the design."

Workmen were plastering narrow spaces beside doorways. "It's no use to paint there," he commented. "I'm going to leave that blank. I don't believe in covering every inch. Sometimes I wonder if there is not too much paint here."

Squares of plaster here and there bore dates, where he was trying out formulas, for resistance: iron oxide and other pigments in varying proportions. He didn't want to have to do this work over again, as he had done in the University. There, magnesium worked through from the lime, obscuring the picture with a white veil.

He was proud of his red: done with black and white beneath, and a transparent red added while the colors were still wet, it produces a peculiar brilliance which shows up even in competition with direct sunlight.

May not all his work, I fancied, be an allegory of the unending struggle of Mexico, through bloodshed, toward freedom;

the repeated human failures of its long history of blood sacrifices, and the undying hope that the spirit typified by Hidalgo will yet prevail? "From night, through blood, to light?"

"Your interpretation is as good as any," was all Orozco would say.

LIII · ART OF THE HUMBLE

MEXICO," says Frances Toor, an authority on the subject, "surpasses any other country on the American continent and many elsewhere, in the variety and artistic quality of its popular arts."

"Mexico," says Jean Charlot, "is esthetic to the core."

I have touched, briefly, on some of the art-crafts of the villages, in discussing the localities where they are practised. Their interest, for me, derives to a large extent from their expression of native artistic instinct and their traces of heritage from pre-Conquest times.

There is, of course, comparatively little of that heritage recognizable. The Conquest disrupted native life. In a time of chaos and oppression, old arts decayed; some, such as the iridescent feather mosaic, disappeared.

Friars, to rehabilitate their Indian wards, reorganized and encouraged some of the existing crafts, and introduced new ones. More recently, the government has interested itself in them. Hence, as Ixca Farías, head of the State Museum of Jalisco, told me, virtually all the popular arts of to-day are more or less "post-Cortesian."

However, styles change, even without such shattering upheavals as the Conquest. Pre-Spanish pottery, for instance, of a single people shows many different periods, involving distinct developments in decoration and form. The crafts of Mexico, had they been left undisturbed, might well have differed to-day from what they were in the time of the Feathered Snake or the Archer of Heaven. And craftsmen have made borrowed motifs their own, adapting them with Mexican touch.

Pottery, lacquer, weaving are the principal crafts surviving from ancient times.

Some of the relatively plain pottery, used by Indians themselves, is probably not very different from its counterpart of long ago. Much of that sold to visitors has doubtless been modified by the buyers' taste.

Ixca Farías has traced the evolution of pottery design around Guadalajara, a development which may be regarded as roughly typical of popular art history. Pre-Conquest remains are decorated chiefly with geometrical figures. From the Conquest to the revival of native arts after the Revolution of 1910, Farías finds European motifs, such as the double-headed eagle. The trend since then he attributes to the influence of Dr. Atl, who founded a school of design in Tonalá in 1914, and to the theories of Adolfo Best-Maugard as to "Mexican decorative art."

Atl introduced Maya frets; these the Tonaltecas "copied with much perfection, but committed the lamentable error of decorating a vase with ten or fifteen frets of distinct forms, since the ideology of these men is to cover the complete surface of whatever they decorate."

The cacti, peons and burros of Tlaquepaque pottery are doubtless a later notion, in response to demands of the trade. The manager of a pottery, pointing to a piece decorated with conventional forms in parallel and cross-hatching lines of black, told me, "This is what the Indians do when left to themselves. Those picture-book things are done to order."

At San Pedro and other widely visited pottery centers, the wheel is used, but in more remote places, such as Coyotepec, out of Oaxaca, the process follows the method used by North American "Pueblo" tribes, in which the dish is built up entirely by hand, coiling strips of the material on a hand-shaped foundation, and shaping it by revolving the growing piece with one hand around the fingers of the other. The black Coyotepec pottery sold in Oaxaca markets, which is made in this manner, is so fine of texture that, when tapped, it rings like a bell. The ware of Puebla, where friars taught the Indians to imitate the Talavera of Spain, is said to be the strongest, though I was told the green pottery of Santa María Azompa, sold in Oaxaca, could be used as baking-dishes.

In general, the best pottery is the simplest and that in which beauty of form, rather than elaborateness of decoration, commands attention. And that is what the Indians will make, usually, if left to themselves.

Early friars found the Tarascans of Michoacán lacquering wood in simple fret designs, and they marveled at the beauty and delicacy of the art.

The process, basically, has not changed much, though inferior materials and the haste inspired by market demands have caused some deterioration. But connoisseurs complain of a decline in design.

Old pieces in museums already show foreign influences, attributable perhaps to Bishop Vasco de Quiroga, who revived

THE COUNTRYSIDE THRONGS IN TO THE OPEN-AIR MARKET

the native arts to improve the economic status of the people. But these examples are better in design and color than most of those in the markets to-day.

Oriental influences also entered, with Colonial trade from China, and may still be traced. Ixca Farías said a Frenchman in 1900 introduced new European designs. And later, Miguel Othon de Mendizábal, when director of popular arts, introduced stylizations of flowers, leaves, and birds which are prominent in Uruápan lacquer to-day. Although purists have objected to these designs as not in harmony with the indigenous genius, the best Uruápan and Olinalá work is attractive in its gaiety of color and quaintness of form. The worst we saw was at Quiroga, near Pátzcuaro, where decoration had run wild in sprawling flower-shapes, too large for the background, and in glaring color combinations. The pottery was as bad. Both reminded me of Ixca Farías' criticism of modern lacquer decoration as "an ignorant copy of a chromo."

But it is in the processes that the unscrupulous commit the worst sins. True lacquer work is a long and patient task. Three weeks is the minimum time for producing a small and simple piece. Some of the more complex take months. With increasing commercialism, some pieces are not allowed to dry long enough between applications of color. These may look just as good in the market. The visitor carries them away in delight. In a few weeks or months the oil has soaked through, ruining the color, or the lacquer has cracked. The only security I know is to find the oldest lacquer-painter in town, show an interest in the process, and then take the pieces he recommends. Or buy from a reputable big-city dealer pieces that have been in his shop long enough to begin to show any imperfections that may exist. Lacquer can't be hurried.

The horizontal loom, I am told, was introduced from Spain; the vertical loom is Indian, but the product of both is genuine hand work. An increasing amount of Mexican textile work, however, comes from motor-driven machinery.

This craft, too, has deteriorated. The old-time sarapes of Saltillo are museum pieces; their like is not made to-day. The gaudy ones, with the eagle sitting on the cactus, or the "calendar stone" emblazoned across the back, are for the foreign trade. The Indian in most regions wears more sober colors and less flamboyant designs.

The best sarapes, Ixca Farías tells his students in Guadalajara, are made in the vicinity of Oaxaca, in Texcoco, and in Santana Chautempan, on the south slope of the mountain Malinche. Their forerunners were of cotton, for wool was introduced by the Spaniards. Wool is now the most frequent material, sometimes mixed with cotton or with goats' hair. Genuine Indian designs are in stripes or geometrical motifs, occasionally with stylized animal forms. Each town or district has its characteristic colors and patterns. Santana Chautempan, for instance, makes two types: the "Cholula" sarape is gray, with a design in white; the "Tlaxcala" sarape is of coffee-color with Indian motifs in white.

Teotitlán del Valle, near Mitla, is the most celebrated center of the Oaxaca textile craft. The characteristic Teotitlán sarape is in soft grays and whites, sometimes with a stylized animal form against a red ground in the center. Another Oaxaca type is white, with blue, gray, or black border. But, as I have said, every district has its own.

As Mexican now as the sarape, although introduced originally from Spain, is the rebozo—three yards or so of cloth, half a yard wide, worn by women around head or shoulders. In Colonial times, when the rebozo was worn by both upper and lower classes, peons were restricted by law to brown, blue, or dark green, with white. Those who sought distinction within those limitations added silver and gold threads and wove the fabric so fine that, according to legend, the whole garment could be passed through a finger ring. Most rebozos to-day are dark blue, with a fine pattern in white, produced, in the best pieces, by tying knots in the material before it is dipped in the dye. For festal occasions, women of Michoacán wear a more elaborate rebozo, usually in a brilliant blue, sometimes with stripes.

Embroidery is another flourishing textile craft. We saw many embroidered blouses, particularly in the market at Orizaba, less ornate but more tasteful ones worn by women in Yucatán, and barbaric ones adorning the sturdy Tehuanas. There are sashes, too, varying from district to district, some relatively plain, some with geometrical designs in contrasting colors, very "Indian."

Textiles that have changed least are probably the *ayate,* or carrying-cloth, and the *petate,* or mat of palm leaf or reeds— both said to be virtually the same in material and design as in pre-Spanish times. And nearly every visitor brings home a basket—now usually in the Mexican national colors of red, green, and white and often bearing the maker's name worked in the material.

Other popular arts are mostly of Colonial or modern origin. There was fine pre-conquest work in precious metals, most of which was melted up to swell the royal treasury of Spain, though a few exquisite pieces, found more recently in tombs, survive in museums. Some fine gold filigree, owing perhaps more to European than to native models, is done in Yucatán.

Silver work for the market is said to date from about the time of Maximilian. I was told in the Capital that silver, being plentiful, was not considered in Colonial times a worthy material for jewelry. Most of the designs, however, another authority said, are Colonial. Recently, some craftsmen have been adapting to silver ancient Indian motifs from other arts —pottery, textiles, stone carving.

Work in tin and copper has had a similar history. The onyx of Puebla is worked into paper-weights, little "Guadalupe" images, and a host of objects of tourist-bait. There is also a great deal of gaudily painted furniture: leather, commonly of inferior quality and workmanship, and ubiquitously stamped with the Calendar Stone or the perennial eagle and cactus. There is some glassware, of Colonial origin, still made almost entirely by hand. Tiny glass figures of animals, human beings, and so forth, often are exquisite.

In such places as the Capital, one may find clever wax sculptors, whose caricatures are often very amusing, and who will also essay a serious portrait. Mme. Calderón de la Barca tells the story of a general who had such a portrait made. One of his friends, inspecting it, remarked: "The features are like him, but don't you think the color of the skin is too light?"

"The general washed his face before he sat for the portrait," the artist replied.

There are ingenious toys made of straw or of palm-leaves; dance masks of wood or tin, still used by certain tribes— lacquered masks of Michoacán, papier-mâché false faces worn at fiestas; musical instruments and carved chocolate-beaters made especially at Paracho. Even quaint and rather repulsive "dressed fleas" are common in the curio shops along the Avenida Juárez.

One of the strangest arts, however, is the fabrication of figurines of chicle (the raw material of chewing-gum). A center of this craft is Talpa, at the western edge of the central plateau. The gum, extracted from a tree, is softened with hot water and cast in clay molds into shapes of baskets, flowers, animals, and reproductions of sacred images, tinted with aniline dyes.

One of the roots of the sophisticated art of Mexico is the mural of the *pulquería*.

A *pulquería* is a shop which retails pulque, beverage of the lowly, which, according to legend, brought about the downfall of those in high places: the exile of Quetzalcoátl, the decay of the Toltec empire. So has pulque fallen from its high estate.

Art of the Humble

Once its use was restricted to the old and noble, and the maguey, of whose juice it is a fermentation, was a sacred plant.

Now, pulque is the drink of the humble, as well as a source of the fortunes of the mighty. The beverage invented by the gods has become a commercial product. Yet something of its ancient sacredness lingers. It is said that the man who sucks the juice through a gourd into the vessel in which it is collected, murmurs, as he does so, a prayer. When he empties it into the vat of hide in which, with the addition of miscellaneous garbage, it is to ferment, he takes off his hat. At the end of the fermenting-shed, a saint presides behind lighted candles and colored paper decorations—a sacred emblem from the ancient time.

Pulque is unobtainable in *cantinas*—the bars of Mexico. It is sold only in *pulquerías*. They bear names heroic, poetic, whimsical: "The Deeds of Obregón," "The Gate of Heaven," "Let's See What Will Happen." Colored paper hangs over the doors and inside. The walls bear murals, in violent, quickly deteriorating colors. It is said that the Health Department once forbade these paintings, requiring that *pulquerías* be whitewashed. Trade fell off so alarmingly that upon petition of the *pulquería* owners (who marched in protest), the prohibition was removed.

These murals are a kind of glorified sign-painting, done by professionals, but considered a folk art. Subjects may be classical or historical or genre; I saw one that was almost surrealist. But the majority, apparently, are sentimental. The best of them express the life of the land; they are of the people.

Another root of modern Mexican art is in the *retablo* or "miracle painting" attached to a church wall. These are usually small, painted in oils, most often on tin, but sometimes in water color or crayon on cardboard. They are, in great part, the votive offerings of the poor.

Almost anything, in Mexico, may be regarded as a miracle.

411

Pattern of Mexico

To recover from illness: surely that could happen only if a saint intervened. An escape from bandits—even escape with one's life but without one's property—is a clear case of divine aid. The Revolution filled the churches with battle scenes. Factory and railway and traffic accidents, fire, flood, earthquake, storm, or the humbler accidents of daily life—all equally are material. A common theme is release or escape from prison.

The picture may be painted by the recipient of divine favor himself, or by a hired professional who specializes in ex-votos. If the latter provides the picture, he doesn't sign it. The inscription merely sets forth the place, date, circumstances, and name of the donor, and that of the saint by whom the miracle was performed.

The prevailing style is a primitive realism, simplified to essentials. The technic may be crude, but surprisingly often a just proportion, a balanced, coördinated design, are achieved —as Rivera has said, "complete and national art."

It is, of course, an exaggeration to say, as I have often heard: "Everything the Indian touches is artistic." The Indian is not infallible, especially when adapting foreign material or seeking to satisfy foreign taste. But on ground with which he is familiar, in works that are related to the life he knows, he seldom errs. Mexico produced anciently, and still produces to-day, folk art of a peculiar and valid beauty.

APPENDIX
Practical Considerations

AROUND, NOT THROUGH

MANY practical details of Mexican travel—such as customs regulations and other border formalities, money exchange, transportation and accommodations —are subject to change, and it would be of little value to discuss them here save in the most general terms. In any case, they should be checked with authorities or with transportation or travel agencies.

One may suggest, however, a few broad principles applying to travel in any foreign country, and some of them applying particularly to Mexico.

Mexico has been inclined, on the whole, to make travel easy for foreigners. Usually in the past no passport has been required of United States citizens who come for travel *per se*, but only a "tourist card" issued by a Mexican consulate or obtainable often through transportation or travel agencies. Persons traveling on business, however, have been considered subject to Mexican immigration regulations, and special documents have been required of them. On the United States side of the border, it is wise to register objects of foreign manufacture, such as cameras, before crossing, to avoid question of duty on reëntry. For those taking automobiles across the border, there are Mexican formalities required.

Medical men commonly advise precautions, such as immunization from typhoid and the like, and vaccination against smallpox, which, however, is not as prevalent as it once was. They will also offer advice on proper care to avoid ailments for which immunization has not been developed.

Dysentery is the visitor's principal hazard, though it should not be allowed to induce a phobia. It does not seem to be preventable with any certainty, and the stranger lacks the partial immunity which a resident may have acquired. If contracted, it is likely, in most cases, to be annoying rather than serious, resulting in a few days of discomfort, and responding to treatment which a physician can advise in advance. There is a virulent type which may require more serious measures, but in places tourists are likely to visit, this is somewhat less frequent.

Travelers are usually advised to avoid, in general, raw vegetables, especially lettuce, and raw fruits except those with protective skins or shells; to drink boiled, electrically purified, or bottled water, or where these are not obtainable, beer. The Mexican press, several times while I was there, called attention to poisoning from adulterated soft cheeses of the perishable sort. (Dry cheeses are safe enough.) Raw milk is under suspicion, though I drank it with impunity.

The water supply in most cities frequented by tourists is, however, reasonably safe, as is food in the better hotels and restaurants. For emergencies, drugstores sell tablets which are intended to chlorinate small quantities of doubtful water.

Around, Not Through

I was assured in each town: "Señor, our water is absolutely pure. You can drink it in entire security." Then my informant would warn me earnestly of the next town: "The water there, señor, is very bad." And in the next town I would be assured that its water was of unblemished purity, whereas that of the town I had just left was practically deadly.

This recalls the story of the stranger who inquired: "What do you do to purify the water here?"

"First we boil it," was the reply. "Then we filter it. And then, señor, we drink pulque."

Visitors, especially in high altitudes, are commonly advised to eat lightly at night, slow down the pace to which they have been accustomed, and not try to do too much in a day. All Mexico takes its siesta for an hour or two after the midday meal, and the visitor is better off if he does likewise. If he tries to keep going, he finds there is little he can do in that time, anyhow. Most places he wants to go are closed.

Aside from that, the altitude of the Capital, in particular, is believed to affect the nervous system, causing susceptible persons to become irritable or depressed. Some one has even attributed the ancient Aztecs' warlike habits, and their propensity for human sacrifice, to their residence at that height.

In general, the more one can go into slow motion, the better off he is. If Mexico is that way, there's undoubtedly a reason.

There is malaria in tropical districts, especially on the east coast. It is preventable by avoiding bites of nocturnal mosquitoes that carry the infection. Hotels in such districts usually provide mosquito nets, or screen their windows. The doubly cautious may carry their own nets and fortify themselves, on their physicians' advice, with preventive drugs.

It is all very well to be careful, but one shouldn't occupy one's mind with it to the extent of detracting from one's enjoyment. Thousands of North Americans visit Mexico every year without serious trouble. Many go back again and again.

Pattern of Mexico

Exchange varies, but for many years has been "favorable." That is, one may expect to get several pesos, the Mexican monetary unit, for one dollar. This doesn't necessarily mean that, if one gets, for example, five pesos for a dollar, those five pesos will buy five dollars' worth of food, shelter or merchandise. In most cases, they won't. Money will go farther in Mexico than at home, but not as far as that. There is local variation, and another variation among different kinds of commodities and services: prices are higher in the larger cities and places more frequented by tourists; articles in which labor is the main element of cost range closer to the peso scale, and those in which the main factor is material approach more nearly the dollar scale. In practice, normal expenses have tended to run between one-half and two-thirds what one would pay in the United States.

The time has gone by when one had to carry around a weight of silver pesos, except in remote districts. We found that travelers' checks were accepted in any city of reasonable size and in any place where visitors are frequent. Banking in Mexico is slow and inconvenient, and when sufficiently familiar with Mexican currency one may, by dealing with professional money-changers, save time and also often get a slightly better rate than at banks or hotels.

It is possible to tour most of Mexico speaking only English, as the language is understood and spoken sufficiently in tourist centers; however, a knowledge of Spanish, even if only slight, heightens the interest and enjoyment of one's visit, and may at times be of practical value. Spanish is one of the easiest foreign languages in which to acquire adequate, if not fluent, ability to express one's self.

One time of year is about as good as another to visit Mexico. One takes one's choice of conditions. Between May and October, for most parts of the country, is the "rainy" season. This doesn't mean continuous downpour. In the Capital, for instance, the rain gathers in the afternoon, at the edge

of the valley, moving darkly over the city. It falls gustily, in
large drops, commonly not very hard or very long. People pay
it little heed. One rarely sees an umbrella—there isn't room
for them on the narrow sidewalks—and only occasionally a
raincoat. Groups stand in doorways and under awnings, waiting for the shower to pass. They have time to wait, in Mexico.
It passes; the air is fresh and fragrant.

In the dry season—between October and May—there is, in
most places, no rain to interfere even slightly with sightseeing,
but one must reckon with dust—dense clouds of it in some regions—and possibly with dust-borne infections.

In selecting clothing, one should prepare for rain or for
dust; for a moderate degree of cold in the highlands, and for
heat in the low country. Most people take too many clothes
and too much baggage, which is difficult to handle in Mexico.
"Check and wreck" is a rule to remember. Most things one
may need can be bought there, except shoes—for Mexican
shoes are not made to fit non-Mexican feet. Clothing should be
substantial and not too delicate; many Mexican laundresses
and cleaners are destructive.

Organized tours conducted by dependable agencies save
time and effort, but independent travelers have more freedom
and often more interesting and genuine experiences. Motorists
can move about freely, within the limits of the rather few
good roads. But a car is a care, and many visitors prefer to
rely upon the transportation systems of the country. Airways,
where they go, are on the whole the most comfortable as well
as the quickest means of travel. Mexican rail service, though
not as luxurious—except on a few crack trains of certain lines
—as in the United States, is reasonably dependable. Trains
may be delayed, but they probably will take one to more places
one wants to go than any other mode of conveyance. Moreover, railroads pass through some of the finest scenery. In
our own travels in Mexico, we used the railroads wherever
possible, supplementing them with bus lines, occasionally with

rented cars or organized local tours, but flying to and from Yucatán.

We visited Teotihuacan and near-by points with Wells-Fargo and with Aguirre's Guest Tours, as well as privately, and found that each method had its advantages; Cook's-Wagons-Lits gave similarly pleasing service to other localities outside the Capital; we went to Yucatán under the joint conduct of Miss Brenner's Pan-American Tours in Mexico City and Mayaland Tours of Mérida, via Compañía Mexicana de Aviación, certainly the most efficient way if time is limited.

In cities that had them, we never hesitated to use the streetcars, which are frequent and inexpensive and safer than taxicabs, whose rates, however, are surprisingly reasonable, if one establishes the price in advance.

In the most active tourist seasons—midsummer and midwinter—it is well to obtain hotel reservations in advance. At other times this is not ordinarily necessary, except as special local conditions may arise. Though guidebooks are valuable, the best of them become obsolete, and a hotel listed therein as "best" may have undergone change or even be no longer in existence. We found the best hotel guide, in the interior, to be the ubiquitous traveling salesman.

Among hotels which cultivate high standards of comfort, however, may be mentioned particularly Southern Pacific's Playa de Cortés, near Guaymas; Wells-Fargo's Rancho Telva at Taxco; the Mexican-owned Posada de Don Vasco at Pátzcuaro, and Virrey de Mendoza at Morelia. I have kind memories of the Diligencias at Vera Cruz, the Mirador at Uruápan, and Mayaland Lodge at Chichén Itza, and have been quite comfortable at many a more obscure hostelry. In any sizable city on tourist routes, there are pleasant abodes for visitors, although in rural regions and those less frequented by foreigners, accommodations often can be described only as "primitive."

In the Capital, the leading hotels are too well known to re-

Around, Not Through

quire comment. We spent some time in the more modest Monte Carlo, of Mexican and European flavor, "discovered" some years ago by D. H. Lawrence and Witter Bynner and frequented by artists and writers because of its convenient situation near the National Library, as well as for the kind helpfulness of Señor Faustino Forte, its host.

One must expect a degree of discomfort at times, and in some places. No travel is as comfortable as staying at home. A traveler anywhere is sure to meet with minor annoyances, due to differences of customs and accommodations, and local peculiarities. If these are accepted in a reasonable spirit, as part of the experience, one usually finds that the interest and pleasure outweigh the fatigue and irritation.

It should not be necessary to remind any one that courtesy, in any country, is more effective than bluster, and nowhere is this more true than in Mexico. Mexicans are courteous and also sensitive; their social manners are in general more formal than ours, and they expect courtesy. In most cases, the humblest Mexican will go blocks out of his way to be helpful to a stranger, if the stranger is not rude or overbearing. Even a complaint can be made in a reasonable spirit. Patience and human tolerance bring their rewards. The way out of difficulties in that country is usually around, rather than through.

Little need be said of physical safety. Most North Americans now know that in normal times the worst that is likely to happen in Mexico is having one's pocket picked. The two visitors who were wounded in the disturbances attending the 1940 election in Mexico City were accidental victims who inadvertently got between rival political factions on the Avenida Juárez while obtaining a close-up view of the rioting, and one of them while photographing it.

Even then, Mexico was mindful of its guests. A Mexican small boy rushed out amid the crossfire, shouting: "Don't shoot that man; he's a tourist!"

BIBLIOGRAPHY

"There are," replied the Dean of the Summer School of the National University of Mexico, "no good books on Mexico."

Thinking he might be referring to books by foreigners, I inquired: "What books can you recommend that have been written by Mexicans?"

"Those written by Mexicans," he answered, "are the worst of all."

Perhaps the Dean didn't mean his words to be taken literally. A number of works recommended later by the Dean and his colleagues to their classes are included among these sources, of which, however, there probably are few, if any, to which Mexicans of one or another social viewpoint would not object.

Ábside: Revista de Cultura Mexicana, periodical (Mexico, 1939)

Acosta, José de.—*The Natural and Moral History of the Indies* (1608; translated by Edward Grinston, London, 1880)

Alamán, Lucas.—*Historia de México* (Mexico, 1849)

Anales de Cuauhtitlan, translated from *Nahuatl,* by Sánchez y Solis, *Anales del Museo Nacional de Mexico III* (Mexico, ap. 1885)

Anales de la Escuela Nacional de Ciencias Biológicas, Vol. I, No. I (Mexico, 1938)

Anonymous Conqueror, The: Narrative of Some Things of New Spain, translated and annotated by Marshall H. Saville (New York, 1917)

Atl, Dr.—*Las Artes Populares en México* (Mexico, 1922)

——— *Iglesias de México*

"Atlantic Presents, The: Trouble Below the Border," symposium pamphlet (Concord, N. H., July, 1938)

Atlas Arqueológico de la República Mexicana, Formado por el Instituto Nacional de Antropología e Historia de la Secretaría de Educación Publica (Mexico, 1939)

Bibliography

AZUELA, MARIANO.—*Los de Abajo, Novela de la Revolución Mexicana* (Mexico, 1938)

———— *Pedro Moreno, el Insurgente* (Santiago de Chile, 1935)

BACHE, FEDERICO.—*México en cifras*

———— and DE LA PEÑA, M.—*México y su Petroleo* (Mexico, 1938)

BANCROFT, HUBERT HOWE.—*History of Mexico* (San Francisco, 1881-1888)

———— *The Native Races of the Pacific States of North America* (New York, 1875)

BANDELIER, ADOLPH F.—*Art of War and Mode of Warfare of the Ancient Mexicans* (Cambridge, 1877)

———— *Social Organization and Mode of Government of the Ancient Mexicans* (Cambridge, 1879)

BARONI, ALDO.—*Yucatán* (Mexico, 1937)

BAXTER, SYLVESTER.—*Spanish Colonial Architecture in Mexico* (Boston, 1901)

BEALS, CARLETON.—*Mexico: An Interpretation* (New York, 1923)

BENAVENTE MOTILINIA, FRAY TORIBIO DE.—*Historia de los Indios de la Nueva España* (Mexico, 1887)

BEST-MAUGARD, ADOLFO.—*A Method of Creative Design* (New York, 1926)

———— *Tradición, Resurgimiento y Evolución del Arte Mexicano* (Mexico, 1923)

Boletín de la junta auxiliar Jalisciense de la Sociedad Mexicana de Geografía y Estadistica, Tomo V, Numeros del 1 al 12 (Guadalajara, 1937-1938)

BORACRÈS, PAUL.—*El Petroleo Mexicano,* ies "Cosa Robada"? (Paris, 1939)

BOURBOURG, ABBÉ BRASSEUR DE.—*Histoire des Nations Civilisées du Mexique et de l'Amérique Centrale durant les Siècles Antérieurs á Cristophe Colomb* (Paris, 1857)

BRENNER, ANITA.—*Idols Behind Altars* (New York, 1929)

Bulletins of the Friends of Mexico (1939-1940)

Bulletins of the Workers' University of Mexico (Mexico, 1938-1940)

CALDERÓN DE LA BARCA, MME.—*Life in Mexico* (London, 1843)

CALLCOTT, WILFRID HARDY.—*Santa Anna* (Norman, Okla., 1936)

Bibliography

CAMPOS, RUBÉN.—*Aztlan, Tierra de las Garzas* (Santiago de Chile, 1935)

CARILLO, ALEJANDRO.—*Mexican Resources for Livelihood* (New York, 1938)

CARILLO Y ANCONA, CRESCENCIO.—*Historia Antigua de Yucatán* (Mérida, 1881; 1937)

CASCALES MUÑOZ, JOSÉ.—*Francisco de Zurbarán—su Época, su Vida y sus Obras* (Madrid, 1931)

CASO, ALFONSO.—*Exploraciones en Oaxaca, Quinta y Sexta Temporadas 1936-37* (Tacubaya, 1938)

―――― *The Religion of the Aztecs* (Mexico, 1937)

―――― *Trece Obras Maestras de Arqueología Mexicana* (Mexico, 1938)

CHAPMAN, CHARLES EDWARD.—*Republican Hispanic America: A History* (New York, 1937)

―――― *Colonial Hispanic America* (New York, 1933)

CHARLOT, JEAN.—*Art from the Mayans to Disney* (New York, 1939)

CHASE, STUART.—*Mexico: A Study of Two Americas* (New York, 1931)

CLAVIGERO, FRANCESCO SAVERIO.—*History of Mexico* translated from Italian by Charles Cullen (London, 1787)

CORNEJO FRANCO, JOSÉ.—*Guadalaxara Colonial* (Guadalajara, 1938)

CORONA NUÑEZ, JOSÉ.—*Rincones Michoacanos—Leyendas y Datos Históricos* (Mexico, 1938)

CORTÉS, HERNÁN.—*Account of the City of Mexico, from His Second Letter to the Emperor Charles V* (Boston, 1892)

―――― *Cartas y Relaciones de Hernán Cortés al Emperador Carlos V* (Paris, 1866)

―――― *The Five Letters of Relation from Cortés to the Emperor Charles V,* edited by Francis Augustus MacNutt (New York, 1908)

CORTI, COUNT EGON.—*Maximilian and Charlotte of Mexico* (translated from German by Catherine Alison Phillips, New York, 1928)

CORZO, ANGEL M.—*Ideario del Maestro Indoamericano* (Mexico, 1938)

COSÍO VILLEGAS, DANIEL.—"Importancia de Nuestra Agricultura," *El Trimestre Económico,* Vol. I.

―――― "La Riqueza Legendaria de México," *El Trimestre Económico,* Vol. VI, No. 1.

Bibliography

Cossío del Pomar, Felipe.—*Haya de la Torre, el Indoamericano* (Mexico, 1939)

Creelman, James.—*Díaz, Master of Mexico* (Mexico, 1910)

Cuevas, Father Mariano.—*History of the Catholic Church in Mexico*

Danzel, Theodor-Wilhelm.—*Kultur und Leben im alten Mexiko* (Darmstadt, 1923)

—— *Grundzüge der Altmexikanischen Geistekultur* (Darmstadt, 1922)

Departamento Autónomo de Prensa y Publicidad.—*México en Acción* (Mexico, 1938)

—— *The Mexican Government and the Solution of the Agrarian Problem in "La Laguna" District* (Mexico, undated [about 1939])

—— *Primera Exposición Objetiva del Plan Sexenal* (Mexico, 1937)

Díaz del Castillo, Bernal.—*The Discovery and Conquest of Mexico, 1517-1521,* edited from the only copy of the original manuscript translated by A. P. Maudslay (London, 1928)

Diez Relaciones de los Encomenderos de la Provincia de Yucatán, Escritas en el Año de 1579 (Madrid, 1898-1900). Appendix, Landa: *Relación de las Cosas de Yucatán,* first Yucatán edition (Mérida, 1938)

Dirección de Monumentos Coloniales.—*Edificios Coloniales, Artísticos e Históricos de la República Mexicana que han sido Declarados Monumentos* (Mexico, 1939)

Escuela Nacional de Ciencias Biológicas, Instituto Politécnico Nacional—*Prospecto de Información* (Mexico, 1939)

Esquivel Obregón, Toribio.—*Influencia de España y los Estados Unidos sobre México* (Madrid, 1918)

Evans, Rosalie.—*Letters from Mexico,* edited by Daisy Caden Pettus (Indianapolis, 1926)

Excelsior, daily newspaper (Mexico, various dates)

Farías, Ixca.—*Artes Populares* (Guadalajara, 1938)

Fernández, Boyolí, and Marrón de Angelis.—*Lo que no se sabe de la Rebelión Cedillista* (Mexico, 1938)

426

Bibliography

FERNÁNDEZ, JUSTINO.—*El Arte Moderno en Mexico,* Siglos XIX-XX (Mexico, 1932)

FERNÁNDEZ DE LIZARDI, JOSÉ JOAQUÍN.—*El Periquillo Sarniento* (Mexico, 1816)

FLANDRAU, CHARLES MACOMB.—*Viva Mexico!* (New York, 1924)

FOREIGN POLICY ASSOCIATION.—*Mexico's Challenge to Foreign Capital* (1937)

FRAZER, SIR JAMES.—*The Golden Bough* (London, 1922; New York, 1940)

FUHRMANN, ERNST.—*Über die religiösen Kulte Tonatiu, Mexikanische Gebete* (Darmstadt, 1924[?])

GAGE, THOMAS.—*A New Survey of the West Indies* (London, 1648; New York, 1929)

GALINDO Y VILLA.—*Geografía de Mexico*

GAMIO, MANUEL.—*Forjando Patria* (Mexico, 1916)

—— *La Población del Valle de Teotihuacan* (Mexico, 1922)

GANN, THOMAS.—*Ancient Cities and Modern Tribes* (New York, 1926)

GARCÍA CUBÁS, ANTONIO.—*El Libro de mis Recuerdos* (Mexico, 1934)

GARCÍA ICAZBALCETA, JOAQUÍN.—*Colección de Documentos para la Historia de México* (Mexico, 1858-66)

GODOY V., BERNABÉ.—*Corrientes Culturales que definen al Periquillo* (Guadalajara, 1938)

GOLDSCHMIDT, ALFONS.—*Mexiko* (Berlin, 1925)

GONZÁLEZ OBREGÓN, LUÍS.—*The Streets of Mexico,* translated by Blanche Collet Wagner (San Francisco, 1937)

GREEN, GRAHAM.—*Another Mexico* (New York, 1939)

GRUENING, ERNEST.—*Mexico and Its Heritage* (New York, 1928)

GUTIÉRREZ CRUZ, C.—*El Brazo de Obregón* (Mexico, 1924)

GUZMÁN, MARTÍN LUÍS.—*El Águila y la Serpiente* (Madrid, 1932)

—— *La Sombra del Caudillo* (Madrid, 1939)

HAGUE, ELEANOR.—*Latin American Music, Past and Present* (Santa Ana, Calif., 1934)

HEMINGWAY, ERNEST.—*Death in the Afternoon* (New York, 1932)

HERRING, HUBERT CLINTON, and WEINSTOCK, HERBERT.—*Renascent Mexico* (New York, 1935)

Bibliography

HEWETT, EDGAR LEE.—*Ancient Life in Mexico and Central America* (Indianapolis, 1936)

Hoy, periodical (Mexico, various dates)

HUMBOLDT, ALEXANDER VON.—*Essai Politique sur le Royaume de la Nouvelle Espagne* (Paris, 1811)

HUXLEY, ALDOUS.—*Beyond the Mexique Bay* (New York, 1934)

Indoamerica, periodical (Mexico, various dates)

IXTLILXÓCHITL, FERNANDO DE ALVA.—*Cruautés Horribles des Conquérants du Mexique* (Paris, 1829)

—————— *Relación de la Venida de los Españoles y Principio de la Ley Evangélica,* in SAHAGÚN, BERNARDINO DE.—*Historia General de las Cosas de Nueva España,* Vol. IV (Mexico, 1938)

JONES, CHESTER LLOYD.—*Mexico and Its Reconstruction* (New York, 1921)

JOYCE, THOMAS A.—*Maya and Mexican Art* (London, 1927)

—————— *Mexican Archeology* (London, 1914)

KINGSBOROUGH, E. K.—*Antiquities of Mexico* (London, 1831-1848)

KLUCKHOHN, FRANK L.—*The Mexican Challenge* (New York, 1939)

KROEBER, A. L.—*Archaic Culture Horizons in the Valley of Mexico* (Berkeley, 1925)

—————— *Anthropology* (New York, 1923, 1933)   .

LANDA, FRAY DIEGO DE.—*Relación de las Cosas de Yucatán* (Paris, 1864; Mérida, 1938)

LAS CASAS, FRAY BARTOLOMÉ DE.—*Historia de las Indias* (Madrid, 1875)

LAWRENCE, D. H.—*Mornings in Mexico* (New York, 1927)

—————— *The Plumed Serpent* (London, 1926)

LÓPEZ Y FUENTES, GREGORIO.—*Campamento* (Mexico, 1938)

—————— *El Indio* (Mexico, 1935)

—————— *Mi General!* (Mexico, 1932)

—————— *Tierra: la Revolución Agraria en México* (Mexico, 1933)

LÓPEZ-ROBERTS, MAURICIO, MARQUÉS DE LA TORREHERMOSA.—*Impresiónes de Arte* (Madrid, 1931)

LOYO, GILBERTO.—*La Demografía Política de México* (Mexico, 1935)

LUMHOLTZ, CARL.—*Unknown Mexico* (London, 1903)

Bibliography

MacLeish, Archibald.—*Conquistador* (Boston, 1932)

Mapa, periodical (Mexico, various dates)

Martínez del Río, Pablo.—*Los Orígenes Americanos* (Mexico, 1936)

Mason, Gregory.—*South of Yesterday* (New York, 1940)

McBride, George McCutchen.—*The Land Systems of Mexico* (New York, 1923)

McConnell, Burt.—*Mexico at the Bar of Public Opinion* (New York, 1939)

Méndez de Cuenca, Laura.—*Alvaro Obregón* (1918)

Mendieta, Fray Gerónimo de.—*Historia Eclesiástica Indiana* (Mexico, 1870)

Mendizábal, Miguel Othon de.—*Ensayos sobre las Civilizaciones Aborígines* (Mexico, 1924)

Menéndez, Carlos R.—*Noventa Años de Historia de Yucatán 1821-1910* (Mérida, 1937)

Mérida, Carlos.—*Modern Mexican Artists: Critical Notes* (Mexico, 1937)

Merriam, Charles.—*Machete* (Dallas, 1932)

Mexican Art and Life, periodical (Mexico, various dates)

Mexican Folkways, periodical (Mexico, various dates)

Mexican Life, periodical (Mexico, various dates)

Modern Mexico, periodical (Mexico, various dates)

Molina Enríquez, Andrés.—*Los Grandes Problemas Nacionales* (Mexico, 1909)

——— La Revolución Agraria de Mexico (Mexico, 1937)

——— Mexico's Defense, in *Atlantic Monthly,* Boston, March, 1939

Morris, Earl H.; Charlot, Jean; and Morris, Ann Axtell.—*The Temple of the Warriors at Chichen-Itza, Yucatán* (Washington, 1931)

Muñoz, Rafael F.—*Vámonos con Pancho Villa!* (Madrid, 1935)

Nacional, El, daily newspaper (Mexico, various dates)

Oglesby, Catherine.—*Modern Primitive Arts of Mexico, Gautemala and the Southwest* (New York, 1939)

Orozco, José Clemente.—*Pinturas Murales en la Universidad de Guadalajara,* preface by Luís Cardoza y Aragón (Mexico, 1937)

Bibliography

OROZCO Y BERRA, MANUEL.—*Historia de la Conquista de México* (Mexico, 1880)

—— *Los Conquistadores de México,* in Vol. IV, Sahagún, 1938 edition (Mexico, 1938)

O'SHAUGHNESSY, EDITH.—*A Diplomat's Wife in Mexico* (New York, 1916)

—— *Intimate Pages of Mexican History* (New York, 1920)

PALACIO, LUCAS DE.—*Mesones y Ventas de la Nueva España*

PALACIOS, ENRIQUE JUAN.—*Arqueología de México* (Mexico, 1937)

—— *Guía Arqueológica de Chichen Itza* (Mexico, 1935)

PANI, ALBERTO J.—*La Higiene en México* (Mexico, 1916)

PARKES, HENRY BAMFORD.—*A History of Mexico* (Boston, 1938)

PAYNO, MANUEL.—*Los Bandidos de Río Frío* (Mexico, 1889)

PINCHON, EDGCUMB.—*Viva Villa!* (New York, 1933)

PLENN, J. H.—*Mexico Marches* (Indianapolis, 1939)

PRESCOTT, WILLIAM H.—*History of the Conquest of Mexico* (Boston, 1834)

PRIESTLEY, HERBERT INGRAM.—*The Mexican Nation: A History* (New York, 1923)

—— and SÁENZ, MOISES.—*Some Mexican Problems* (Chicago, 1926)

Proceedings of the 27th Congress of Americanists (unpublished, Mexico, 1939)

RADIN, PAUL.—*The Sources and Authenticity of the History of Ancient Mexico* (Berkeley, 1920)

REDFIELD, ROBERT.—*Tepoztlan: A Mexican Village* (Chicago, 1930)

Revista de Educación, periodical (Mexico, various dates)

Revista Mexicana de Sociología, periodical (Mexico, various dates)

RICARD, ROBERT.—*La Conquête Spirituelle du Mexique* (Paris, 1933)

RIVA PALACIO, VICENTE, ed.—*México á Través de los Siglos* (Mexico, 1887-89)

RIVERA, DIEGO, and WOLFE, BERTRAM D.—*Portrait of Mexico* (New York, 1937)

ROBERTS, W. ADOLPHE.—*The Caribbean: The Story of Our Sea of Destiny* (Indianapolis, 1940)

Bibliography

ROMERO FLORES, JESÚS, editor.—*Leyendas y Cuentos Michoacanos* (Mexico, 1938)

ROSS, EDWARD ALSWORTH.—*The Social Revolution in Mexico* (New York, 1923)

RUÍZ, GENERAL B. MARIANO.—*Leyandas Históricos de los Estados de Michoacán, Jalisco y Nayarit* (manuscript in collection of Don Aurelio Guerrero, Mexico, 1927)

SAHAGÚN, FRAY BERNARDINO DE.—*Historia General de las Cosas de Nueva España* (Mexico, 1829; 1938)

SALAZAR, ROSENDO.—*Mexico en Pensamiento y en Acción* (Mexico, 1926)

SALM-SALM, FELIX.—*My Diary in Mexico in 1867* (London, 1868)

SÁNCHEZ DE AGUILAR, PEDRO.—*Informe Contra Idolorum Cultores del Obispado de Yucatán* (Madrid, 1639; Mérida, 1937)

SECRETARÍA DE EDUCACIÓN PÚBLICA.—*Monografía de las Escuelas de Pintura al Aire Libre* (Mexico, 1924)

———— *Archeological Monuments of Mexico* (New York, 1923)

SELER, EDUARD.—*The Tonalamatl of the Arbin Collection* (Berlin and London, 1900)

SIMPSON, EYLER N.—*The Ejido: Mexico's Way Out* (Chapel Hill, N. C., 1937)

SIMPSON, LESLEY BYRD.—*The Encomienda in New Spain* (Berkeley, 1924)

SOUSTELLE, JACQUES.—*Mexique, Terre Indienne* (Paris, 1936)

SPINDEN, HERBERT J.—*Ancient Civilizations of Mexico and Central America* (New York, 1928)

SPRATLING, WILLIAM.—*Little Mexico* (New York, 1932)

STARR, FREDERICK.—*In Indian Mexico* (Chicago, 1908)

STEININGER, G. RUSSELL, and VAN DE VELDE, PAUL.—*Three Dollars a Year* (New York, 1935)

STEPHENS, JOHN L.—*Incidents of Travel in Central America, Chiapas and Yucatan* (New York, 1841)

STEVENSON, SARA YORKE.—*Maximilian in Mexico* (New York, 1899)

TANNENBAUM, FRANK.—*The Mexican Agrarian Revolution* (New York, 1939)

———— *Peace by Revolution* (New York, 1933)

Bibliography

TEJA ZABRE, ALFONSO.—*Historia de México: Una Moderna Interpretación* (Mexico, 1935)

TERRY, T. PHILIP.—*Terry's Guide to Mexico* (Boston, 1923, 1938)

TEZOZÓMOC, F. DE A.—*Crónica Mexicana,* edited by Manuel Orozco y Berra (Mexico, 1878)

THOMPSON, JOHN ERIC.—*Mexico Before Cortés* (New York, 1933)

THOMPSON, WALLACE.—*The Mexican Mind* (Boston, 1922)

—— *The People of Mexico* (New York, 1921)

TOOR, FRANCES.—*Frances Toor's Guide to Mexico* (Mexico, 1934)

—— *Mexican Popular Arts* (Mexico, 1939)

TOOR, FRANCES, editor.—*Mexican Folkways,* periodical (Mexico, various dates)

TORRES, TEODORO.—*La Patria Perdida* (Mexico, 1935)

Twenty Centuries of Mexican Art, compiled by The Museum of Modern Art in collaboration with the Mexican Government (Mexico, 1940)

Universal, daily newspaper (Mexico, various dates)

VAILLANT, GEORGE C.—*Artists and Craftsmen in Ancient Central America* (New York, 1935)

VALLE-ARIZPE, ARTEMIO DE.—*Historia de la Ciudad de México segun los Relatos de sus Cronistas* (Mexico, 1939)

VASCONCELOS, JOSÉ, and GAMIO, MANUEL.—*Aspects of Mexican Civilization* (Chicago, 1926)

VELÁSQUEZ CHÁVEZ, AGUSTIN.—*Contemporary Mexican Artists* (New York, 1937)

WEYL, NATHANIEL and SYLVIA.—*The Reconquest of Mexico: The Years of Lázaro Cárdenas* (London, 1939)

WILLARD, T. A.—*The City of the Sacred Well* (New York, 1926)

WILSON, HENRY LANE.—*Diplomatic Episodes in Mexico, Belgium, and Chile* (New York, 1927)

WOLFE, BERTRAM D.—*Diego Rivera, His Life and Times* (New York, 1939)

WORKERS' UNIVERSITY OF MEXICO.—*The Oil Conflict in Mexico* (Mexico, 1937-38)

INDEX

433

Index

Index

Index

Index

Index

438

Index

Index

Index

Index

(I)